RIGHTS OF CHILD

RIGHTS OF CHILD

SUBHASH CHANDRA SINGH

SERIALS PUBLICATIONS
NEW DELHI (INDIA)

First Published - 2007

ISBN: 81-8387-085-6

Published by

SERIALS PUBLICATIONS
4830/24, Prahlad Street, Ansari Road
Darya Ganj, New Delhi-110002 (India)
Phone : 23245225. Fax : 91-11-23272135
E-mail: serials@satyam.net.in

CONTENTS

PREFACE

The different experiences of girls and boys make it important to integrate gender concerns into child labour research, advocacy, programmes and policies. Research that reflects gender disparities will provide a more frozen basis for actions aimed at reducing child labour. Gender-sensitive programmes and policies that combat and prevent child labour are essential to fulfilling the rights of boys and girls, including the right to an education, a healthy childhood, protection from violence, abuse and exploitation, and rest and recreation. Working in the privacy of individual homes, child domestic workers are often invisible to the outside world and thus particularly vulnerable to violence, exploitation and abuse. These children are exploited economically and often physically, including sexually. They are forced to do heavy work, work overtime, are often deprived of food, schooling and rest, and work in unhealthy and unsafe conditions. Domestic labour becomes even more hazardous when children are trafficked into another town or country to take up service, especially when they do not speak the local language. There is a close correlation between gender and the reasons for trafficking, with girls being trafficked mainly for domestic service and commercial sexual exploitation. Child labour, in particular its worst hazardous forms (including slavery, trafficking, debt bondage and other forms of forced labour, forced recruitment of children for use in armed conflict, prostitution and pornography, and illicit activities), need to be seen in the larger context of development since its reduction depends on improved household incomes, economic empowerment and infrastructure development for education and health.

Often children are trafficked for reasons including sexual exploitation; adoption; entertainment and sports; marriage; labour; begging, organ trade; drug peddling, armed conflicts and smuggling. Domestic violence, illiteracy, unemployment, poverty, unsafe migration and child marriage are the root causes that explain the increasing rate of illegal human trafficking. Disabled children are not benefiting from equal rights to others in developing economies due to strongly entrenched stigma and discrimination, and are certainly not receiving any further help to assist with their disabilities. A disabled child is a matter of shame even for educated families in India. Until recently, disability and child policies have been paternalistic, based on charitable interventions as opposed to rights. Society has strong negative attitudes of children, especially disabled children, and made assumptions of their ability to express their views and participate in policy and planning.

There are hundreds of millions of children and young people around the world who are imprisoned, not in physical jails, but in a state of bondage more permanent than locks or bars alone could create. These are children who labour at tasks that harm their bodies and minds, their spirits and future. Only estimates exist, but at least 250 million children between the ages of 5 and 14 work for a living in developing countries, nearly half of them full time. Many millions more are uncounted and uncountable. They are everywhere but invisible, toiling as domestic servants in homes, labouring behind the walls of workshops, hidden from view in plantations.

It has often been the case that child soldiers have been thought of as a common category of children who would possess the same characteristics and needs. The unique individual features and characteristics of the children were often overlooked or ignored. There was a time when the prevailing opinion was that all child soldiers were boys. It is now recognized that child soldiers include girls as well as boys and that demobilization and reintegration programs must take into account the unique needs of girls. The fundamental needs of girls who have been child soldiers have not been very well documented, understood and addressed. It has only been recently recognized that girls are used in many different ways by the armed groups. Their demobilization and reintegration needs are directly related to the specific ways that they were used.

In the present volume the authors have identified the major objectives and triumphs in the area of recognizing children as bursting focus of human rights and getting rid of impunity for gender crimes.

Subhash Chandra Singh

ABUSE OF CHILDREN IN THEIR HOMES DURING DISCIPLINE PRACTICES: A VICTIMOLOGICAL ANALYSIS

K. Jaishankar & C. Kannan**

INTRODUCTION

Although the vulnerability of children to abusive practices is recognized in the Indian constitution, most research to date has focused on children's survival needs and societal abuses, such as malnutrition, child labor, child beggary, child marriage, and child prostitution (Banerjee, 1979; Bhattacharyya, 1979, 1983; Gupta, 1977; Jabbi, 1986; Mehta, Lokeshwar, Bhatt, Athavale, and Kulkarni, 1979). A few early clinical studies of child injuries suggested that some maltreatment of children may be the result of harsh discipline from family members (Bhattacharyya, 1983; Dave, Dave, and Mishra, 1982). At around the same time, Poffenberger (1981) offered one of the first candid observations of parental discipline practices in his report of child rearing in rural India. In this qualitative investigation, parents described discipline practices they deemed acceptable and unacceptable. Whereas physical punishment was the norm and considered necessary for the socialization of children, the villagers spoke of punishments that they considered to be overly harsh including threats to send children away, invocations of ghosts and evil spirits to do the child harm, holding burning sticks to penises to control masturbation, branding, and hanging by hands or feet. Threats of death were also common.

Suman (1985), noting the paucity of systematic and quantitative data related to child physical and emotional abuse in India, called for research to document the prevalence of these phenomena and to identify the interacting factors that support or discourage child maltreatment within the family environment. In response, several investigators have conducted small studies investigating the extent to which harsh and

* Department of Criminology and Criminal Justice, Manonmaniam Sundaranar University, Tirunelveli, Tamil Nadu, India

abusive practices occur within the context of normal child rearing and socialization (Segal, 1992, 1995; Segal and Ashtekar, 1994). Because there are no universal standards related to optimal child rearing or what might be considered child maltreatment, these early studies confronted the need to balance cultural norms against the well-being of children (Hunter et al 2000).

Segal's progression of empirical studies has shed considerable light on the extent of harsh child discipline practices and the perceptions of the public and professionals regarding what constitute abusive behavior (Segal, 1992, 1995; Segal and Ashtekar, 1994). Investigating cultural definitions of child abuse in India, Segal found very little difference in the perceptions of severity for different forms of child abuse among social workers, other human service workers, and other service workers (Segal, 1992). Cross-cultural comparisons with a similar U.S. study (Giovanonni and Bercarra, 1979) indicated that while both Indian and U.S. samples perceived sexual abuse as highest on an abuse scale and inadequate housing conditions as lowest, the rankings of the remaining forms of abuse were influenced by recognition of abuse, national norms, expectations, and the socioeconomic conditions of each country. Although the U.S. sample ranked physical abuse second in severity in terms of its detrimental effects on the child, the Indian sample ranked it sixth, after sexual abuse, fostering delinquency, medical neglect, poor supervision, and exposing children to parental sexual mores (Hunter et al 2000).

A subsequent study that used the Conflict Tactics Scale (Straus, 1979) to investigate the discipline practices of middle-class professionals in India found that 57% engaged in "normal" corporal punishment (spanking, slapping), 42% in "abusive" forms of discipline (kicked, bit, or hit with fist; hit or tried to hit with something; beat up child), and 3% in "extreme" forms of violence (threatened with, or used, a knife or gun on child) (Segal, 1995). Segal observed that these relatively high rates of harsh discipline may reflect societal sanction of violence toward children and the perception that physical abuse has fewer detrimental effects than other forms of abuse (Hunter et al 2000).

Yet some parents, like those in Poffenberger's study (1981), may resort to practices that they feel are inappropriate and potentially harmful. Identification of risk and protective factors related to different levels of severity in discipline practices used in India may help address the question of whether severe practices are normative or whether they, at some point, cross a line to become unacceptable or abusive. In this study, risk and protective factors have been conceptualized using an ecological model that attributes family interactions (including child abuse and other family violence) to characteristics of the nested social ecology including the larger society, the local community, the family itself, and finally the characteristics of the involved individuals (Belsky, 1980; Cicchetti and Lynch, 1993; Garbarino, 1977).

As in all societies, the treatment of children in India is likely a function of deepseated cultural norms. Few would deny that there is societal tolerance for the use of corporal punishment, a cultural factor theorized as a risk factor for physical abuse (Zigler and Hall, 1989). In addition, India is a patrilineal society in which the spiritual, economic, and social norms of everyday life reflect an extreme preference for male offspring and a corresponding denigration of female children. As a result, female children have been at higher risk for selective feticide, infanticide, poorer nutrition, poorer health care, poorer educational opportunities, kidnapping, and forced prostitution (Poffenberger, 1981; Wadley, 1993). However no data indicate that females are more likely to experience harsh parental discipline than their male counterparts. Although Singh and Kaur (1981) found that rural Indian mothers felt that girls need more instruction and discipline than boys, they did not analyze the harshness or severity of actual childrearing practices by gender. In China, another country where sons are venerated because they are seen as insurance against old age and poverty, boys are more strictly disciplined, perhaps because the stakes connected to their behavior and success are much higher (Ho, 1996; Tang, 1998; Wu, 1996). It is reasonable to expect that the same family dynamics might contribute to harsher punishment of sons in India (Hunter et al 2000).

At the community level, social isolation, lack of social support, and social change, such as migration away from family of origin, have been identified in the United States as risk factors for child abuse (Egeland and Brunquell, 1979; Garbarino and Gilliam, 1980; Starr, 1988). In studies outside the United States, Levinson (1989) found that child abuse is less likely in extended family households where child care responsibilities can be shared. Increasing mobility of Indian families and movement away from extended family structures may increase the parenting stresses once absorbed within the joint family (Sinha, 1984). Other types of stresses that occur at the family level (e.g., alcohol abuse, marital conflict or violence, large family size, and parent psychological problems) have been shown to increase the probability of child abuse (Whipple and Richey, 1997). In a 1985 survey of American families, Straus and Gelles (1990) found that mothers who were victims of partner violence were at least twice as likely to physically abuse their children as mothers who were not (Hunter et al 2000).

Harsh discipline and child abuse have also been linked with family or parent socioeconomic characteristics, especially low income (Straus, 1980), low maternal education (Brown, Cohen, Johnson, and Salzinger, 1998; Egeland and Brunquell, 1979), closely spaced children (Holden, Willis, and Corcoran, 1992), and a high household crowding index (Youssef, Attia, and Kamel, 1998). Characteristics of the child may increase the likelihood of severe discipline or abuse, especially when other risk factors are present. Wolfe has reported that the average age of abuse victims in the United States tends to be younger than the average age of all children (Wolfe, 1987). Others have found age related to discipline practices, with parents more likely to physically discipline younger children and more likely to use nonphysical discipline techniques including verbal abuse with older children (Jackson et al., 1999). Children perceived as being difficult to parent or manage have been identified as being at higher risk (Blackson, Tarter, and Mezzich, 1996; Korbin, 1991; Youssef et al., 1998), especially when the mother is depressed and has few available supports (Hetherington, 1989). Poor health and handicapping conditions have also been found to be associated with child abuse (Dubowitz, Hampton, Bithoney, and Newberger, 1987; Youssef et al., 1998), possibly because the child is perceived as different or as the source of increased stress (Kotelchuck, 1982).

SCOPE OF THE STUDY

The scope of the present study is restricted to child abuse in homes, particularly physical abuse, verbal abuse and mental abuse by parents. Other forms of child abuse in the homes such as abandonment, child Labor etc, are not included in this study. Other forms of child abuse in schools and various other institutions are not included in this study. The aim of this study was to determine the type and severity of child abuse in homes during discipline practices used in Tirunelveli district, Tamil Nadu.

NEED AND SIGNIFICANCE OF THE STUDY

Child abuse is increasing in the modern world. Particularly child victimization has been increasing in the homes. The parents who abuse the children may feel that they are in their control and deserve the abuse. The children usually have poor self esteem, in addition to physical injuries that may be the result of abuse; child victims may develop eating disorders, or sleep disturbances, nightmares. Though the incident of child abuse sons an increasing trend, many of such incidences were not reported. In this context, it was felt by the researchers to conduct an empirical investigation to study the problems of child abuse by parents in homes.

METHODOLOGY

The universe of the study comprised of the children of Sankar nagar area, Tirunelveli district, Tamil Nadu. Purposive sampling method was adopted to choose the sample for this study. A total of 40 respondents were selected for this study. Due to non-cooperation from the parents only a lesser number of samples were possible to be collected from the victims. 6 respondents were chosen from age group of 9-12 and 34 respondents were chosen from age group of 13–18. An Interview schedule constructed by the researchers was used to elicit the required data pertaining to the present study. The research tool consisted 15 items pertaining to the objectives of the study. The tool was divided into 6 parts. Part 1 had items relating sex and age of the respondents. Part 2 of the tool had items relating to family details. Part 3 had items relating to physical abuse of the respondents. Part 4 of the tool had items relating mental abuse. Part 5 had items relating verbal abuse. Part 6 of the tool had items relating to draw back of the respondents.

RESULTS AND DISCUSSION

Socio Economic Characteristics

Table 1
Sex

Sex	*N*	*%*
Male	22	55.0
Female	18	45.0
Total	40	100.0

55% of the respondents were male and the 45% were female.

Table 2
Age

Age	N	%
9-12	6	15.0
13 18	34	85.0
Total	40	100.0

This above table (2) shows that children under the age group of 13-18 are more abused. The reason is that they start thinking which result in disobeying. They want more free time to play which result in getting abused.

Table 3
Educational Background of Parents

Educational background of parents	*N*	%
Literates	24	60.0
Illiterates	16	40.0
Total	40	100.0

60% of abused children's parents were literate. Even with their education they feel that their wards can be corrected only by beating.

Table 4
Economic Background

Economic background of parents	*N*	%
Low	13	32.5
Medium	15	37.5
High	12	30.0
Total	40	100.0

This table (4) shows that medium income group family's children's are more abused than low and high income. The reason is that the medium income families feel that, only if they study well they would be successful in life. So to make them successful they have to be beaten and made to study hard.

Table 5
Family Structure

Family structure	*N*	%
Joint family	21	52.5
Single family	19	47.5
Total	40	100.0

The above table (5) shows that joint family children are more affected by this problem. The reason is that, in joint family more than one family live under one roof, so when a child commits some mistakes even if his or her parents are not serious, other family members complain about this. This makes the parents get irritated and they show their anger on their children.

The table (6) shows that the most common physical abuse is slapping. The reason is that it is immediate and spontaneous reaction for any mistake and easy way to punish.

The children are more abused while getting corrected when they commit mistakes. The reason would be that, parents feel that they children can be corrected only by beating when they do not follow routine or parent's advice or does some wrong acts.

Typology of Abuses

Table 6
Type of Abuse–Physical Abuse

Physical Abuse	*Yes*		*No*	
	N	*%*	*N*	*%*
Slapping	37	92.5	3	7.5
Beating with stick	32	80.0	8	20.0
Pinching	3	7.5	37	92.5
Branding with hot wood or iron etc	13	32.5	27	67.5
Making to fast	18	45.0	22	55.0

Table 7
Abuses take place during this period

Duration	*Yes*		*No*	
	N	*%*	*N*	*%*
Playing	23	57.5	17	42.5
Studying	25	62.5	15	37.5
While doing mistake	35	87.5	5	12.5

Table 8
Type of Abuse–Mental Abuse

Mental Abuse	*Yes*		*No*	
	N	*%*	*N*	*%*
Forcing to study more	25	62.5	15	37.5
Not allowing to play	36	90.0	4	10.0
Not allowing to see T.V	35	87.5	5	12.5
Lodging in a room to study	17	42.5	23	57.5
Comparing others for scolding	39	97.5	1	2.5

This table (8) shows that children are more abused not for their mistakes but of short comings compared to other neighboring children. The mental torture is more because they are forced to study without any entertainment and kept under constant watch. Their freedom is much restricted and comparison is made with respect to those who are better at studies. Marks become measuring scale of good and bad children.

The table (9) shows that children are not provided freedom and also about the time of mental torture. The reason is that they are always stressed to study more and more with tuitions even after attending schools, so never get their mind diverted from studies, even if they play for sometimes their mind would always be thinking of their parent's scolding for not studying and teachers beatings. This would put mental strain on them and negative attitude towards the studies.

Table 9
Time of Mental Torture

Duration	*Yes*		*No*	
	N	%	*N*	%
Getting low marks in studies	26	65.0	14	35.0
During Heavy study load	26	65.0	14	35.0
Confining in home without leisure	39	97.5	1	2.5

Table 10
Type of Abuse–Verbal Abuse

Verbal Abuse	*Yes*		*No*	
	N	%	*N*	%
Scolding related to studies	25	62.5	15	37.5
Scolding related to mischief	39	97.5	1	2.5
Scolding related to disobedience	39	97.5	1	2.5
Scolding related to late wakeup	19	47.5	21	52.5
Scolding related to food habits	38	95.0	2	5.0

This table (10) shows that scolding relating to mischief and disobedience tops in the list of reasons for abuse. The reason is that the parents want their children to be under their control. They also want their children to obey them.

Impact and Reactions Towards Abuse:

Table 11
Physical Abuse—Victim reaction

Reactions	*Yes*		*No*	
	N	%	*N*	%
Crying	39	97.5	1	2.5
Fasting	38	95.0	2	5.0
Getting locked into a separate room	18	45.0	22	55.0
Will not speak with others	39	97.5	1	2.5
Will not mingle with others	40	100.0	0	0

This table (11) shows that, the children react by isolating themselves more than any other reaction. The reason is that they feel this is the way to exhibit their feelings and get sympathy from others.

Table 12
Mental Torture—Victim reaction

Reactions	*Yes*		*No*	
	N	*%*	*N*	*%*
Hatred with studies	34	85.0	6	15.0
Hatred with parents	39	97.5	1	2.5
Try to escape from home	25	62.5	15	37.5
Decide to commit suicide	20	50.0	20	50.0
Unwilling to go to school	32	80.0	8	20.0

This table (12) shows that the reaction shown by the children towards their parents is too negative and hatred behavior is also shown. This is because that they feel parents are the controlling agents who restrict all their liberty and freedom resulting in dislike towards the studies.

Table 13
Verbal Abuse—Victim reaction

Reactions	*Yes*		*No*	
	N	*%*	*N*	*%*
Don't care about it	25	62.5	15	37.5
Making low interest in studies	37	92.5	3	7.5
Spending more time with friends	29	72.5	11	27.5

This table (13) shows that most react towards the studies in negative manner. This is because the verbal abuse is more when it is related to studies. So they loose their interest towards studies, as it is forced on them. To escape from this mental torture, they spend more time with their friends.

Table 14
Acceptance of Abuses

Victim Response	*Yes*		*No*	
	N	*%*	*N*	*%*
Accept	0	0	40	100

This table (14) shows that none wants to get abused in any form. This is universal that no person would like to get hurt in any form.

Table 15
Lack of care (Types)

Victim response	*Yes*		*No*	
	N	*%*	*N*	*%*
Love and affection	39	97.5	1	2.5
Proper caring	40	100	0	0
Recreation facilities	40	100	0	0

This table (15) shows that most children wanted proper caring and recreation facilities. This is also universal that no person can live alone or with out a friend, so naturally as a child he or she would need caring. Only proper care augments positive and good growth of child.

MAJOR FINDINGS

- Majority of the victims (92.5%) were physically abused by their parents by slapping.
- Majority of the victims (80.%) were physically abused by their parents by beating with stick.
- Majority of the victims (87.5.%) were physically abused by their parents when they commit mistake.
- Majority of the victims (90.%) were mentally abused by their parents by the way of not allowing to play.
- Majority of the victims (97.%) were mentally abused by their parents by the way of comparing with others and scolding.
- Majority of the victims (97.5.%) were mentally abused by their parents by confining in home without providing leisure.
- Majority of the victims (97.5%) were verbally abused by their parents by the way scolding which is related to mischief committed by the victims.
- Majority of the victims (97.5%) were verbally abused by their parents by the way scolding which is related to disobedience of the victims.
- Majority of the victims (95%) were verbally abused by their parents by the way scolding which is related to food habits of the victims.
- Majority of the victims (97.5%) reacted to the physical abuse by crying and (95%) reacted by fasting.
- Majority of the victims (97.5%) reacted to the physical abuse by not speaking with others and (100%) reacted by not mingling with others.

- Majority of the victims (85%) reacted to the mental abuse by hating studies and (97.5%) reacted by hating their parents.
- Majority of the victims (80%) reacted to the mental abuse by showing their unwillingness to go to school.
- Majority of the victims (80%) reacted to the mental abuse by showing their unwillingness to go to school.
- Majority of the victims (92.5%) reacted to the verbal abuse by showing low interest in studies.
- No victim (100%) accepts to be abused.

CONCLUSION

The present study has found out the marginal phenomenon which is normally considered as trivial in India i.e. Child abuse in homes by parents. Because in Indian culture parents are considered to be equivalent to God and it is believed that whatever they will do for the child will be for their progress. However, in the process of rising the children parents forget their role and they become tyrannical. The study would help providing the empirical information about the child abuse to the parents, and the society to take appropriate measures to curb the child abuse menace. The future of every nation solely depends on its children. Therefore, efforts must be taken to address the issue of child abuse by parents at homes. This study however cannot be generalized because of the sample size and duration of the study. More studies are still needed to document the magnitude of the problem of child physical and psychological abuse across India; studies are also needed that examine the impact on children's physical, social, and emotional well-being.

REFERENCES

Banerjee, S. (1979), *Child labour in India*. London: Anti-Slavery Society.

Bauman, L.J., and Adair, E.G. (1992), The use of Ethnographic Interviewing to Inform Questionnaire Construction. *Health Education Quarterly*, 19, 9-23.

Belsky, J. (1980), Child Maltreatment: An Ecological Integration. *American Psychologist*, 35, 320 335.

Bhattacharyya, A.K. (1979), Child abuse in India and the Nutritionally Battered Child. *Child Abuse and Neglect*, 3, 607-614.

Bhattacharyya, A.K. (1983), Child abuse and Neglect (CAN): Indian Perspective. *Indian Pediatrics,* 20, 803-810.

Blackson, T.C., Tarter, R.E., and Mezzich, A.C. (1996), Interaction between Childhood Temperament and Parental Discipline Practices on behavioral Adjustment in Preadolescent Sons of Substance Abuse and Normal Fathers. *American Journal of Drug and Alcohol Abuse*, 22, 335-348.

Brown, J., Cohen, P., Johnson, J.G., and Salzinger, S. (1998), A Longitudinal Analysis of Risk Factors for Child Maltreatment: Findings of a 17-year Prospective Study of Officially Recorded and self-reported Child Abuse and Neglect. *Child Abuse and Neglect*, 11, 1065-1078.

Cicchetti, D., and Lynch, M. (1993), Toward an Ecological/transactional Model of Community Violence and Child Maltreatment: Consequences for Children's Development. *Psychiatry*, 56, 96-118.

Dave, A.B., Dave, P.B., and Mishra, K.D. (1982), Child Abuse and Neglect Practices in the Durg District of Madhya Pradesh. *Indian Pediatrics*, 19, 905-912.

Dubowitz, H., Hampton, R.L., Bithoney, W.G. and Newberger, E.H. (1987), Inflicted and non-inflicted Injuries: Differences in Child and Familial Characteristics. *American Journal of Orthopsychiatry*, 57, 525-535.

Egeland, B. and Brunquell, D. (1979), An at Risk Approach to the Study of Child Abuse: Some Preliminary Findings. *Journal of the American Academy of Child Psychiatry*, 18, 219-235.

Frick, P.J., Christian, R.E., and Wooten, J.M. (1999), Age Trends in Association between Parenting Practices and Conduct Problems. *Behavior Modification*, 23, 106-128.[Abstract/Free Full Text]

Garbarino, J. (1977), The Human Ecology of Child Maltreatment: A Conceptual Model for Research. *Journal of Marriage and the Family*, 3 721-735.

Garbarino, J. and Gilliam, G. (1980), *Understanding Abusive Families*. Lexington, MA: Lexington Books.

Giovannoni, J.M., and Bercerra, R.M. (1979), *Defining Child Abuse*. New York: Free Press.

Gupta, S. (Ed.) (1977), *Child in India*. New Delhi: Indian Pediatrics.

Hemenway, D. Solnick, S. and Carter, J. (1994), Childrearing Violence. *Child Abuse and Neglect*, 18, 1011-1020.

Hetherington, E.M. (1989), Coping with Transitions: Winners, Losers, and Survivors. *Child Development*, 60, 1-15.

Ho, D. (1996), Filial Piety and its Psychological Consequences. In M.H. Bond (Ed.), *The handbook of Chinese Psychology* (pp. 155-165). Hong Kong: Oxford University Press.

Holden, E.W., Willis, D.J. and Corcoran, M. (1992), Preventing Child Maltreatment During the Prenatal/perinatal Period. In D.J. Willis, E.W. Holden, and M. Rosenberg (Eds.), *Prevention of child maltreatment*. New York: John Wiley.

Hughes, D. and DuMont, K. (1993), Using Focus Groups to Facilitate Culturally Anchored Research. *American Journal of Community Psychology*, 21, 775-806.

Hunter Wanda M., Dipty Jain, Laura S. Sadowski, and Antonio I. Sanhueza (2000), Risk Factors for Severe Child Discipline Practices in Rural India *Journal of Pediatric Psychology*, Vol. 25, No. 6, 2000, pp. 435-447.

Jabbi, M.K. (1986), Child marriages in Rajasthan. *Social Change*, 16, 3-9.

Jackson, S., Thompson, R.A., Christianson, E., Colma, R.A., Wyatt, J., Buckendale, C.W., Wilcox, B.L., and Peterson, R. (1999), Predicting Abuse-Prone Parental Attitudes and Discipline Practices in a Nationally Representative Sample. *Child Abuse and Neglect*, 23, 15-29.

Kelley, M.L., Power, T.G., and Wimbush, D.D. (1992), Determinants of Discipline Practices in Low-income Black Mothers. *Child Development*, 63, 573-582.

Korbin, J.E. (1991), Cross-cultural Perspectives and Research Directives for the 21st Century. *Child Abuse and Neglect*, 15, 67-77.

Kotelchuck, M. (1982), Child abuse and Neglect: Prediction and Misclassification. In R.H. Starr (Ed.), *Child Abuse Prediction: Policy Implications* (pp. 67-104). Cambridge, MA: Ballinger.

Kotch, J.B., Browne, D.C., Ringwalt, C.L., Stewart, P.W., Ruina, E., Holt, K., Lowman, B., and Jung, J.W. (1995), Risk of Child Abuse or Neglect in a Cohort of low-income Children. *Child Abuse and Neglect*, 19, 1115-1130.

Levinson, D. (1989), Family Violence in a Cross-cultural Perspective. *Frontiers of Anthropology*. Vol. 1. Newbury Park, CA: Sage.

Maharashtra State Government (1991), *1991 Statistics*. State of Maharashtra, India.

Mehta, M.N., Lokeshwar, M.R., Bhatt, S.S., Athavale, V.B., and Kulkarni, B.S. (1979), Rape in Children. *Child Abuse and Neglect*, 3, 671-678.

Noh, S., Avison, W. R., and Kaspar, V. (1992), Depressive Symptoms Among Korean Immigrants: Assessment of a Translation of the Center for Epidemiologic Studies-Depression Scale. *Psychological Assessment*, 4, 84-91.

Poffenberger, T. (1981), Child Rearing and Social Structure in Rural India: Toward a cross-cultural Definition of Child abuse and Neglect. In J. Korbin (Ed.), *Child abuse and Neglect: Cross-cultural Perspectives* (pp. 71-95). Berkeley, CA: University of California Press.

Qasem, F.S., Mustafa, A.A., Kazem, N.A., and Shah, N.M. (1998), Attitudes of Kutwaiti parents toward physical punishment of children. *Child Abuse and Neglect*, 22, 1189-1202.

Radloff, L.S. (1977). The CES-D Scale: A Self-report Depression Scale for Research in a General Population. *Applied Psychological Measurement*, 1, 385-401.

Salgado de Snyder, V.N., Cervantes, R.C., and Padilla, A.M. (1990), Gender and Ethnic Differences in Psychosocial and Generalized Distress Among Hispanics. Special Issue: Gender and Ethnicity: Perspectives on Dual Status. *Sex Roles*, 22, 441-453.

Segal, U.A. (1992). Child Abuse in India: An Empirical Report on Perceptions. *Child Abuse and Neglect*, 16, 233-232.

Segal, U.A. (1995), Child Abuse by the Middle Class? A Study of Professionals in India. *Child Abuse and Neglect*, 19, 217-231.

Segal, U. A., and Ashtekar, A. (1994), Detection of Intrafamilial Child Abuse: Children at Intake at a Children's Observation Home in India. *Child Abuse and Neglect*, 18, 957-967.

Singh, M.B., and Kaur, S. (1981), Mother-child Interaction in Rural and Urban areas. *Indian Psychological Review*, 20, 1-16.

Sinha, D. (1984), Some Recent Changes in the Indian Family and their Implications for Socialization. *Indian Journal of Social Work*, 45, 271-286.

Starr, R.H., Jr. (1988), Physical Abuse of Children. In V.B. Van Hasselt, R.L. Morrison, A.S. Bellack, and M. Hersen (Eds.), Handbook of Family Violence (pp. 119-147). New York: Plenum.

Straus, M.A. (1979), Measuring Intrafamily Conflict and Violence: The Conflict Tactics (CT) Scales. *Journal of Marriage and the Family*, 41, 75-88.

Straus, M.A. (1980), Stress and Child Abuse. *Child Abuse and Neglect*, 4, 75-88.

Straus, M.A., and Gelles, R.J. (1990), *Behind Closed Doors: Violence in the American Family*. New York: Anchor Press.

Straus, M.A., Hamby, S.L., Finkelhor, D., Moore, D.W., and Runyan, D. (1998), Identification of Child Maltreatment with the Parent-Child Conflict Tactics Scales: Development and Psychometric Data for a National Sample of American Parents, *Child Abuse and Neglect*, 22, 249-270.

Suman, S.K. (1985), Child Abuse in India. *Social Welfare*, 21-23.

Tang, C.S. (1998), The Rate of Physical Child Abuse in Chinese Families: A Community Survey in Hong Kong. *Child Abuse and Neglect*, 22, 381-391.

Wadley, S.S. (1993), Family Composition Strategies in Rural North India. *Social Science and Medicine*, 37, 1367-1376.

Whipple, E.E., and Richey, C.A. (1997), Crossing the Line from Physical Discipline to Child Abuse: How much is too much? *Child Abuse and Neglect*, 21, 431-444.

Wolfe, D.A. (1987), *Child Abuse: Implications for Child Development and Psychopathology*. Newbury Park, CA: Sage.

Wu, D. (1996), Chinese Childhood Socialization. In M.H. Bond (Ed.), *The Handbook of Chinese Psychology* (pp. 143-154). Hong Kong: Oxford University Press.

Youssef, R.M., Attia, M.S.-E.D., and Kamel, M.I. (1998), Children Experiencing Violence I: Use of Corporal Punishment. *Child Abuse and Neglect*, 22, 959-973.

Zigler, E., and Hall, N.W. (1989), Physical Child Abuse in America: Past, Present, Future. In D. Cicchetti and V. Carlson (Eds.), *Child Maltreatment: Theory and Research on the Causes and Consequences of Child Abuse and Neglect* (pp. 38-75). New York: Cambridge University Press.

Zuravin, S.J. (1989), Severity of Maternal Depression and Three Types of Mother-to-child Aggression. *American Journal of Orthopsychiatry*, 59, 377-389.

BAN ON EMPLOYMENT OF CHILD LABOUR IN HOMES AND DHABAS: AN UPHILL TASK

*Neera Bharihoke**

From October 10, 2006, the Government has prohibited employment of children aged below 14 as domestic workers or in tea shops and dhabas 13 occupations and 57 processes were already prohibited under the Child Labour (Prohibition and Regulation) Act, 1986. The gazette notification of October 10 prescribes a fine of Rs. 20,000 and imprisonment of upto one year against employers and establishments found engaged in child labour.

Child labour covers those children who are of the age of 14 years and below who are employed and exploited at the cost of their opportunities for development like education and recreation. Their needs for nutrition and health are also neglected or abused by their employer for low wages and in hazardous tasks. The phenomenon of child labour existed much before industrial revolution, but has become more visible during post-industrial revolution period. Children are exploited through wage, quasi wage employment and through self employment.

Despite Constitutional directives and enacted law, millions of children have been working in India in a variety of hazardous occupations ad no serious effort to remedy the situation has been in evidence so far. The notification of October 10, 2006 banning child labour in the domestic/ employment sector is not going to make much change in the employment of child labour in the time to come.

CONSTITUTIONAL PHILOSOPHY OF CHILD LABOUR

Article 21 A: Right to Education

The State shall provide free and compulsory education to all children of the age of 6 to 14 years in such manner as the State, by law, may determine.

---

* Lecturer Faculty of Law University of Delhi.

Article 24: Prohibition of Employment of Children in Factories, etc.

No child below the age fourteen years shall be employed in work in any factory or mine or engaged in any other hazardous employment.

Article 39: The State shall, in particular, direct its Policy towards securing

(e) that the health and strength of workers, men and women, and the tender age of children are not abused and that citizens are not forced by economic necessity to enter avocations unsuited to their age or strength.

(f) that children are given opportunities and facilities to develop in a healthy manner and in conditions of freedom and dignity and that childhood and youth are protected against exploitation and against moral and material abandonment.

Article 45: The State shall endeavor to provide, within a period of ten years from the commencement of the Constitution, for free and compulsory education until they complete the age of fourteen.

Article 21 A and Article 24 are under the heading of Fundamental Rights in the Constitution and Article 24 is better known as Right against Exploitation. Article 39 and 45 find its place in Directive Principles of the State Policy, Chapter IV of the Constitution of India.

Article 24 recognises child labour in non-hazardous employments. Constitution has not defined the term "Child" or "hazardous employments" thus leaving many hazardous employments from prohibition of child labour. Article 24, therefore, partially prohibits child labour.

LEGISLATIVE PROVISIONS

Apart from these Constitutional rights/ provisions, State has passed a number of number of Acts such as the Children (Pledging of Labour) Act, 1933, the Employment of Children Act, 1938 which has been repealed by Child Labour (Prohibition and Regulation) Act, 1986, the Factories Act, 1948, Shops and Establishments Act in various States and Union Territories, Child Labour (Prohibition and Regulation) Act, 1986 etc.

Legislative measures relating to child employment met with little success in ameliorating conditions of work of child labour[1]. Child labour's presence is visible in small industries and unorganized sector. There are often children employed below minimum age for employment, exploited by hiring for long hours of work with least payments, with no rest periods or leave provision. Legislation to uplift children's welfare in India exists only on paper with lip service being paid to Directive Principles.

Legislation to abolish or regulate child labour is already flooding the statute books. Today there are more than 250 central and State enactments relating to children, dealing with marriage, adoption, criminal law, reformatory service, probations, children homes, child welfare, education of children and other miscellaneous matters. Various legislations have been passed for uplifting, protecting, safeguarding and ameliorating labour conditions of child labour. But the existence of child labour is evident and that too with blatant violation of all these laws and safeguards.

IMPACT OF NOTIFICATION ON CHILD LABOUR BAN

As per the Child Labour (Prohibition and Regulation) Act, a"child" means a person who has not completed his 14th year of age.

- The Act prohibits employment of children in 13 occupations (now 15 after Gazette Notification of October 10, 2006) and 57 processes contained in Part A & B of the Schedule to the Act (Section 3).
- Under the Act, a Technical Advisory Committee is constituted to advice for inclusion of further occupations & processes in the Schedule.
- The Act regulates the condition of employment in all occupations and processes not prohibited under the Act (Part III).
- Any person who employs any child in contravention of the provisions of section 3 of the Act is liable for punishment with imprisonment for a term which shall not be less than three months but which may extend to one year or with fine which shall not be less than Rs 10,000 but which may extend to Rs 20,000 or both. ((Section 14).
- The Central and the State Governments enforce the provisions of the Act in their respective spheres.

The gazette notification of October 10, 2006, has been issued by the Central Government as an amendment by way of addition to the Schedule of the Child Labour (Prohibition and Regulation) Act, 1986. The Schedule provides for Occupations wherein a child cannot be employed. Earlier it consisted of 13 entries. Now the fourteenth entry wherein child labour is prohibited from 10 October, 2006 is *Employment of Children as Domestic Workers or Servants* and the fifteenth entry is *Employment of*

Children In Dhabas (Road Side Eateries), Restaurants, Hotels, Motels, Fee-shop Restaurants, Resorts, Spas Or Other Recreational Centres.

This implies that whatever provisions existed in Constitution or other legislative enactments relating to employment of child labour, be that of States or of the Centre, have been left untouched. Therefore the notification provides no relief to child labour employed in non hazardous factories or in unorganized sector or other places which was permissible under the various enactments like the Mines Act, 1952, the Factories Act, 1952, the Beedi and Cigar Workers (Condition of Employment) Act, 1966 etc. And as mentioned above these laws have failed to deliver any results in regard to abolition of child labour. There has been no amelioration in their working conditions or otherwise regulation of engagement of child labour.

CHILD LABOUR: A PLETHORA OF FACTORS FOR ITS EXISTENCE

Child labour is considered to be a necessary evil and economic necessity. There exist many social, economic and administrative obstacles in a progressive policy on child labour. A sophisticated trafficking of children is developing which involves children from both industrialized countries and third world nations.

Child labour is a socio-economic problem. Karl Marx observed that the result of buying the children and young persons of underage by the capitalist is physical deterioration and moral degradation.[2] Childhood is the most important period of life and is considered to be the base of the life. During this period, moulding and shaping of the life takes place and the behaviour, conduct and sentiments are moulded. Tomorrow's citizens of India are on the brink of collapse in the building stage itself.[3]

Most of the children from poor families are forced to work for their livelihood as well as to lend a hand towards the finances of the family. However, children are most vulnerable victims. They have no political lobby to campaign for their rights. They do not have any avenues of protest. Child workers cannot form any union to fight for their demands. They work more and charge comparatively less than adult workers. The abolition of children as domestic servants or in dhabas is not going to eradicate child labour in these sectors.

INEFFECTIVE IMPLEMENTATION OF LAWS

The reasons for failure of child labour abolition laws are as many as are the factors or causes for their existence. First and foremost is that there is no provision for rehabilitation of displaced children. This may lead to breeding of juvenile criminals.[4] Ban on their being employed as domestic servants will force them to look for alternate avenues of employment which may be more or equally ghastly as regards working conditions, exploitation or hazardous for them as compared to their employment as domestic servants or in dhabas. Examples of such industry could be glass industry or even slate industry. In glass industry, children are forced to work near furnaces kept at 1400 degree Celsius. In slate industry slate dust results in thousands of silicosis deaths.

Further the government has shown no commitment to implement the Act effectively over the period of last twenty years. Mere enhancement of the punishment for employing children does not fulfill the object of the Act unless it is effectively implemented. Children are exploited not only by their employers but also by their own parents. They are deprived of education. In spite of laws, exploitation and neglect continues and miseries are suffered. Children are employed under uncertified employment or false certificates.

The exploitation continues except that those who employ these children are unashamed about the fact and hide them from the authorities. According to government estimates[5], there are about 2,56,000 children working in areas coming under the ban-1,85,000 as domestic labour and over 70,000 in dhabas and restaurants.. But NGOs monitoring working children put their population at 2 crore, with 10 lakh children estimated to working in Delhi alone.

THE NEED FOR REHABILITATION

At such a large figure of child workers, the process to rehabilitate the rescued children is essential. Else the enactments passed for benefit of children will continue to be violated by beneficiaries because the enactments do not make any provision for them against starvation. There is a need to implement the ban and rehabilitate the children. But given the strange division of responsibilities in the government too much is being ask for. The legislation came from the labour ministry because "Work" is out of the purview of Women and Child Department (WCD). The WCD's concern is child care, not child labour. And education that's the burden of the HRD ministry. Is it any wonder a travesty is made of the implementation or enactment of the legislation?[6]

Millions of children have no access to food, drinking water, shelter, timely medical facilities and education. For them our constitution and Acts having main objective of protecting children from exploitative and hazardous employments has remained a myth. The notification of abolition of child labour has given birth to a haunting question as to how is government going to rehabilitate the children, to be rescued from city's dhabas, restaurants and homes Though that raises another issue as to how would the authorities come to know about children employed as domestic servants. And there is also the problem of those employers who claim that the children working in the dhabas, restaurants, tea shops or repair shops are their own.

The stark reality is that even if the officials rescue child labourers, there is not enough infrastructure and mechanism to rehabilitate them. At present there are only 20 Transition Educational Centres (TEC) for rescued child labourers.[7] At best they can accommodate 1000 children at a time, whereas according to some NGOs, the number of child labourers in New Delhi is in lakhs.

It would take months to restore the children to their homes in cases where they have families[8] and much more time to provide them shelter or to be sent to institutional care to rehabilitate children where they don't have homes or families. One voluntary organisation[9] estimates that to rehabilitate all kids would account for Rs. 50 crore for food alone and in all, it takes Rs 2, 000 per month to shelter, food, clothe and educate a child.An action plan is the need of the hour so as to dole out tasks to various departments so that all of them work in harmony for the eradication of child labour from the city. It is not clear which department of government is responsible for the rescued child, the labour ministry, the WCD or the social Welfare Ministry. There is also a need to increase the number of TECs. The enforcement of a law for compulsory universal primary education is the first step towards elimination of child labour. But the issue is far too complex for one single solution to suffice. A blanket ban will not serve the purpose.

Mere legislation on papers cannot assure implementation of teaming millions of these helpless souls. The political will to bring up all children, whatever be their economic background, as healthy, honest and useful child is needed. Unless all forces of society are integrated to produce composite results, social justice as envisaged by our Constitution will remain a dream. In order to attain progress, social justice must be coordinated with Rule of Law and various sociological aspects and then alone it will lead to a better understanding of various human problems.

NOTES

1. S. Kumar Sharma in Right Against Exploitation and the Bonded Labourers in India: A study in Distributive Justice Perspective, 1987, Aca LR, 311-26.

2. Karl Marx in Das Kapital. Chapter XV. Sec 3 (a).
3. Dev Singh Negi, in Bonded Labour, 1976 at p 94-108.
4. Mohd. Aqther in An Overview of Child Labour (Prohibition and Regulation) Act, 1986, 1989 (3): 61 An LT 35-38.
5. Census 2001.
6. Anuradha Raman in Life is an offence, Outlook, October 30, 2006.
7. Amitabh Shukla in Child Workers Face Rehab Blues, Oct 13, 2006, The Times of India.
8. According to newspaper reports, many of the children are from Jharkhand, West Bengal and Bihar.
9. Quality Institutional Care.

CHILD WORKER-POVERTY AND HUNGER: A STUDY AMONG THE STONE CRUSHERS OF BALASAN RIVER BED

*Samar Kumar Biswas**

INTRODUCTION

In all societies, irrespective of caste, race or area, children occupy a very important position. They are considered as an extremely valuable asset for society. The importance of a child in the life of most people can be seen from the fact that the birth of a child is heralded with much fanfare and celebration. The importance of children is stated in Vedas also. When we look into a child's eyes expect to see hope, trust and innocence but when these signs of childhood are replaced by betrayal, hunger, fear and suspicious, we need to take stock of ourselves and the society we have created. For every labour there is a reason and a child for every labour under heaven: a child to hoist and a child to tow, a child to hire out and to lock in, a child to reap and a child to sow, a child to push and a child to pull. He is every where.

The phenomenon of child workers is global and is as old as the history of mankind. Child workers continue to be a problem of enormous dimensions through out the world. Deprivations are his daily lot. He has lot to narrate about losses than gains and in many cases he is not even aware of the losses. He is a child deprived of physical, intellectual, social, spiritual and psychological growth. However in practice, socio-economic condition of large majority of the children of today's developing countries is very tragic. In many instances, children are seen as a source of cheap labour to augment profits/incomes in various enterprises and families. Children have been the victim of the prevailing social, economic and political systems that exploit and suppress them. As a result, remarkably high proportions of children are being deprived of minimum basic facilities needed for their overall development. India has the dubious distinction of having the highest child worker population in the world.

* Lecturer , Department of Anthropology, North Bengal University, Darjeeling-734013.

Poverty coupled with illiteracy and unawareness on the part of parents and constitutional provisions which forbid employment of children below 14, the practice of child labour exist in almost all sectors of Indian economy, like the Agrarian, Industrial and the Service sectors. There are several forms of child labour—migrant labour, invisible labour, bonded labour, wage-based labour, self-employed and so on. UNICEF has classified child worker into three categories: (a) with-in the family: children helping in the domestics chores or family occupations like agriculture/pastoral work, handicraft, khadi and cottage industries etc. (b) with-in the family but outside home: children do local agricultural work, assist in shops, help in construction, harvesting crops, laundry/recycling of waste and so on. (c) Outside the family: children are employed in bonded work, doing errands for the rich land lord; various works in the village industries, skill trades, industrial unskilled occupations and informal sector like shoe shining, car washing, begging, prostitution and so on. Here the child worker those who are engaged in stone based work and in different type of related activities like- stone crushing, stone collection, sand gathering and loading.

The Concept of Child Worker: In the studied area, the working conditions of the child workers are–they do not work under any 'Malik' or 'Sardar' (Master), they work with their family and by other means. Here all the family members are part of the production unit. The supply of child worker is solely governed by the living standard of a family and children are sent to work to meet on the demand.

A distinction is often made between child work and child labour. The Operation Research Group (ORG) based in Baroda defined child worker as: "a working child is one who was enumerated during the survey as a child falling within the 5-14 years age group and who is at remunerative work, may be paid or unpaid and busy in any hour of the day, within or out side the family" (Rehman, 1992: 297).

Child work refers to occasional light work done by children, which, in most societies, is considered to be an integral part of the socialization process of the child. While helping parents at home and in family farms, children learn to take up responsibilities, acquire certain skills and prepare themselves for the tasks of adulthood. According to the ILO most children work but all the works by children cannot be considered child labour. 'Child labour', on the other hand implies something different in which young people are being exploited, or overworked or deprived of their rights to health, education, or just to childhood. United Nation (1990) also defines child labour in the similar fashion. In some instances, 'child worker/labour' is defined as a person in the age group of 5-14 employed for hire or reward, on a full time basis and includes a self-employed child and a child assisting his/her parents in their occupations for two or more hours a day.

The distinction between both child work and child labour may be stated as follows—

	Child Work		*Child Labour*
1.	Light work (children learn to take responsibilities).	1.	Hard and hazardous work, exploitation.
2.	Respect of children's right to health and education.	2.	Deprivation of rights to health and education.
3.	Occasional.	3.	Constant and for long hours.
4.	Legal	4.	Illegal

Source: T.M. Dak, (ed.), 2002, 'Child Labour in India'.

The present article is primarily based on a field study among the 72 (100%) stone crusher families near the Siliguri town, named as 'Tari Jot' of Balasan Colony under Atharokhai Gram Panchayet of Siliguri-Naxalbari C.D. Block in the Darjeeling District of West Bengal. The 'Balasan' is an important river of North Bengal that passes from near Siliguri town with natural resources, like sand, stones/pebbles, boulders etc. The said colony was developed near by Balasan river depend on stone based economy, because manual labour force is the main capital for earning. Most of the family members are engaged in this work where children too are not exempted from that. Here different aspects of children, mainly, who are engaged partly or fully in stone based work, particularly their socialization, early development, education and health situation have been highlighted in this article.

DEMOGRAPHIC COMPOSITION

Child worker is a problem of the whole world and it is more acute in the poor countries belonging to the third world, mainly due to economic backwardness of the families. Thus, economic reason move the whole family to work as a production unit. The children too get engaged in such work by any means. In the rural areas the children belonging to the poor agro-based families generally work with their family members. On the contrary, in the sub-urban/ urban slum areas, most of the poor children have to work either with their family members or individually, or under any person on daily wage basis or on monthly basis.

The incident of child labour in India is one of the highest in the world (Geeta, Lal-1997). As per the estimates of the 55th round of the NSSO

Survey, 1999-2000, the estimated number of working children in the country was 10.4 million. However the ILO study in 2002 puts the number of working children at 246 million out of whom 110 million works in the mining and chemical sectors. Within India, the highest number of child workers is found in the state of Andhra Pradesh, that is 14.70 per cent, and the lowest number is found in Kerala, that is 0.31 per cent (Census-1991). The 1991 Census showed that the total number of working children in West Bengal was 593,387 and it was highest in the district of Midnapur, that is 14.72 per cent (Census-1991). It may also be noted that Midnapur had the highest population compared to the other districts of West Bengal, its total population being 8331912. On the other hand, Darjeeling had the lowest population rank with a total of 1299919, but at the same time one sixth of the total working children of West Bengal was in this district (Census-1991). As per Census 2001, Darjeeling district had 10,122 working children of whom 5582 were males and 4540 were females. In this studied area all the able members of the stone crushing families are engaged in this work and most of the children too are not exempted from that. Where 76.25 per cent children belonging to 5-14 years from 55 (76.39%) families do the same [Table 1]. This per centage of involvement of child work may be higher than the general statistics of any state or countries.

Table 1
Distribution of Stone Based Work Families on the basis of Child Workers (Primarily or Secondarily)

Total Family	*Child Working Family*	*Absentee Child Worker Family*
72 (100.00)	55 (76.39)	17 (23.61)

FAMILY BACKGROUND OF CHILD WORKER

The family background of the child workers, namely caste, religion, type of family, educational status of parents, occupation of parents, number of members in the family, levels of income and tenurial pattern of occupation are the most important determinants of child working or the involvement of children in different jobs to assist in family income.

All the families of this colony are migrants who came from the adjoining districts, states and countries also and among them 79.34 per cent families came from Bangladesh from time to time. The people of this colony are mainly rural, and most of them have a very poor economic (87.27%) and educational background [Table 5]. They migrated to this place as homeless, landless, and moneyless groups of people. Previously they resided in remote areas and they had a poor knowledge about the outside world. Poverty being the common feature of all the people, most of them are living in a poor socio-economic condition.

All of the studied people are Hindu Rajbanshi belonging to an important scheduled caste of North Bengal. In case of family type, out of 55 (100%) families, nuclear family is higher (67.27%) than that of joint family (32.73%), [Table 2]. The educational status of the child workers and their parents is not remarkable and it is quite low. Among the parents, 13.64 per cent are illiterate, 45.45 per cent can sign only and 40.91 per cent have the formal school education. Formal education among the fathers and mothers is 45.45 per cent and 36.36 per cent respectively. Here 64 per cent fathers and 55 per cent mothers upgraded upto primary level, that is, I - IV class standard ; while only 36 per cent fathers and 45 per cent mothers have the education upto the secondary level, that is, V–VIII class standard [Table 3].

Table 2
Distribution of Child Worker Families on the Basis of Type of Family

Total No. of Families	*Type of Family*	
	Nuclear Family	*Joint Family*
55 (100)	37 (67.27)	18 (32.73)

Table 3
Distribution of Educational Level of the Parents of the Child Workers

Category	*Number of Persons*	*Illiterate*	*Can sign only*	*Literate (Formal education)*	*Educational category of the Literate persons (Formal Education)*	
					Primary level (I-IV)	*Secondary level (V-VIII)*
Father	55 (100.00)	3 (5.45)	27 (49.09)	25 (45.45)	16 (64.00)	9 (36.00)
Mother	55 (100.00)	12 (21.82)	23 (41.82)	20 (36.36)	11 (55.00)	9 (45.00)
Total	110 (100.00)	15 (13.64)	50 (45.45)	45 (40.91)	27 (60.00)	18 (40.00)

In case of occupational background of the fathers a higher proportion (92.73%) is engaged in stone crushing as primary occupation, and 3.64 per cent are engaged in day labour and the same in businesses. Among the mothers, 74.55 per cent are engaged in stone crushing as a primary occupation [Table 4]. All of the family members work through out the day but earn a very little. Where 34.55 per cent of the families earn up to Rs. 1000/-; 52.73 per cent of the families earn upto Rs. 1001-2000/- per month; and only 12.73 per cent families have a monthly income above Rs. 2000/- per month [Table 5]. With such low level of income it is very difficult to lead a normal livelihood of their average five member's family. By this poor income they can not fulfill their minimum requirements of the basic amenities and as a result, they go under poverty, poor health condition and poor residential situation. They do not get sufficient food, purified drinking water and so on. As such, most of them suffer from malnutrition and various diseases. These adverse conditions also affect the children. But they have not any alternation. The parents being unable to give proper care and guidance as well as the minimum basic facilities and living conditions to their children. The children are debarred from many facilities and are forced to take up stone crushing along with their family members.

Table 4
Distribution of Father and Mother on the basis of their Occupation

Category	*Primary Occupation*				
	Stone Crush	*Day Labour*	*Business*	*Household work*	*Total*
Father	51 (92.73)	2 (3.64)	2 (3.64)	-	55 (100.00)
Mother	41 (74.55)	-	-	14 (25.45)	55 (100.00)

Table 5
Distribution of Child Worker Family on the basis of Monthly Income

Monthly Income (in Rupees)	No. of Families	Percentage
Upto 1000	19	34.55
1001-1500	21	38.18
1501-2000	8	14.55
2001-2500	5	9.09
Above 2500	2	3.64
Total	55	100.00

NATURE OF WORK OF THE CHILDREN

In the studied area, 76.25 per cent children are engaged in stone based work. Their nature of work, duration of work and activities are varied.

Some are partly engaged, while the others are fully engaged in this work and all are treated as 'Child Worker'. On the basis of their nature of work, the child workers of Tari Jot can be divided into three categories. The first category consists of those—who work individually; the second, who work with their families; and third one is comprised of workers who work in a group. Among the total child workers 94.12 per cent work along with their families, 3.92 per cent work individually and 1.96 per cent work in groups. It has been reported that all the female child workers work with their family members and they do not work individually or in a group [Table 7].

Table 6
Distribution of Child Workers

Age group (Years)	*Male*	*Female*	*Total*
5-9	16 (41.02)	23 (58.97)	39
10-14	33 (52.38)	30 (47.62)	63
Total	49 (48.04)	53 (51.96)	102

Table 7
Distribution of Child Workers on the Basis of Nature of Participation

Age (in years)	*Nature of Participation*								
	Individually			*With Family*			*Group Wise*		
	Male	*Female*	*Total*	*Male*	*Female*	*Total*	*Male*	*Female*	*Total*
5-9	-	-	-	16	23	39	-	-	-
10-14	4	-	4	27	30	57	2	-	2
Total	4	-	4	43	53	96	2	-	2
	(8.16)		(3.92)	(87.76)	(100.00)	(94.12)	(4.08)		(1.96)

Another point worth notice is that 86.27 per cent child workers work on part time basis and the rest (13.73%) of them are full time workers. Most of the part time workers are school going children. After returning from school again they find some engagement in stone based work. It is reported that 63.73 per cent child workers work in the morning and afternoon sessions while 22.55 per cent children have no fixed time. The working hours for the part time male and female child workers vary from 1-4 hours in a day [Table 8]. Most of the child workers (44.12 %) are engaged in stone crushing; while sand gathoring 12.75 per cent; stone collection 19.61 per cent; and others 23.53 per cent have not any specifications, they do all types of work [Table 9]. Most of the children are forced to do this work either part time or full time to support their families as well as themselves.

Table 8
Distribution of Child Workers on the Basis of Duration of Work

No. of Child Workers					
Part time worker (1-4 hours)				*Full time worker (5-8 hours)*	
Male		*Female*		*Male*	*Female*
Morning / Afternoon	*No Fixed time*	*Morning / Afternoon*	*No Fixed time*		
29 (72.50)	11 (27.50)	36 (75.00)	12 (25.00)	9 (18.37)	5 (9.43)
40 (81.63)		48 (90.57)			
88 (86.27)				14 (13.73)	

The economic condition of the child worker's family is quite low. As such it is very difficult for them to maintain their minimum livelihood. Despite of their hard physical labour they are unable to earn any surplus income. That's why, each and every member of the family is engaged in this work and the children are working to support their family as labour forces as well as economic forces.

Table 9
Distribution of Child Workers on the Basis of Type of Work

Type of Work	*Number of Child Workers*					
	Male		*Female*		*Total*	
	No.	*%*	*No.*	*%*	*No.*	*%*
1. Only Stone Crushing	21	42.86	24	45.28	45	44.12
2. Only Sand Gathering	6	12.24	7	13.21	13	12.75
3. Only Stone Collection	11	22.45	9	16.98	20	19.61
4. All Type	11	22.45	13	24.53	24	23.53
Total	49	48.04	53	51.96	102	100.00

PROBLEMS RELATED TO CHILD WORKER

Several types of problems have been noticed among the child workers and it is perhaps largely due to their teenage engagement and other related factors. The problems include their personal grooming, school attendance, duration of work, social and economic insecurity and so on. The major problem of the child workers is that they do not get the minimum educational facilities. As the major constraint of the parents is illiterate or belong from primary level of educational background, the children are unable to get the proper guidelines of education from them. The lack of minimum infrastructural facilities in the houses and the poor income level as well as economic uncertainty of the families are the factors owing to which most of the poor parents are not able to provide tuition or coaching or any other guidelines to their children for better results as well as their education. A large proportion of child workers (24.72%) have not got any formal schooling as during school-time mostly they are busy in collecting stones, sand or crushing stones, this involvement is necessary for their economic needs as well as survival. Child workers are mostly first generation learners. Most (59.09%) of their parents are illiterate or can sign only. Though some (40.91%) have school education, this is mostly limited to primary level (60%)and secondary level (40%) [Table 3]. Due to this poor educational background most of the parents are not well aware or fail to understand about the significance of their children's education. Non-attendance or absenteeism in school is mainly due to the fear of losing family income. Among the child workers 75.51 per cent males and 73.58 per cent females face a major economic crisis [Table 10]. The study also reveals that 72.73 per cent of the families have a monthly income of only up to Rs. 1500/- [Table 5]. Besides these the social environment is another major cause for which educational progress gets seriously affected. It has been seen that alcoholism, gambling, inter-familial and intra-familial conflicts among the adults, have a tremendous effect on the practices of non enrolment, dropout or absenteeism or irregular participation in school which again seriously affecting the educational environment.

Table 10
Distribution of Child Workers on the Basis of Problems Faced by Them

Age group	*Type of Problems*											
	Economic				*Social Insecurity*				*Others*			
	Male		*Female*		*Male*		*Female*		*Male*		*Female*	
	No.	*%*	*No.*	*%*	*No.*	*%*	*No.*	*%*	*No.*	*%*	*No.*	*%*
5-9	12	24.49	16	30.19	2	4.08	4	7.55	2	4.08	3	5.66
10-14	25	51.02	23	43.40	2	4.08	3	5.66	3	6.12	4	7.55
Total	37	75.51	39	73.58	4	8.16	7	13.21	5	10.20	7	13.21

The other problems faced by the child workers are insufficiency of nutritious food, unhygienic health condition, malnutrition and other diseases. The people in the studied area mainly take rice, vegetables and pulses for lunch and dinner; regular breakfast and tiffin are a mere dream to them. Most of the people are unable to buy sufficient nutritious food like animal protein, milk and fruits. A major section of the people use the polluted river water for their daily necessities like cleaning, bathing, washing, cooking and worst even for drinking. Besides these, the lack of drainage system and poor sanitation also affect their health system. Most people use the open river bed for defecating. That is why, waterborne and other infectious diseases are very common in this area and child health as well as child growth has been seriously affected. Due to these several causes, the problem of the children are in very bad shape. The overall situation does not permit them to avail of proper education, health facilities and others, and ultimately, this situation force them to take up work with their families or outside the families at such early ages.

OBSERVATION AND CONCLUDING REMARKS

Education is the right of every child and 'Education for all' is the slogan, but most of the child workers are debarred from it. Though some of them have received education but it is mostly confined in the primary level. They do not get the minimum educational facilities, infrastructure and minimum requirements. Thus, from very early childhood the fundamental right of education is lacking among the children. Though children are getting enrolled to the primary schools the expense of higher education is becoming unaffordable to the parents. Recent initiatives of local panchayat are trying to redress the situation but proper educational awareness is lacking to the present parental generation thus the whole effort of the local administrative body is not reaching to its proper implementation. Most of the children of Tari Jot, Balasan colony go to the work field and take part in work with their parents because it has become obligatory to them. Several complex factors are responsible for this particular involvement. Firstly, the stone based economy requires more and more labour force. This nature of work entices the child to get involved as a worker. Secondly, the parents think that the involvement of the child in this work can bring some money and here the importance of education has become secondary to them. Ultimately this practice of sending their children to earn at a very young age is affecting their development potentials.

During the partition of India and Pakistan in 1947, and at the time of independence of Bangladesh in 1971, these migrants were forced to leave their own homes, land and property and became landless, rootless and homeless. Subsequently they settled in different parts of West Bengal and also in other states of India. Many of them came to North Bengal and settled down here and this process is continuing till now. Most of them being undocumented migrants, they are facing a serious economic setback which is forcing them to get engaged in this work along with their children. The children are supposed to do this work as their whole family participates as a production unit. And this is the common scenario in most of the poor families belonging to the Third World Countries because the poor economic infrustucture of these families forced them to engage in any type of work.

Though the above discussed picture is that of only 55 stone crushing families it is near about the same as the other stone crushing families of North Bengal and so on. Economic hardship is not only confined to the stone crushing families, it is also true for the other landless, rootless as well as poor families of both rural and urban areas. A huge number of children are forced to get engaged in different works with their parents, or individually, or group wise. Some also work under the owners of tea stalls, hotels, sweet shops, grocery, many small industries etc. and it is only due to acute economic crisis. Hence the children work not only for their ownselves but also for their families. Being economically, educationally and socially backward, they face several difficulties like higher percentage of child mortality and other health hazards. Most of the parents are unable to provide the required medical treatment to their children. Thus, their ill health and diseases are not getting its full prevention. Generally they have a single dwelling room along with kitchen. Proper drainage system is lacking very much. Even the basic requirements of sanitation and hygienic drinking water is also absent in their daily livelihood. From an early childhood a child needs a homely affection from where his psychological development occurs. But here a child grows up with acute poverty, improper care of his parents and with the feature of hard struggle for the survival. Thus, from early childhood his psychological feelings also turns into the way of serious complexities. They face major constraints in their daily life. Their standard of living is very poor. Due to working involvement, the children are debarred completely from enjoying their childhood. They are not able to spend enough time in the play-ground or in educational activities; modern health facilities or sufficient nutritious food are a mere dream to them. Sometimes they also get involved in many unfair, unsocial and illegal activities. They do not get proper love, affection, and guidance from their parents and that is why, they grow up with out learning the proper value system of the life as well as the society. It should not be forgotten that "child is father of man and citizen of tomorrow". So, in this context there is a great need for the proper development of both the mental and physical health as well as all aspects of the social and cultural life of the children and it is necessary not only for the future development of the societies as well as for the nation. In concluding remarks it may be said that development of a child should be given the first priority through proper education, health care facilities and poverty alleviation. Otherwise this scenario will be continued generation after generation and the child worker would not only be the obligation in stone crushing families of Balasan river bed but also be the same of other landless, rootless poor families of both rural and urban areas.

To solve the problem, Government has taken a number of initiatives, like Child Labour Abolition Act, 1986; and again in October, 10, 2006, Supreme Court has given the verdict to abolish Child Labour. But to eradicate the root cause of the said problem, first of all those families should be provided the economic security and education. Otherwise their poverty and hunger would force them to send their children in hard manual labour either along with the family which we generally call child worker or outside of the family under any master known as child labour.

In this regard Confucius remarked that "if you want to improve society, improve family", and it should be through the proper development of child as because "child is father of man and citizen of tomorrow".

REFERENCES

Ahuja, R. (1997), 'Social Problem in India'. New Delhi: Rawat Pubications.

Burra, N. (1995), Born to Work: Child Labour in India'. New Delhi: Oxford University Press.

Biswas, S.K. and S. Bhattacharjee (2005), The Stone Crushing Women of Balasan River Bed An Appeal From Humanitarian Perspective, *South Asian Journal of Human Rights*. Vol. 1(1-2), January- December-2005. New Delhi: Serials Publications.

Biswas, S.K. and S. Bhattacharjee (2006), Effect of Land Alienation: A Study between a Scheduled Caste and A Primitive Tribal Group, in Swapna, H. Samel (ed.), Rights of Dalit. New Delhi: Serials Publications.

Case Study, The ETI Child Labour Project (2001- 2002).

Census of India (1991), New Dellhi: Government of India.

Census of India (1991), West Bengal, Part–II A, Series-26. New Delhi: Government of India.

Census (2001), Working Children in India-An Analysis.New Delhi: Government of India.

Choudhary, D.P. (1995), 'A Dynamic Profile of Child Labour in India'. New Delhi.

Dak, T.M. (ed.) (2002), 'Child Labour in India'. New Delhi:Serials Publications.

Devi, P.A. and Meenakshi, N. (2003), Working Children in Coimbatore City, A Case Study, *Social Welfare*: 8-12.

Gupta, R., M.K. Dhilon., N. Mehrotra (1998), Female Child Labour in Domestic Work, *Indian Journal of Social Research*. Vol. 99 (1): pp. 49-53.

Jaya, N. and T.V. Yamuna (2001), Socio-economic Profile of Child Workers of Hosiery Industries in Tirupur Town, Tamil Nadu, *Man in India*, Vol. 81 (152) : 123-137.

Kar, J. (2002), The Issue of Child Labour in Orissa: A Developmental Approach, *Indian Social Science Review*, Vol. 4 (1) : 117-131.

Kabeer, N. Geetha, B. Nambissan. and Ramya Subrahmanian (2003), Child Labour and the Right to Education in South Asia. New Delhi: SAGE Publication.

Lal, Geeta. Child labour in India: An overview, *Social Change:* September-December 1997: Vol. 27 No. 3-4, Pg. 57-65.

The Indian Child-A Profile (2002), Ministry of Human Resource Development. New Delhi: Govt. of India.

Misra, L.D. (2000), 'Child Labour in India'. New Delhi: Oxford University Press.

Misra, S. (2003), Combating Child Labour in India, *Social Welfare*: 4-7.

Mittal, Sujata (2004), *Child Development* Vol. 1,2 and 3. Delhi: Isha Books Publications.

Sharma, V.K. (1990), Child Labour and Urban Informal Sector. New Delhi: Deep and Deep Publishers.

Singh, A.N. (1990), Child Labour in India: Socio-economic Perspective. Delhi: Shipra Publications.

Sinha, S.K. (1991), 'Child Labour in Calcutta'. Calcutta: Naya Prakash, Sumangala, M. and B.S. Nagarjan, 1993. 'Economics of Child Labour and Fertility'. Delhi: B.R. Publishing Corporation.

Pasayat, C. (2002), Child Labour and Child Rights, *Social Welfare*.

Tikoo, S. (2003), Urban Slums and Child Labour, *Social Welfare*: 14-18.

UNICEF (1997), *The State of World's Children*.

UNICEF (1994), *The Right to be a Child*: UNICEF Indian Background Paper. Unpublished Paper, UNICEF, New Delhi.

AN EMPIRICAL STUDY ON CHILD RAGPICKERS IN WARANGAL CITY

Lal B. Suresh & T. Joga Chary***

INTRODUCTION

Child Labour is a global phenomenon. It exists both in the developing and the developed countries though with a difference in cause and magnitude. Its prevalence is more in the developing countries as compared to the developed ones, because the families, to which the working children belong, are in an urgent need of income of child labour for their subsistence, whereas children in the developed countries are often working for pocket money.

Informal sector of the rural and urban economies of the developing countries is an important source of employment for a major chunk of labour force particularly child and women labour. Though the sectoral distribution of working children differs from country to country yet the child labour is predominantly confined to agricultural sector followed by services and industry.

The working children themselves may not be productive but are capable of relieving the adults for productive employment by engaging themselves in domestic chores and looking after younger children in the home. This way, they allow their parents to spend more time on income generating activities.

In the urban areas child labour exists both in the formal as well as informal sector enterprises, though its presence in the latter is more frequent. In small manufacturing enterprises, which are spread over wide locations and can ignore legal restrictions, the children often work along with their elder relatives and friends. They are possibly not paid directly but indirectly through a supplementary wage paid to the main worker. The main occupations where the children are employed in the

* Asst. Professor of Economics, Dept. of Economics, University Post-Graduate College, Kakatiya University, Karimnagar-505001 (A.P.)

** Professor of Commerce, University Post-Graduate College, KU, Karimnagar (AP).

urban sector are those, which don't require heavy labour. The packing, pasting, labeling, wrapping etc., are the main activities of the children working in small industries. Domestic servants, workers in hotels and restaurants, canteens, wayside shops and establishments or as hawkers, rag pickers, newspaper-sellers, peddlers, coolies, shoeshiners, vendors, helpers in repair shops are the main categories of the working children in the urban areas. The construction work is another activity, which also attracts children. In this context, child labour is considered a source of cheap labour and means of quick profits by their employers. The supply of child labour always exceeds the demand for labour. Consequently, child labourers do not have any bargaining power and are more easily exploited by their employers. They are employed at much lower wages than adults and made to work for longer periods.

Amongst various causes of child labour, unemployment, poverty and indebtedness of the households are the most important. Many parents secure advances from the landlords or the employers and repay the loans in terms of their child labour. In some cases the children are compelled to migrate temporarily to the nearest cities or the urban areas of adjoining states to earn the necessary subsistence.

In most of the developing countries, parents depend on their children to assist them in performing important work at home or outside. In absence of any social security measures, dependence on children increases and in many cases the working children are the main or the only support for many parents. In this way, children of the poor are economically valuable to their parents as a source of labour contributing to household income and social security in their old age also.

OBJECTIVES AND METHODOLOGY

The present study seeks to investigate into the "Socio-economic conditions and problems of Child Ragpickers in Warangal city" with the following objectives.

1. To study Socio-Economic conditions of Child Ragpickers.
2. To Estimate their Earning patterns.
3. To examine their consumption patterns.
4. To examine the effects of Environment on their health condition.
5. To identify the factors responsible for poor conditions of the Child Ragpickers.
6. To identify their problems at work.

150 Ragpickers have been selected randomly from different parts of Warangal city in A.P. for purpose of collecting data. A structured schedule has been used in which questions and items regarding the socio-economic background and other problems of the child rag pickers are included. Efforts have been made to elicit their free and frank views.

PROFILE OF WARANGAL CITY

The study area, the Warangal city was once the capital of the Kakatiya Dynasty. It is an ancient town after which a district, a commissioner's division in the erstwhile Hyderabad state and again is a district in the present Andhra Pradesh state. Warangal city is one of the oldest urban settlements of Andhra Pradesh and has had a chequered history since ages. It is now the second largest urban centre, next to metropolitan Hyderabad in the Telangana region of Andhra Pradesh. After 1953 October 1st, a few taluks were separated from it and was formed into the Khammam district. The district of Warangal lies on the North-East of the state between 17-49 (degrees) and 80-43, (degrees) East. The geographical total area is 12, 846 square kilometers. It is bounded on the North by Karimnagar district, on the South by the Nalgonda district. It is located between the river Godawari and Krishna along the trunk Railway line connecting Madras with Delhi. It is situated in the heart of the Telangana region of Andhra Pradesh. The ancient town of Waranagal is situated on the South Central Railway, about 138 km. North of Hyderabad city.

POPULATION

Warangal district occupies an area of 12,846 sq. kms and has a population of 28,18,832 of which 14,36,666 are males and 13,82,166 are females. Of the total population, 22,72,210 live in rural areas whereas 5,46,622 live in urban areas.

About 93 per cent of population are Hindus, 5 per cent Muslims and below two per cent Christians. There are a few Jains and Sikhs.

WORLD SCENARIO

In India, the extent of child labour is not as large as in Turkey, Thailand, Bangladesh, Brazil, Pakistan, Indonesia, Mexico, and Egypt. It is estimated around 5.2 per cent of the total labour force in India as against 27.3 per cent in Turkey, 20.7 per cent in Thailand, 19.5 per cent in Bangladesh, 18.8 per cent in Brazil, 16.6 per cent in Pakistan, 12.4 per cent in Indonesia, 11.5 per cent in Mexico and 8.2 per cent in Egypt.

However, in Srilanka the child labour accounts for only 4.4 per cent of the total labour force. Even the workforce participation rate of children in the age group 10-14 years in India (10.4 per cent) is less than Bangladesh (33.3 per cent), Nepal (22 per cent) and Pakistan (11.6 per cent), but greater than Indonesia (8 per cent) and Srilanka (1.8 per cent).

In India, as elsewhere, no proper estimates of child labour are available. Various social scientists and non-governmental organizations have estimated their own figures depending upon their methodology and definition of child labour. Thus, the estimates of child labour are not exact and vary from source to source. However, according to the ILO India contributes to about a third of Asia's child labour and a fourth of World's working children. According to various social scientists, with estimates varying between 60 to 115 million, India has the largest number of working children in the world. An important feature of child labour in India is that nearly eleven to eighteen million working children are street children and approximately fifteen million children work as bonded labourers.

Historically, child labour has been prevalent in Germany in: (a) workshops as well as factories of the Proto-Industrial and early Industrial Phases between 1750-850 (b) Factories during the peak phase of industrialization. Even as early as in the 16th and 17th centuries, child labour was practiced in orphanages and workhouses. In 1667, for instance, children worked together with convicts at the loom in the orphanage of Basel, in order to turn out products of sale. One of the first to criticize the cruel exploitation of children in workshops, particularly in the workshops run for orphans, was Christian Gotthilf Salzmann, a representative of the Enlightenment movement. His criticism is voiced in his novel "Car Von Carlsberg or on Human Misery" which appeared in 1783. The portrayal of the scene wherein five children are "tortured" in a worship for orphans because they had not "spun up all the wool and cotton given to them", "though fictitious, probably does hear some degree of authenticity since surrogate parents at the orphanages were often discharged because they were torturing the children too much during work or because the mortality rate in the orphanages had risen too high as result of child labour".

In Ancient India, it was the duty of the king to educate every girl and boy and parents could be punished for not sending their children to school called Ashrams, which were really residential schools under a Guru (a learned sage). Child labour existed only in the form of child slaves. Children sometimes even less than 8 years of age were purchased to do so-called "low and dishonorable" work. Kautilya (4th century B.C.)

considered it degrading to make children work on such jobs and hence prohibited the purchase and sale of slave children below 8 years (Kautilya: Arthshastra III).

In the late 17th century, the most significant change was the growth of organizations involving the employment of large number of artisans. The Dutch silk factory at Kasimbazar in Bengal employed 700-800 weavers. But the characteristic unit of production was still the small unit. "The persistent dominance of family based work units indicated that any disciplined organization of an industrial society was not in sight."

In the middle of the 19th century, there was an enormous growth of European industry in India especially during 1860-70 as seen by the growth of the tea, coffee, indigo, and jute industry. At this time, the factory industry began taking the place of handicrafts. It was in the fifties that the cotton and jute industry and coal mining were started in an organized way. However, even in 1880 the number of people employed in these industries was rather small, even though people were quickly being driven out from their old crafts.

It was in the early 19th century that a change started taking place. Factory type units started springing up. Agriculture became more mechanized and small land holdings were no longer economically viable. Small landowners left their lands and started working as farm labourers on bigger farms. Factories required cheap and plentiful labour. Children were employed both on farms and in factories because they provided a cheap, uncomplaining labour force as against adults who could be more demanding and hence more difficult to handle. In the course of the 19th and early 20th century, people especially in the European countries, became conscious of the evils of this exploitation of children and the International Labour Organization (ILO) was setup in 1919 to formulate guidelines to improve the working conditions of children and ban their employment before the age of fourteen. In the preamble to the constitution of the ILO, it is stated that in many regions the conditions of Labour are such as to result in untold misery, which disturbs the peace and harmony of the world. Children and young persons must be protected. At the very first session of the International Labour Conference, a convention was adopted fixing the minimum age as 14 years for children in industrial employment. Between 1919 and 1965, there were 10 conventions on the minimum age. Finally in 1973, the convention concerning Minimum Age for admission to Employment (No 138) and the Recommendation (No. 146) were adopted and these replaced all the recommendations of earlier conventions. However, much needs to be done through national legislation in the various countries. According to the ILO, the number of working children, the world over increased from 43 million to 52 million between 1970 and 1979 of these approximately 29 million were from south Asia, 10 million from Africa, 9 million from East Africa, 3 million from South America and about 1 million from the developed countries.

THE CHILD RAGPICKERS

Society, as a whole, regards ragpickers as antisocial elements, an embarrassment to the community, and unfits to live. However their useful contribution to society and ecology is little understood and generally ignored. The waste collected by these children is recycled and produces 25% of the paper, the packing materials, egg trays, plastic and metal household items, etc., used in homes. This benefits the society and world ecology enormously by the production of cheaper household goods, and the slowing down of the destruction of the already threatened forests. It also helps to prevent the waste materials piling up as mountains in city centers. The ragpicker's valuable contribution to society should not be ignored and taken for granted.

As a street children, between five and eighteen years of age, they earn their livelihood by polishing shoes, washing cars, finding parking spaces, ragpicking, selling lottery tickets and news papers, etc. They also work as coolies and helpers in automobile repair shops, construction sites, and hotels. Their average earnings vary between Rs. 15 to 20 per day, while the more experienced ones earn Rs. 25 to 40. The Girls are forced into prostitution at an early age. Arising at dawn, the ragpicker children start their rounds, with feet bare and backs aching, they carry heavy gunny bags that contain the day's pickings. Sometimes on foot they travel over 20 kilometers each day for the best pickings. Their clothing is filthy, tattered, ill fitting, and wholly inadequate for protection especially, when the weather is wet and cold.

Life is very hard as they rummage (competing and fighting with stray dogs and cattle) through every filthy garbage heap in railway stations, bus stations and other locations, etc. All recyclable garbage is collected and sorted into: paper, plastic, bottles, bones, metals etc. If the day's collection is bad, they resort to stealing for survival, if good, they rush to the nearest wayside shop to fill their starving bellies. They receive a meager pittance from the scrap dealers for their collections and sometimes this pittance is withheld to recover previous loan. Very often they starve. If another dealer negotiates a better price, the child is frequently beaten and tied up by the dealer who holds them almost as bonded slave for collection of scrap items.

A major part of their income is spent on drugs, alcohol, solvent abuse (sniffing solvents), and gambling. They frequently become involved in street fights. With little money and too much freedom, they are vulnerable and fall prey to any kind of situations and exploiters.

After sorting and selling their day's collection at the scrap dealer, they spend their nights on the streets, in graveyards, railway stations etc, where they are exploited and abused. Older ragpickers and perverted people give them drugs or threaten them for sexual purposes, thus exposing them to AIDS, and other diseases.

A ragpicker is not a beggar. He works hard and considers ragpicking as a source of livelihood and a profession of his choice. It enables him to earn money, and gives him ample amount of free time. The ragpicker feels proud and considers that he is master of his own life. Ragpickers socialize among themselves, share food, money, problems and love with children of their age group.

They are involved in drugs, alcohol, smoking, gambling, and unhealthy sexual habits. Since their income is less than their expenses, due to bad habits, they are perpetual debtors to the retail scrap dealers. They participate in stealing, street-fighting, and delinquent activities. They are unwelcome guests at weddings, social gatherings, and shopping zones. They are physically vulnerable to health problems and infectious skin diseases. They are victimized socially through poverty, illiteracy, and rejection. With no facilities available for bathing or laundry, they are forced to live in filth and squalor. They are tempted to live with anti-social gangs for security and survival. It is very difficult to isolate one member and group pressure is strong to retain them in gangs, to perpetuate their old habits.

They soon become dependent, both physically and mentally, on their readily available addictions, enabling them to forget for a while their pitiful existence. This is a huge problem, and expert help is needed to treat their physical and psychological dependence and addiction. There are many disappointments for the worker, as relapses are very common. Their integration into society is difficult, as the public has preconceived ideas about the ragpickers not to them.

Though the majority of the street children manage to earn their daily bread, in many cases, the street children are: Abused and exploited, Deprived: lacking job, money, food and shelter, they are forced into begging, thieving, drug peddling, pimping, and prostitution. Regarded as juvenile delinquents and antisocial elements, they are often falsely accused of crimes and sent to secure homes of correction, or worse, put into adult prisons. Engaged in gambling, a popular pastime on the street, denied education, cut off from parental care and guidance. Most importantly, the children on the streets remain deprived of their basic needs of food, shelter, clothing and the security of family love and a home. With no one to care for them, these children have to fend for themselves and cope with the problems of the world.

Street children and ragpickers suffer from diseases like scabies; lice; chronic dysentery; lung, ear, nose and throat infections; cuts; and abrasions. These are caused by poverty, malnutrition and the unhygienic surroundings in which the children are forced to work and live.

SUMMARIZED FINDINGS OF THE STUDY

Following are the summarized findings of the empirical study conducted in Warangal town on 150 child ragpickers.

1. The Socio-economic background of the sample respondents shows that majority of the child ragpickers are male, belonging to age group 11-20 years.
2. Nearly 66% of them i.e., 99 out of 150 are illiterates.
3. 68 per cent belong to schedule caste, 20 per cent to schedule tribe and 12 per cent to backward class.
4. Majority of the ragpickers is from rural areas of the same district. Other ragpickers came from the urban areas of neighbouring districts like Khammam, Nalgonda.
5. Majority of the child ragpickers' family type is nucleus, and size of the family is identified as one of the important reasons for ragpicking, as children of bigger families are forced more to go in for ragpicking.
6. 73 per cent child ragpickers' place of staying is railway station and bus stations.
7. Nearly 58 per cent of them have taken to ragpicking for last five years.
8. Illiteracy, poverty, indebtedness, other economic factors are important reasons for their ragpicking.
9. 97 per cent are earning below Rs. 1200 per month, while the highest and lowest earnings are Rs. 1600 and Rs. 400.
10. Nearly 80 per cent of child ragpickers' families are still having huge debts and source of debt is moneylenders.

11. Majority of child ragpickers goes for collection of garbage on foot.
12. Nearly 90 per cent of the respondents are facing different problems at the time of ragpicking and they suffer from infections and ill health.
13. About 70 per cent of the ragpickers are not getting reasonable price from the garbage buyers.
14. Majority of child ragpickers are having bad habits such as consumption of alcohol, tobacco, and gutka in various forms and some have tendency to go in for homosexuality.
15. Majority of the ragpickers do not purchase significant consumer durable items.
16. Majority of child ragpickers are spending money on consumable and unproductive items, such as beedi, wines, tobacco and cinema.

CONCLUSION

The problem of child ragpickers has to be addressed from at least two angles. The first one is the attitudinal change of the society. Street children represent the end point of a complex set of factors, which require a multitude of resources and efforts to address the problem. A situation that has been created due to the existing social, political, and economic pressures in society and needs to be addressed at the root of the problem, through an attitudinal change in the society.

However, change is not an easy process. A change that demands a modification in attitudes, as well as change in the social, economic, and political situation, is a slower process. Policy makers, industry, society need to view the street children with compassion and sensitivity.

Concentrated and specific efforts of the NGOs, Philanthropists and the Govt. are needed in this context. Counseling, informal talks and befriending, Non-formal education setting up training centers, teaching marketable and useful skills, will change their life for better.

NOTES AND REFERENCES

1. UNICEF, The state of world's children (1997), Oxford University Press-New Delhi.
2. Dingwaney, Manjari, et.al, (1988), Children of Darkness; A manual on child labour in India (Rural Labour Cell-New Delhi).
3. Bhatty, Kiran (1996), Child Labour Breaking the Vicious Cycle, Economic and Political Weekly, Vol. XXXI, No. 7, Feb. 17.

4. Sharma, B.K. and Vishwa Mittal (1990), Child Labour and Urban Informal Sector, Deep and Deep Publications, New Delhi.
5. Kaul, A.J. (1998), Child Labour Law-An Overview (V.V.Giri National Labour Institute, Noida).
6. Rodgers, Gerry and Standing, Guy (1981), Economic Role of Children in low-Income Countries, International Labour Review, Vol. 120, No. 1, Jan-Feb.
7. Naidu, D.A. (1978), Child Labour Participation in India A State wise Census Analysis, International Institute for Population Studies, Bombay.
8. Government of India, (1975); National Policy for Children, New Delhi.
9. Gokhale, S.D. and Shani, N.K. (ed),(1979), Child Labour in India, Somiya, Bombay.
10. Khatu, K.K. (1983), Working children in India-Operation Research Group, Baroda.
11. Lal, A.K. (1977), Politics of Poverty A study of Bonded Labour, Chetana, New Delhi.
12. Muthayya (1992), Child Welfare–Existing Conditions and Parental Attitudes, Hyderabad.
13. Ministry of Welfare Child Labour in India a Statistical Profile, Government of India, New Delhi.
14. Narayana Reddy, G. (1992), Women and Child Development Some Contemporary Issues, Ashish publications, Allahabad.
15. Naidu, Usha A.K. and Amini, R. Kapadia (1985), Child Labour and Health Problems and Prospects, Tata Institute of Social Sciences, Bombay.
16. District Profile of Warangal –2001, 2002, and 2003.

STATUS OF TUIKUK MINORITY CHILDREN IN MIZORAM WITH SPECIAL REFERENCE TO BAWNGVA AND DARLAK VILLAGES IN MAMIT DISTRICT

*Y. Nilachandra Singh**

INTRODUCTION

High fertility and prodigious numbers of surviving children may be economically rational propositions from the point of view of parents in many parts of the developing country like India. During the period when children are adherents of their parents' household the significant cogitation with respect to the micro allusions of high fertility is the economic roles and productive endowments of children and their production has been ruled by their parents[1]. The primordial finding from ongoing research furnishes a basis for investigating the work endowment of children to their parents' household. The results intimate that male children may become the net producers as early as age 13, indemnity for their own cumulative assumption by age 15, and indemnity for their own and one sister's cumulative consumption by age 21.

The data are collected from Bawngva and Darlak villages of Mamit District situated in the western part of Mizoram lying between the latitude 23˚.52' to 24˚.30' north and the longitude 90˚.22' to 92˚.30' east[2] by interviewing 396 couples and 763 unmarried children living in 205 households[3]. This district was formerly under Aizawl District. The villages have been chosen as a study area because in respect of its economy, ecology, population density and high fertility, they seemed not atypical of the country[4]. The villages have the Tuikuk population of 1558 in 2006. They are scheduled tribe and a member of the Mongoloid groups. In Mizoram there are mainly three communities, namely the Mizos, the Chakmas and the Tuikuks. All these communities living in the state are found only in this district. In the context of Mizoram the latter two are

* Principal, Mamit College, Mamit, Mizoram.

the minority communities. Hence,the Tuikuk community in these villages of Mamit District is selected for the study area. Given the land area for Bawngva and Darlak villages of 202 acres, the population density is about 7.71 persons per acre. The age structure of Bawngva and Darlak villages casts back the high population growth rate – 763 out of 1558 persons are less than 16 years old.

Similar to other hill tribes of North Eastern Region of India, agriculture is the mainstay of the Tuikuks. About 90.00 per cent of the total work potency of these villages in this district is engaged in agriculture and its allied activities, i.e., shifting cultivation[5] (locally it is known as jhuming). As it is true for most of rural Mizoram especially the Tuikuk community, the village hings on the cultivation of rice, maize, yam, pumpkins, beans, cucumbers, brinjals, chillies, tobacco, cotton etc. for subsistence[6]. These crops are the main well–head of the family income for the preponderance of village households, either through production on their own holdings or as wage employment. Farmable or cultivable land tantamounts to the bulk of the total cornucopia in the village. In the midst there is hardly enough land support the present population and the subsisting land is immensely unequally doled out, despite that the cultivable lands in the villages are evenly assigned among all households, each would have only a few acres and this area hardly ample to meet subsistence desideratum for an average size household with 7.60 members and unample to light upon the desideratum of more prodigious households. Hence, the most villagers of this community in Bawngva and Darlak are penniless by any touchstone[7]. Besides, the dropped out rate of school going Tuikuk children is very high in the state.

The continued rapid population growth is likely to whet the coercion on resources and excoriate over all economic welfare from the point of view of the villages. However, the village is not the locus of doggedness influencing human reproduction in the context of Mizoram. Such decisions have been made by households and individuals in riposte to the socio-economic predicament they front onto; and from the micro point of view of the household, the economic welfare allusions of continued high fertility and prodigious numbers of surviving children are not nearly as clear-cut as they appear to be from the macro allusion[8].

In the context of household economic organization the welfare presumption of fertility consequences to parents are to a large scale dependent on the productivity of children. The present paper investigates the roles of Tuikuk children in the household detachment of labour in the villages of Bawngva and Darlak and attempts to determine their net productivity while living as minor members of their parents' household.

The economic activities of children in these two villages-the amount and nature of labour they supply-can best be appreciated in the circumstances of the household's demand for labour[9].

DEMAND FOR HOUSEHOLD LABOUR

In Bawngva and Darlak villages of Mamit District of Mizoram household activities compel a large scale of labour. Labour since qua non can be somewhat capriciously pooled into the two: labour mandatory for the nurture and upkeep of the household, that is not directly productive in the sense of creating the family income to the capital formation physically; and labour mandatory for creating the family income and capital, what it is known as productive work. Incorporated in the first type, which it typifies as enabling labour insofar as it sets free other household members to occupy in activities which are directly productive, are housework activities such as cleaning and sweeping house as well as compound, washing clothes and utensils, preparing food, cooking, providing cooking fuel and water, looking after young children and for other dependents and incalculable other small domestic works. The second type, productive work is made up principally of activities associated to agricultural cultivation, incorporating animal husbandry[10].

There is a taut detachment of labour between the sexes in the Tuikuk community of Bawngva and Darlak villages as there is rural Mizoram in general. Women are out-of-the ordinary in work which keeps them within or else to the homestead and men are out-of-the ordinary in field work and other activities compelling physical mobility. The high degree of sex role specialization is embedded in this community. Owing to the fact that most productivity activity materialize away from the homestead, a main result of the sequestration task roles by sex is that men are the primary producers of income in the general household.

(a) Upkeep of the Household

The chores related with food preparation and arrangement incorporating proviso of fuel and water, are the most time-consuming forms of household nurture work. Food commonly flows into the household in forms that compel substantial operating before consumption, and the technology available to household for food processing or operating is primitive. For example, unhulled rice must be dried, husked and cleaned. Husking is effectuated using a cumbersome, a heavy wooden plank with a pestle on one end that is operated see-saw style. One woman compels about four to five hours to husk 40 kg. of paddy. Therefore, presuming that a household having 7 members takes about 7 or 8 kg of rice a day, a full day of husking is called for, on average, every 5 or 6 days. The Tuikuks take food thrice in a day; sun rise food, noon food and evening food respectively. Rice processing also requires repeated winnowing and drying. During the long summer drizzly season, because of inadequate grain storage facilities, paddy must be brought and dried at every opportunity. Such other food crops as chillies compel equally time intensive processing but the large scale of households are forced to engage in the less time-consuming searches to meet fuel needs. Common source of the family fuel is dried bamboos.

Many of the activities typified as an enabling labour could possibly be construed as productive. Husking, for example, adds a computable amount of market value to paddy. Husking is mulled over housework in this context, however, because rice is most often marketed unhusked by cultivators (i.e. jhumias), and husking at home is virtually always for the purpose of home consumption rather than sale. These subtleties become comparatively insignificant when one observes the interdependence of housework and unobscurely productive work. Both types of work are mandatory and within limits recommended by the nature of social organization and levels of technology and opulence, both must to a great extent be satisfied by household labour.

(b) Income–Generating Activities

In these villages the main well–head of the family income for households are crops production on own land, agricultural wage work, non–agricultural wage work, petty trading and fishing. The present study observes that crop production is the most important well–head of the family income for 81.00 per cent of all Tuikuk households and the second most important well–head for an additional 11.00 per cent. The cropping patterns are dictated by the slope of hills and the monsoon climate. The main crops in these villages are rice, chillies and sesame, and virtually all the land holdings in the villages are planted with the mixed cropping pattern. None of the Tuikuk land is irrigated, and the variety of paddy grown are all local; no high yielding varieties are tilled. The technology employed in crop production is very simple[11] and production is dovetailly labour intensive. The estimates of the man–days of labour mandatory for holding one acre area of each of the three main crops are presented in the Table 1. The total labour requirements for rice cultivation is more than chillies and sesame in view of the fact that under the multiple cropping pattern the jhumias spend on the selection of site, cutting trees, bushes, etc. and set the fire while no labour is engaged on the first three items (Table 1) for the cultivation of chillies and sesame. These crops are the depended crops. Rice is the main food. Generally, the bulk of shifting cultivating households incur some labour costs in their production owing to the fact that labour demand for certain operations is congregated in brief time periods. The range to which labour must be hired to meet these requirements hinges on the size of the shifting cultivation area and the size of the household labour force. There are substantial advantages to households supplying most or all of their cultivating labour.

Table 1
Estimated Labour Requirements, Production Cost and Output for Bawngva and Darlak Villages of Mamit District of Mizoram

Particulars	*Rice*	*Chillies*	*Sesame*
Labour (man-days)			
Selection of site	1	na	na
Cutting trees etc.	8	na	na
Fire	1	na	na
Dibble the seeds	8	1	1
Wedding (3 times in a year)	24	18	21
Harvest	8	5	5
Carrying charge	8	2	4
Thresh	6	5	4
Total man-days	64	31	35
Variable costs			
Mean wage rate (Rs. Per head and day)	37.39	37.39	37.39
Labour costs (Rs.)	2392.96	1159.09	1308.65
Seeds (in kg.)	16	2	5
Seeds (Rs. Per kg.)	2.81	100	20
Seeds (Rs.)	50	200	100
Gross output			
Yield (in kg.)	960	100	200
Price per kg.	2.81	100	20
Gross output (in Rs.)	2698	10000	4000

Note: na = not applicable
Source: The data are computed from the primary data collected for the present study.

A high cost for labour may be complication for a family to mop, even though the labour is a must to help yield the family income. Most households face persistent cash flow difficulties and acts for which labour is true–to–typely cash reserves are already low for many households in view of the fact of the long time since the previous harvest. A high wage bill at the harvest time may force the jhumias to sell yield at unenthusiastic prices in order to pay labourers or repay loans from the neighbouring Mizos. In general wage labour needs more administration than family labour and are probably less efficient. Moreover, while it is simple in shifting cultivation accounting to value family labour at the market price of labour, the opportunity cost of family labour is conventionally less than the market wage rate[12]. A household in which the only bodily competent children are female has to hire male wage labourers rather than employing female family members in field operations especially in cutting the trees etc.

Among other well–heads of the family income in these villages agricultural wage employment–fundamentally in the crop production of the neighbouring Mizos–is one more important well–heads of the family income for 11.00 per cent of the households in Bawngva and Darlak villages. The opportunities for such employment and the wage rate differ with the seasonal timing of major operations in the shifting cultivation. The culminated periods in the villages and surrounding areas are during the month of April and May for sowing; June, July and August for weeding and the last part of September and October for harvesting respectively. In sluggish periods some men and women leave their villages ephemerally to be on the look out for employment in other Mizo villages with various crop cycles.

Non–agricultural wage employment is the most important well–head of the family income for 2.00 per cent of all households. For both sexes, the opportunities for temporary, non-agricultural wage work are fewer than for agricultural work. One important well–head is the PWD road maintenance, an activity that is congregated in the rainy season. For this some young boys are engaged. For women, almost the only opportunity for nonagricultural employment is as maid servants in the households of the Mizos.

Trading supplies the primary well–head of income for 3.00 per cent of the Tuikuk households in these two villages and is an extra well–head of income for many more. The scale of operation is invariably small, and the commodities traded are for the most part food stuffs. They have established stable dealings with clients and suppliers of Damchhora (Tripura) that secure a relatively steady stream of the family income. Part–time traders flow into the market for brief periods, usually during the eve of Christmas festival and other festivals as well as deal in seasonal commodities such as chillies, sesame, etc. whose prices approach to yo–yo promptly. Hence, they act at a higher level of risk than full time Mizo traders.

Fishing is an extra well–head of income for a large segment of households. The fishing season extends over the period from late summer through December when the monsoon waters move further off. For a very few households fishing is the most important well–head of income, however the great majority of households fish on a small scale and only for home consumption.

CONTRIBUTIONS OF TUIKUK CHILDREN TO BE HOUSEHOLD ECONOMY

Casual finding of children in the villages leaves a clear impact of pensive, tenacious activity beginning at a very young age. One is struck by the seemingly precipitate metamorphosis in Tuikuk children's status, from quitely dependent recipients of parental satiation and amity to subordinate, responsible economic factors. The full metamorphosis from dependent child to adult–equivalent worker, regardless of how, comes about a long period of time. Consigned that most parents work out direct control over their children for a limited, notwithstanding the fact that not insubstantial, period of the Tuikuk children's productive lives, the timing of the metamorphosis is an important determinant of the net economic value of children to parents.

A child's productive life cycle within the parental household can be viewed as having four distinct stages. After an initial period when the child is quitely dependent, the child becomes more and more economically active but yields less than she/he consumes. Then comes a period during which the child yields more than she/he consumes but less than an adult yields. Finally the child's productivity becomes identical to an adults.

The rate at which a child's total productivity increases hings on: the rate at which the child begins working; the relevant amount of time the child puts in working; the apposite competency of children in doing economic activities; and the productiveness of the chores to which children to allot their time. These factors are highly interrelated; nonetheless, to decipher the parley, they will be dealt with independently.

(a) Age at Which Tuikuk Children Begin Work

Physical maturity and force of the Tuikuk child, the ability stands in need of carrying out the activity, and the culturally specified detachment of labour all impact the age at which a child sets about to engage in specific work activities. Table 2 shows the mean and minimum ages by sex at which the Tuikuk children set about a multifariousness of economic activities.

Table 2
Economic Activities of Unmarried Tuikuk Children Aged 4 and Older Residing in Parents' Household for Bawngva and Darlak Villages of Mamit District of Mizoram

Activity	*Males (485)*			*Females (361)*		
	Work Participation (%)	*Mean Age (years)*	*Lowest Age (years)*	*Work Participation (%)*	*Mean Age (years)*	*Lowest Age (years)*
Cultivation						
Cutting trees etc.	36.68	12.17	11.00	a	a	b
Weed	48.82	10.09	8.00	2.32	a	b
Harvest	51.31	9.77	8.01	2.35	a	b
Carry	59.28	8.90	6.00	13.08	a	8.00
Thresh	54.00	9.73	7.00	6.22	a	b
Harvest other crop	65.52	8.47	6.00	63.11	7.05	6.00
Animal husbandry						
Graze	59.62	8.32	6.00	10.00	a	9.00
Cut fodder	54.00	8.54	8.00	9.38	a	b
Tend fowl	34.11	a	5.00	64.62	6.83	5.00
Tend goats	26.20	a	7.00	25.41	a	6.00
Fishing						
Fish	59.70	8.54	8.00	20.82.	a	7.00
Make nets	22.00	a	9.00	3.80	a	b
Operate boats	62.74	8.15	6.00	15.52	a	8.00
Home maintenance						
Repair floors	5.51	a	11.00	47.73	9.30	6.00
Repair thatch	7.40	a	14.00	0.81	a	b
Repair walls	19.54	a	11.00	0.00	a	b
Clean tools	40.20	12.11	8.00	24.65	a	6.00
Marketing						
Purchase	49.41	10.38	8.00	6.17	a	b
Carry goods	54.00	8.92	8.00	6.20	a	b
Tend sale	48.21	10.57	8.00	3.11	a	b
Housework						
Food preparation						
Dry	12.28	a	8.00	49.22	9.31	6.00
Husk	5.57	a	b	39.00	10.28	8.00
Clean	0.66	a	b	50.07	9.41	7.00
Wash food	2.43	a	b	61.49	8.10	6.00
Cook	0.67	a	b	46.17	9.60	7.00
Serve meal	15.88	a	8.00	52.33	9.08	7.00
Wash dishes	8.53	a	b	74.61	6.98	6.00
Collect fuel	68.32	6.50	5.00	78.44	6.91	5.00

Activity	*Males (485)*			*Females (361)*		
	Work Participation (%)	*Mean Age (years)*	*Lowest Age (years)*	*Work Participation (%)*	*Mean Age (years)*	*Lowest Age (years)*
Sweep	20.67	a	5.00	78.40	6.42	6.00
Wash clothes	38.47	a	4.00	83.65	5.70	5.00
Fetch dater	79.34	5.83	4.00	83.67	5.74	5.00
Carry message	84.68	5.29	4.00	80.83	4.81	4.00
Care child	73.28	5.95	5.00	85.40	5.76	5.00

Note: a – indicates that proportions ever having participated did not coverage to 100.00 per cent at older ages.
b = lowest ages are not reported if overall participation is less than 10.00 per cent

Source: Same as Table 1, and in this Table the number of cases are given in parentheses.

An investigation of the all–embracing involvement rates of male and female children indicates that the sexual division of labour presents itself instantly. For male children there is little general involvement in housekeeping or food preparation; likewise for females there is very little involvement in marketing activities or with the oddity of harvesting chillies and sesame in shifting cultivation. For every type of assignment, specialization is obvious. With regard to animal husbandry, boys take care cattle, that entails large grazing and searching fodder, while girls look after chickens. With regard to home upkeep men and boys mend mat walls and thatched roofs, while young girls mend bamboo floors.

Children of both sexes set about their economically effective lives about age 6, doing such assignments as collecting fuel, fetching water, carrying messages, and looking after young children. Physical compulsions restrict the age at which they can take on extra duties. For example, a minimum level of physical force is mandatory before a boy can handle a group of bullocks and a minimum weight is mandatory before a girl can act the cumbersome for husking rice.

Boys vow duty for the care of cattle around age 8 or 9. At the same age they set about to engage in fishing and the operation of skiffs, a necessary mode of conveyance during the annual flood. On average, male children set about agricultural task at roughly age 11. The young mean ages are for relatively unable and physically unnagging task and carrying paddy from field to threshing floor. The oldest mean age 14, is for sowing paddy, an activity that stands in need of both great stamina and skill.

Girls are active sweeping, cleaning utensils and dishes, looking after chickens and hand–picking chillies by age 6 or 7. On average they set about to engage in most rice processing and food arrangement activities between ages 9 and 10.

A consequential extra factor for determining a child's age of ingress into an economic activity is opportunity. A great many activities hing for their achievement on such physical assets as land, livestock etc. For households that do not possess the indispensable assets, a child's involvement can only take place through wage employment, for which, in turn, opportunities may also be restricted. Table 3 shows class specific estimates of the ages at which the Tuikuk children set about task. The classes have been ground on the size of landholding. Economic class I is made of households owing to 6 acres and above; Economic class II of households owing to 1 acre–5 acres, and Economic class III of landless households. The activities are grouped according to their dependence on assets.

Table 3
Mean Age of Entry into Economic Activity by Activity, Economic Class and Sex of Unmarried Children Age 4 and Older Residing in Parents' Household for Bawngva and Darlak Villages of Mamit District of Mizoram.

Activity	*Males*		
	Economic Class I 6 acres–& above (63)	*Economic Class II 1 acre–5 acres (151)*	*Economic Class III Landless (271)*
Requiring Assets			
Cutting trees etc.	11.60	11.20	15.59
Weed	10.40	10.33	10.50
Harvest	9.77	9.65	10.57
Carry paddy, Chillies etc.	7.80	10.15	9.80
Thrush	9.49	9.76	10.30
Pick chillies	8.01	8.00	9.71
Livestock			
Graze cattle	7.82	9.61	9.30
Collect and Cut fodder	8.27	9.20	9.22
Other Assets			
Clean tools	11.05	11.93	13.11
Operate boat	8.66	8.05	10.35
Not Requiring Assets			
Fetch water	6.31	6.02	5.27
Carry message	5.36	5.21	4.48
Care child	6.60	6.37	5.92
Collect fuel	7.90	6.40	6.20
Make purchase at Market	11.50	9.47	10.11
Carry goods to market	10.00	8.31	9.64
Tend sale at market	11.87	9.00	11.00

Activity	*Females*		
	Economic Class I (38)	*Economic Class II (102)*	*Economic Class III (221)*
Requiring Assets			
Tend fowl	7.28	6.90	6.63
Husk	11.45	10.06	9.82
Pick chillies	8.50	7.01	6.52
Not Requiring Assets			
Fetch water	6.50	5.02	5.00
Carry message	5.49	5.11	4.68
Care child	5.62	5.11	5.00
Sweep	7.22	6.38	5.49
Wash food	8.55	7.90	7.47
Cook	10.31	9.88	5.69
Serve meals	9.30	9.21	8.65
Wash dishes	7.36	7.28	7.00
Repair floor	10.09	8.75	8.50
Wash clothes	8.90	8.00	7.82
Collect fuel	6.90	5.13	5.54
Winnow Rice	10.01	9.68	8.63

Source: Same as Table 2.

The mean ages at which male children become active in crop cultivation, livestock care and other activities which utilize or hing on a assets are invariably lower for Economic class I than for Economic class III. These age variations are quite substantial, averaging around 1.50 years, nevertheless ranging as high as 4.00 years. They set in owing to the fact that, for the most part, children of the landless can employ in these activities only by being employed for a wage, and wage employment is limited for young children. Children of owners of productive assets, accordingly can set about task at a significantly earlier age in a large number of uncircuitously productive activities having need of assets.

On the other hand the male children of the poor set about task at earlier ages than male children of the better-off for such household maintenance activities as fetching water and collecting fuel. The consistently positive association between the mean age and economic class for activities which do not hing on assets in even increased hiting for female children. The better-off are increased fit and increased likely to engage outside labour to do household works. At the same time the poor have enormous prerequisite for young children to presuppose these comparatively unproductive responsibilities in order to fit parents and older children to employ in income–generating task.

(b) Children's Time Inputs to Work

As juxtaposed with task benchmarks in the midst of the fully-grown population of this community, the sum of time, the Tuikuk children use up working the assignments of their time to various types of task. Table 4 reveals the mean hours worked per day for the spacious groups of activities. The animal care takes account of all activities associated with the looking after and feeding of cattle, chickens, ducks and goats; crop production also embraces all activities associated with the production of field crops and homestead gardening, but the activities of husking, drying and cleaning of paddy have been plopped out from it. Both agricultural and non–agricultural wage employment have been coined as wage work or wage task. The other productive tasks are handicraft production for either home consumption or sale at the market. Besides, the activities of housekeeping and food preparation, housetask necessitates childcare and other useful and necessary, with the exception of not straightforwardly productive work.

The data in Table 4 reveal that, on average, both sexes fully developed aged 22-59 do the work merely more than 9.00 hours per day. The worktime for men has been used up in straightly productive work, i.e., 8.02 hours, at the same time, it is for women in housework (7.63 hours). In case of Tuikuk children both male and female work long hours at every ages.

The children aged 4–6 years do the work approximately one–fifth as long as the fully grown population and their worktime proliferates to one–half a fully grown population workday by ages 7–9, to three–quarters by ages 10–12 and at 13 and above, they do an average, as long as or longer than men and women.

The sum of worktime passed in instantaneously productive work or task intensifies at about the identical rate as total time worked in case of boys. All boys aged below 16.00 years use up comparably more time in the activities of animal husbandry than men. Notwithstanding, by about age 8, boys use up more than half their work time employed in the more instantly productive activities such as crop production, wage work and trading. Despite the fact that they continue to use up comparably more time in animal care than the fully grown, and boys use up the same sum of worktime as men and women in the most productive activities by about age 14. Meanwhile girls use up approximately the same total worktime as boys at each age, they use up invariably less time in diametrically productive work.

Table 5 indicates that, among the male children aged 10 and older those from the landless households do markedly more work than those

Table 4
Mean Number of House Worked Per Day by Age and Sex for Bawngva and Darlak Villages of Mamit District of Mizoram.

Activity	*Age*											
	4-6		*7-9*		*10-12*		*13-15*		*16-21*		*22-59*	
	M	*F*	*M*	*F*	*M*	*F*	*M*	*F*	*M*	*F*	*M*	*F*
Animal care	0.64	0.31	1.48	0.69	2.04	0.60	1.47	0.06	0.79	0.10	0.48	0.08
Crop production	0.43	0.45	0.88	0.40	1.74	0.80	2.25	0.51	2.31	0.35	2.49	0.59
Wage work	0.00	0.00	0.22	0.42	1.90	0.06	3.07	3.00	2.89	0.38	2.38	0.45
Trading	0.00	0.00	0.86	0.00	0.33	0.08	1.50	0.00	0.97	0.00	1.13	0.00
Fishing	0.12	0.00	0.45	0.00	0.40	0.08	0.98	0.00	0.92	0.27	0.30	0.00
Others	0.00	0.00	0.18	0.00	0.46	0.41	0.25	0.38	0.55	0.80	0.55	0.57
Total Productive	1.19	0.66	3.00	1.52	6.87	2.03	9.52	2.24	8.45	1.92	8.02	1.68
Total housework	1.09	1.22	1.18	4.03	0.81	5.80	0.71	6.80	0.76	7.75	1.15	7.63
Total work	2.28	1.88	4.18	5.55	7.68	7.83	10.23	9.04	9.21	9.67	9.17	9.31

Source: Same as Table 3.

from the landed classes. In total workday, the difference between the highest and the lowest economic classes in case of the male children aged 13 and other is about 3.00 hours. The boys aged below 10 years from the landless households do fewer hours overall than boys from the landed households; and they also use up correspondingly less time in promptly productive work. This is undeviating with the unidentical control of productive assets, which restrict the early productive employment of the poor, while acquiesce in such employment in the midst of the better-off. Besides, despite the out and out variations between economic classes in hours engaged by males, hours engaged by children in each class approach the full–grown–homologous workday at similar rates for all economic classes. The boys aged 10–12 work, on average, 9.33 hours, of which 5.00 hours have been used up in wage employment for the landless households. Hence, the male children come into view to be of roughly identical significance in each class with regard to their time inputs relative to the fully grown sexes.

Table 5
Mean Number of House Worked Per Day by Age, Sex for Economic Class for Bawngva and Darlak Villages of Mamit District of Mizoram

Economic Class	*Age*											
	4-6		*7-9*		*10-12*		*13-15*		*16-21*		*22-59*	
	M	*F*	*M*	*F*	*M*	*F*	*M*	*F*	*M*	*F*	*M*	*F*
Economic Class I												
Animal care	0.90	0.60	1.72	0.70	3.61	0.82	2.21	0.00	1.21	0.32	0.91	0.10
Crop production	0.74	0.29	1.20	0.43	2.81	0.69	4.50	0.40	3.42	0.31	3.89	0.79
Wage work	0.00	0.00	0.00	0.00	0.02	0.00	0.00	0.00	1.10	0.00	0.39	0.00
Trading	0.00	0.00	0.39	0.00	0.00	0.00	0.00	0.00	0.00	0.00	0.58	0.00
Fishing	0.01	0.00	0.61	0.00	0.29	0.00	0.00	0.00	0.00	0.81	0.68	0.00
Others	0.00	0.00	0.00	0.00	0.50	0.41	0.10	0.21	0.10	0.78	0.53	0.22
Total productive	1.65	0.89	3.92	1.13	7.23	1.92	6.81	0.61	5.83	2.22	6.98	1.11
Total Housework	0.95	0.82	0.74	3.11	0.53	6.77	0.88	7.59	0.90	8.69	1.20	8.58
Total work	2.60	1.71	4.66	4.24	7.76	8.69	7.69	8.20	6.73	10.91	8.18	9.69
Economic Class II												
Animal care	0.53	0.32	2.01	0.85	1.22	0.27	1.70	0.19	0.70	0.00	0.53	0.14
Crop production	0.44	0.39	1.32	0.38	1.59	1.60	2.01	0.42	2.69	0.42	2.66	0.65
Wage work	0.00	0.00	0.00	0.00	0.68	0.17	3.32	0.35	3.06	0.00	2.11	0.00
Trading	0.00	0.00	1.63	0.00	0.88	0.11	2.13	0.00	1.49	0.00	1.58	0.00
Fishing	0.35	0.00	0.13	0.00	0.82	0.13	0.64	0.00	1.27	0.00	1.02	0.00

Economic Class	*Age*											
	4-6		*7-9*		*10-12*		*13-15*		*16-21*		*22-59*	
	M	*F*	*M*	*F*	*M*	*F*	*M*	*F*	*M*	*F*	*M*	*F*
Others	0.00	0.00	0.43	0.00	0.11	0.49	0.50	0.52	0.44	0.82	0.19	0.58
Total productive	1.32	0.71	5.52	1.23	5.30	2.77	10.30	1.48	9.65	1.24	8.09	1.37
Total Housework	0.81	1.13	1.28	2.90	0.65	5.20	0.88	7.61	0.66	8.01	1.00	7.52
Total work	2.13	1.84	6.80	4.13	5.95	7.97	11.18	9.09	10.31	9.25	9.09	8.09
Economic Class III												
Animal care	0.50	0.00	0.72	0.54	1.29	0.72	0.49	0.00	0.48	0.00	0.00	0.00
Crop production	0.11	0.37	0.12	0.38	0.82	0.11	0.25	0.70	0.82	0.33	0.91	0.33
Wage work	0.00	0.00	0.66	1.27	5.00	0.00	5.89	3.52	4.53	1.15	4.66	1.34
Trading	0.00	0.00	0.58	0.00	0.11	0.13	2.38	0.00	1.43	0.01	1.23	0.00
Fishing	0.00	0.00	0.62	0.00	0.10	0.13	2.29	0.00	1.50	0.00	1.27	0.00
Others	0.00	0.00	0.12	0.00	0.77	0.33	0.15	0.42	1.11	0.82	0.93	0.91
Total productive	0.61	0.37	2.82	2.19	8.09	1.42	11.45	4.64	9.87	2.31	9.00	2.58
Total Housework	1.52	1.72	1.53	6.08	1.24	5.44	0.38	5.20	0.72	6.54	1.26	6.80
Total work	2.13	2.09	4.35	8.27	9.33	6.86	11.83	9.84	10.59	8.85	10.26	9.38

Source: Same as Table 4.

Again, there are clear class variations in the activities to which male children's time is allotted that recommend that the male children of the landed parents work in the more productive activities to a larger expanse than the male children of the landless households. The poor boys use up most of their total worktime in wage employment and fishing, while boys in more well–to–do households use up most of their worktime in animal care and crop production.

(c) Productivity and Labour Efficiency of Children Relative to Fully Grown Population

The efficiency dissimilitudes, i.e., work output per unit time, by age for specific activities have been linked to the age at the means of access into the activity. The activities that are embarked at comparatively young ages require relatively small efficiency distinctions by age, and a child gets come efficiency gruffly after he/she embarks. In the midst of these activities are the fishing including snailing, gleaning paddy from fields and foraging for wild leaves and shoots which are utilized as vegetables. Albeit, it is not doable to apportion a value to efficiency or productivity levels of such activities, they indubitably puff up the overall productivity to some bit by bit.

Table 6 shows the wage rates of labourers aged 8–25 years who are engaged during this research. The similitude of wages for ages over 11 put forward that the male children get a level of efficiency in harvesting that is well–nigh homologous to that of a full grown by age 12 or 13. The age–specific efficiency levels recommended by wage levels should hold true identically for children engaging on own lands. If anything the actual returns to a unit of labour, other things being equal, will usually be higher for children who engage on land owned by their father than children who work for a wage.

Table 6
Mean Daily Wage for Harvest Labour by Age of Worker for Males Aged 8–25 for Bawngva and Darlak Villages in Mamit Districof Mizoram

Age Group	*Number of Cases*	*Mean Daily Wage (Rs.)*
8-9	27	20.00
10-11	32	25.00
12-13	59	30.00
14-15	68	35.00
16-17	74	40.00
18-19	76	45.00
20-25	55	50.00

Source: Same as Table 5.

The male children get efficiency levels on a par to the fully grown population at much earlier ages than for harvesting and other field operations for many other promptly productive activities. This is true of activities related with the looking after cattle and other livestock. Relatively young boys specialize in cattle care, and during seasons of pinnacle, exiguity of paturage may use up many hours each day grazing cattle or collecting and cutting fodder. The value of this kind of work is onerous to calculate nevertheless boys as young as age 8 are engaged on an annual basis by some better–off households to do little else but care for cattle. The wage for perpetual labour for such boys is most often room and board, plus a small sum of money, clothes and care in case of illness.

The calculating age variations in efficiency for females is more byzantine. Wage cannot be manoeuvred, owing to the fact that the scope of wage employment is low amidst females than amidst males, and the market for their labour is more patchy with regard to wage measurement and paroxysm to employment. The suspicion is that for the bulk of activities in which females engage, the efficiency variations by age are not much; that is soon after onsetting to do these activities a child is an efficient as a full–grown. The significant non-inclusions are husking, grinding and cooking. The body avoirdupois is a cut–off–pointing determinant in husking efficiency. As a consequence of husking necessitates acting a colossal cumbersome, as long as a child weighs less than a young adult, she will be less efficient in doing this work. Relatively the unskilled, children compel more administration, relatively few young children do in the wage work, where young girls do the work for a wage, they very oftenly do so in the guild of their mother and are, as a general rule, paid a lower amount of wage for the period of work.

CONCLUSIONS

The preceding assay gives a basis for deducing that, from the point of view of parents in Bawngva and Darlak, high fertility and prodigious numbers of surviving Tuikuk children are economically rational propositions. The children of both sexes set about to work and put in comparatively long hours of work at young ages. The male children come forth to pass into the net producers at least by age 12, indemnity for their cumulative consumption by age 15, and indemnity for their own and one sister's cumulative consumption by age 21. The male Tuikuk children, in particular, may epitomize a means of augmenting income and accruing economic wealth within their parents' lifetime.

The assay in this paper weighs up only the work endowments of the child. Nevertheless, it is worthwhile to mention at this point in the research that the cost of catering for children outshines other children rearing cost, embracing clothing, education and marriage and other ceremonies, regardless of the economic status of the household. The productive task opportunities for women, in tune of women's work and child care and dealing out of child care responsibilities with others in the households.

The assay is also incarcerated to only a allocation of the parents' life cycle, that period during which a child abides a subordinate member of the parents household. Moreover, the assay is called for the economic and social relations between parents and children after children make off their parents' household.

Although the findings bestowed above are titillating, less conjectural conclusions apropos the economic roles and contributions of children await further the assay using households preferably than individuals as units of assay. In the condition of the rural society of Mizoram, it is more suitable to state of household product than individual product, in as much as the activities of individual household members have been synchronized parts of a single household enterprises. An important enquiry to be weighed up is the association between productivity and the size and structure of the households. It is believable that the mean productivity and employment of children reduces as the member of children mounts. This is not mandatorily the case for boys, yet. The mean productivity of male Tuikuk children as observed from the point of view of any presented household may not be influenced by their numbers. Amidst the comparatively well–to–do, if the supply of household labour is greater than the labour mandatory to act a farm, there are opportunities for variegating the household enterprise under the aegis of trading and wage employment, or by educating one or more sons. In amidst of the poor there are impulsions to full employment that are outside to the household, and variations in the number of sons in one household will not abate these impulsions. On the other hand, mounts in the number of daughters may very well reduce their mean productivity in all economic classes both because the amount of house work that calls for to be done in any presented household is curbed and owing to the fact that there are few productive work opportunities for women outside the household. These and other issues abide for supplementary assay.

NOTES AND REFERENCES

1. Singh, Y. Nilachandra, Children Economics of Tuikuk Community in Mizoram with Special Reference to Bawngva and Darlak Villages of Mamit District, Journal of North–East India Council for Social Science Research, Vol. 29, No. 1, April, 2005.

2. Agricultural Finance Corperation Limited, Teirei Watershed Management Project–Mizoram, Part I, North Eastern Council, Shillong, 1984:16.

3. The detailed procedure of methodology–sampling area, selection of villages, sample size and selection, interview schedule, interview techniques, adequacy of the sample etc. are available from the author. See Singh, Y. Nilachandra, Population Dynamics of Mizoram: A Case Study of Differential Fertility in Aizawl District, Ph.D. Thesis (Unpublished), Manipur University, Imphal, 1999: 18–25.

4. A more detailed description of socio-ecnomic conditions of the Tuikuk villages is available from the author. See Singh, Y. Nilachandra, Fertility Behaviuor and Its Correlation: A Case Study of Tuikuk Community in Mizoram, M.Phil. Dissertation (Unpublished), Manipur University, Imphal, 1990: 1–25.

5. Since times unknown the Tuikuks have persued jhuming, i.e., shifting cultivation. Under this method of cultivation first of all a suitable site is selected. This site is cleared of its vegetal cover. The felled trees, bushes, creepers etc. are allowed to dry for some period. Later on the dried mass is set on fire. The ash that collects there gets soaked into the soil with the first rain and acts as fertilizers in the soil. In the later part of April and the first part of May people dibble the seeds after digging the earth with 'dao', a sort of primitive tool. The crops are grown in the mixed pattern. During the south–west monsoon period the jhumias are very busy in weeding process. After the monsoons maize and other vegetables are harvested whereas rice is harvested in the months of September and October; chillies, cotton, sesame etc. in the months of December and January.
6. Chib, S.S., Caste, Tribe and Culture of India: North Eastern India, Vol.8, New Delhi, 1984: 309.
7. Singh, Y.Nilachanmdra, op.cit., 1990: 6–35.
8. Cain, Mead T. The Economic Activities of Children in a Village in Bangladesh, Population and Development Review, Vol. 3, No. 3, 1977.
9. In Bawngva and Darlak and for Mizoram as a whole it is fairly accurate to speak in terms of parents deriving economic benefits from their children's labour because children normally spend a good part of their lives as subordinate members of their parents' households. See Singh, Y.Nilachandra, Differential Fertility, Outlook and Patterns Among Two Economic Variables in Mizoram, Journal of North–East India Council for Social Science Research, Vol. 24, No. 2, 2000; Enke, Stephen, The Economics of Government Payments to Limit Population, Economic Development and Cultural Change, Vol. 8, No. 2, 1960 and Caldwell, John C., Mass Education as a Determinant of the Time of Fertility Decline, Population and Development Review, Vol. 6, No. 2, 1980.
10. Tribal Research Institute, Riang Chanchin, Aizawl, 1996: 64–74.
11. Hunter, W.W., A Statistical Account of Bengal, Vol. 5, London, 1877: 93.
12. Subrahmanyam, K.V. and Ryan, James G., An Analysis of Rural Labour Market in India: Kanzara Village, Maharashtra, ICRISAT, Hyderabad, July, 1976.

HUMAN RIGHTS OF CHILDREN OF WOMEN PRISONERS: AN ANALYSIS

*Gurpreet K. Pannu**

Children are assets of nation. Future of country depends upon growth of children. If there is no proper growth of children of today the future of country will be dark. It is obligation of every generation to bring up children, citizens of tomorrow, in a proper way[1]. It has been rightly said that "child is the father of man". To enable fathering of valiant and vibrant man, the child must be groomed well in the formative years of his life. Every child must receive education, acquire knowledge of man and materials and blossom in such an atmosphere that on reaching maturity he is found to be a man with a mission, a man who matters so far as society is concerned[2].

There are various provisions of Constitution and other statutes, which cast an obligation on the state to look after the welfare of children and provide for social, educational and cultural development of the child with dignity intact and protected from any kind of exploitation. Children are to be given opportunities and facilities to develop in a healthy manner and in a condition of freedom and dignity. The same rights are available to children of women prisoners living in jail, since such children are not prisoners as such but are merely victims of unfortunate circumstances. This paper is humble academic venture to analyse condition of children of under-trial and convicted female prisoners. It is an attempt to analyse rights of such children, who have to stay in jail with their mother without any fault and to suggest certain remedies.

INDIAN LAW AND CHILDREN

The best interest of child has been regarded as primary consideration in our Constitution, so special and specific provisions have been made both in Part III and IV of Constitution and following require mention:

---

* Reader, Law Department, Punjabi University, Patiala.

Article 14: State shall not deny to any person equality before law or equal protection of law within territory of India.

Article 15: Prohibits discrimination on the grounds of religion, race, caste, sex or place or birth etc.

Article 15 (3): Provides that state can make special provision for women and children for their welfare.

Article 21: No person shall be deprived of his life and personal liberty except according to procedure established by law.

Article 21-A: Provides for free and compulsory education to all children of the age of six to fourteen years.

Article 24: Prohibits employment of children below the age of fourteen years in any factory, mine or hazardous employment. We may also note some provisions of part IV of Constitution:

Article 39 (e): Directs the State of ensure that health and strength of workers, men and women and tender age of children are not abused and citizens are not forced by economic necessity to enter avocations unsuited to their age or strength.

Article 39 (f): directs state to ensure that children are given opportunities and facilities to develop in a healthy manner and in conditions of freedom and dignity and that childhood and youth are protected against exploitation and against moral and material abandonment.

Article 45: State shall endeavour to provide early childhood care and education for all children until they complete the age of six years.

Article 46: State shall promote with special care the educational and economic interests of weaker sections of the people, and, in tribes and shall protect them from social injustice and all forms of exploitation.

Article 47: State shall regard raising of level of nutrition and standard of living of its people and improvement of public health among its primary duties and, in particular, State shall endeavour to bring about prohibition of the consumption except for medicinal purposes of intoxicating drinks and of drug which are injurious to health.

Apart from these Constitutional provisions there are so many other laws on issues concerning children, such as Guardian and Wards Act, 1890, Child Marriage Restraint Act, 1929, Factories Act, 1948, Hindu Adoption and Maintenance Act, 1950, Probation of Offenders Act, 1958, Orphanges and Other Charitable Homes (Supervision and Control) Act,

1960 Child Labour (Protection and Regulation) Act 1986, Juvenile Justice (Care and Protection of Children) Act 2000, Infant Food (Regulation of Production Supply and Distribution) Act, 1992, Pre-conception and Pre-natal Diagnostic Techniques (Prohibition of sex selection) Act, 1994 Persons with Disabilities (Equal Opportunities, Protection of Rights and Full Participation) Act, 1995, Immoral Traffic (Prevention) Act 1986. The Juvenile Justice (Care and Protection of Children) Act, 2000 replaced the Juvenile Justice Act, 1986 to comply with provisions of Convention on the Rights of Child which has been acceded to by India in 1992.

In addition to this national policy for children was adopted on August 22, 1974. This policy lays down that State shall provide adequate services for children both before and after birth and during the growing stages for their full physical, mental and social development. The measures suggested include amongst others a comprehensive healthy programmes, supplementary nutrition, for mothers and children, promotion of physical, educational and recreational activities, special consideration for children of weaker section and prevention of exploitation of children[5].

India acceded to U.N. Convention on the Rights of the Child in December 1992 to reiterate its commitment to the cause of the children. Main objective of the Convention is to give every child the right to survival and development in a healthy and congenial environment. In May 2004 U.N. General Assembly Special Session was held on children in New York, it was attended by Indian delegates led by minister of Human Resources Development and consisted of Parliamentarians, N.G.Os and officials. It was a follow up world summit held in 1990. The summit adopted the declaration on the survival, protection and development of children and endorsed a plan of action for its implementation.

The Government of India is implementing various schemes and programmes for benefit of the children. National Charter for Children, 2003[6] has been adopted to reiterate the commitment of Government to the cause of children in order to see that no child remains hungry, illiterate or sick. Government has affirmed by this Charter that best interest of children must be protected through combined action of the State, civil society and families and their obligation in fulfilling children's basic needs. National Charter has been announced with a view to securing every child has inherent right to enjoy happy childhood, to address the root causes that negate the health, growth and development of children and to awake the conscience of community in the wider societal context to protect children from all forms of abuses by strengthening the society and nation. This Charter provides for survival, life and liberty of all children, promoting high standards of health and nutrition, assailing basic needs and security, play and leisure, early childhood care for survival, growth and development, protection of children in distress for welfare and providing opportunity for all around development of personality including expression of creativity etc.

The Government of India is implementing various schemes and programmes for benefit of children. By taking another step ahead The Commission for Protection of Child Right Act, 2005[7] has been enforced. The main object of this Act is to provide for constitutiion of National Commission[8] and State Commissions[9] for protection of rights of children. This Commission can inquire into any matter of violation of child rights and to examine all factors that inhibit the enjoyment of rights to children affected by terrorism, communal violence, riots, domestic violence, HIV/AIDS, trafficking, maltreatment, exploitation, pornography, prostitution etc. Commission is empowered to look into matter relating to children in need of special care and protection including children in distress, marginalized and disadvantaged children, children in conflict with law, juveniles, children without families and to recommend remedial measures. If Commission finds a case of violation of rights of child it can recommend to concerned Government or authority for intiation of proceeding for protection of such person. The Commission can approach the Supreme Court or High Court for such directions, orders or writs as court may deem necessary. The above said Act also provides for constitution of Children's Courts[10] for providing speedy trial of offences against children or of violation of child rights.

Recently Child Labour (Prohibition and Regulation) Act, 1986[11] has been amended by the government to include child domestic work as a form of hazardous labour and action can be taken against those who employ children upto the age of 14 in domestic work including homes, hotels, motels, tea shops, resorts or other recreational carters.

RIGHTS OF CHILDREN OF FEMALE AND PRISONERS

There are many rights which are provided for the development and betterment of the children. There are some of the rights which are provided by Indian Constitution, Universal Declaration of Human Rights, 1948 and National Charter for Children, 2003, like right to nutrition, right to education, right to life and personal liberty etc. are provided for all the children without any discrimination on the ground of sex, religion, caste, race and place of birth etc. But these rights are not prevailed by children of female prisoners due to bad living conditions in the prisons. Sometimes children have to stay in jails with their mothers who are either under-trial prisoners or convicts. Such children stay in prisons due to their tender age, while in other cases, it may be because there is no one at home to look after them or to take care to them in the absence of mother. The jail environment is not congenial for development of children. There are special provisions in Jail Manual to deal with such children and to provide them basic facilities of food, education, recreation etc.

Para 832 of Punjab Jail Manual allows female prisoners to keep their children with them until they are four years of age or with the approval of Superintendent of jail upto six years of age. The Manual provides that as soon as any child admitted or born in jail attains the age of four years or any female prisoners dies leaving a child of that age, the Superintendent of jail shall communicate with Magistrate of District of which the mother was resident, with a view to the child being hand over to the charge of a relative or friend or being placed in an orphanage or being entrusted to some respectable person to be brought to some respected person to be brought up at the expenses of Government, if necessary, until it attains an age to earn livelihood.

DIET

The Manual also provides dietary scale for such children. There is provision for special ration above and beyond the normal labouring ration for nursing mother and for supplementary milk for children under the age of 1 year not receiving sufficient milk from mother. Provision is also made for ration for children from 12-18 months and from 18-24 months. Changes in diet may be recommended by the medical officer. In some of the states like Maharashtara, Jharkhand, Kerla, Manipur, Orissa, Tamil Nadu, Delhi and Bihar clothing is being provided by the jail authorities as per Rules of their states Manuals.

HEALTH, EDUCATION AND RECREATION

The Government of India has ratified the UN Convention on Rights of the Child. Appropriate measures are being taken for implementing the Convention by concerned departments. A national plan for children has been adopted. The plan seeks to cover the programmes in the area of child and maternal health, nutrition, water and sanitation, education of children in different difficult circumstances. A number of child care programmes for improving the nutritional status of children are being implemented and Integrated Child Development Services (ICDS) programme is a major intervention for providing services including nutrition to all the children under six years of age.

In the initial years of life these facilities are very important for the children. The rights of children of women prisoners living in jail are broader, since such children are not prisoners but are helpless victims of the circumstances. It is clearly provided in National Charter for Children, 2003:

(a) State shall take measures to ensure that all children enjoy the highest attainable standards of health and provide for prevention and curative facilities at all levels especially immunization and prevention of micronutrient deficiencies for all children.

(b) State shall take measurers to cover, under primary health facilities and specialized care and treatment, all children of families below poverty line.

(c) State shall take measures to provide adequate pre-natal and post-natal care for mothers along with immunization against preventable diseases.

(d) State shall undertake measures to provide for a national plan that will ensure that mental health of all children is protected.

(e) State shall take steps to ensure protection of children from all practices that are likely to harm the child's physical and mental health.

There is no provision in Jail Manual regarding vaccination & immunization of children of female prisoners and vaccination is required in first four years to every child. In some of the jails polio drops are given to such children on pulse polio day. There is no specialist doctor and full time nurse for such children. Such vaccination is provided from government hospitals.

In majority of the jails there is nursery with care facility for such children and an attendant to take care of such children, when mother is away or on work. Children under 3 years are treated at creche and upto the age of 6 yeas are treated at nursery. Such nurseries are provided with toys, tricycles, swings etc, which are sometimes provided by social service organizations. In jails there is no proper school for such children, although they stay upto the age of 6 years. If few states like Delhi, Maharashtra, Chattisgarh, West Bengal NGOs are providing helping hand for nurseries and elementary education to such children.

National Institute of Criminology and Forensic Sciences conducted a research study of children of women prisoners in Indian Jails in February 2002[12]. The salient features of the study brought to the notice of all Governments are:

1. In majority of jails women inmates with children were not given any special or extra meals. In some cases, occasionally, some extra food, mostly in the form of a glass of milk was provided to children. In some jails, separate food was being provided only to grown up children i.e. over the age of five years. But the quality of food remains same as supplied to adult prisoners.
2. No special consideration was reported to the given to child bearing women inmates in the matters of food or other facilities. The same food and same facilities were given to all women inmates, irrespective of the fact whether their children were also living with them or not.
3. There are no appropriate programmes being run in jails for their proper bio-psycho social development. Their looking after is mostly left to their mothers. No trained staff was found in any jail to take care of these children.
4. No separate or special medical facilities for children were available in jails.
5. Majority of mother prisoners considered that their stay in jails would have a negative impact on the physical and mental development of their children.
6. Crowded environment, lacks of appropriate food, shelter and above all deprivation of affection of other family members, especially the father was generally perceived by mother as big stumbling block for proper development of their children in the formative years of life.
7. Mother prisoners identified six areas where urgent improvement was necessary for proper upkeep of their children. These areas are related to food, medical facilities, accommodation, education, recreation and separation of their children from habitual offenders.
8. No prison officer was deployed on the exclusive duty of looking after such children or their mothers. They had to perform this duty along side many other duties including administrative work, discipline maintenance, security related jobs etc. None of them was reported to have undergone any special training in looking after the children in jails.
9. The general impression gathered was that most of such children were living in really difficult conditions and suffering from diverse deprivations relating to food, health care, accommodation, education, recreation etc.

This report shows the real picture and it is quite clear that provisions of Jail Manuals and other Constitutional and legal provisions for betterment of children remain on papers and in reality these are not being implemented any where.

In August 2002 a field action project prepared by Tata Institute of Social Sciences on situation of children of prisoners[13]. This report shows main problems being faced by minors accompanying their mothers in the prisons:

(a) The prison environment is not conducive to the normal growth and development of children.

(b) Many children are born in prison and have never experienced a normal family life, sometimes till the age permitted to stay inside (four to six years).

(c) Socialization pattern get severally affected due to their stay in prison. Their only image of male authority figures is that of police and prison officials. They are unaware of the concept of a home. Sometimes boys may be found talking in female gender, having grown up only among women confined in the female ward. Unusual scenes, like animals on the road (seen on the way to court with mother) are frightening.

(d) Such children get transferred with their mothers from one prison to another, frequently (due to overcrowding or other reasons) thus unsetting them.

(e) Sometimes such children display violent and aggressive behaivour in prison.

GUIDELINES ISSUED BY SUPREME COURT

Indian judiciary has always, remained concerned with the plight of under-trail women prisoners languishing in various jails, Recently Apex Court in *R.D. Upadhya V. State of A.P.*[14] took notice of plight of children of female prisoners. The Court directed the states and union territories to disclose on affidavit number of female prisoners (under-trail and convicted), period of their detention, children who are with mothers lodged in the jail and whether any facilities are available in the jails concerned for taking care of such children? From the various affidavits submitted it came to light that there were 6496 under-trial women with 1053 children and 1873 convicted women with 206 children[15]. Reports of National Institute of Criminology and Forensic Sciences and Tata Institute of Social Sciences on living conditions of children of prisoners were also placed before the court. However, on the basis of various affidavits submitted by various State Governments and Union Territories, as well as, Union of India, it became clear to Supreme Court that children of women prisoners who are living in jails require additional protection. In many respects such children have to suffer the consequences of neglect. Supreme Court issued following detailed directions to ensure minimum standards of living of children of women prisoners:

1. A child shall not be treated as an under-trial/convict while in jail with his/her mother. Such a child is entitled of food, shelter, medical care, clothing, education and recreational facilities as a matter of right.

2. Pregnancy:

   (a) Before sending a woman who is pregnant to a jail, the concerned authorities must ensure that jail in question has the basic minimum facilities for child delivery as well as for providing per-natal and post-natal care for both, the mother and the child.

   (b) When a woman prisoner is found or suspected to be pregnant at the time of her admission or at any time thereafter, the lady Medical Officer shall report the fact to the superintendent. As soon as possible, arrangement shall be made to get such prisoner medically examined at the female wing of the District Government Hospital for ascertaining the state of her health, pregnancy, duration of pregnancy, probable date of delivery and so on. After ascertaining the necessary particulars, a report shall be sent to the Inspector General of Prisons, stating the date of admission, term of sentence, date of release, duration of pregnancy, possible date of delivery and so on.

   (c) Gynecological examination of female prisoners shall be performed in the District Government Hospital. Proper pre-natal and post-natal care shall be provided to the prisoner as per medical advice.

3. Child birth in prison:

   (a) As far as possible and provided she as a suitable option, arrangements for temporary release/parole (or suspended sentence in case of minor and causal offender) should be made to enable an expectant prisoners to have her delivery outside the prison. Only exceptional cases constituting high security risk or cases of equivalent grave descriptions can be denied this facility.

(b) Births in prison, when they occur, shall be registered in the local birth registration office. But the fact that the child has been born in the prison shall not be recorded in the certificate of birth that is issued. Only the address of the locality shall be mentioned.

(c) As far as circumstances permit, all facilities for the naming rites of children born in prison shall be extended.

4. Female prisoners and their children:

(a) Female prisoners shall be allowed to keep their children with them in jail till they attain the age of six years.

(b) No female prisoners shall be allowed to keep a child who has completed the age of six years. Upon reaching the age of six years, the child shall be handed over to a suitable surrogates as per the wishes of the female prisoner or shall be sent to suitable institution run by the Social Welfare Department. As far as possible, the child shall not be transferred to an institution outside the town or city where the prison is located in order to minimize undue hardships on both mother and child due to physical distance.

(c) Such children shall be kept in protective custody until their mother is released or the child attains such age as to earn his/her own livelihood.

(d) Children kept under the protective custody in a home of the Department of Social Welfare shall be allowed to meet the mother at least once a week. The Director, Social Welfare Department, shall ensure that such children are brought to the prison for this purpose on the date fixed by the Superintendent of Prisons.

(e) When a female prisoners dies and leaves behind a child, the Superintendent shall inform the District Magistrate concerned and he shall arrange for the proper care of the child. If the concerned relatives are unwilling to support the child, the District Magistrate shall either place the child in an approved institution/home run by the State Social Welfare Department or hand the child over to a responsible person for care and maintenance.

5. Food, clothing, medical care and shelter

(a) Children in jail shall be provided with adequate clothing suiting the local climatic requirement for which the State/U.T. Government shall lay down the scales.

(b) State/U.T. Governments shall lay down dietary scales for children keeping in view the calorific requirements of growing children as per medical norms.

(c) A permanent arrangement needs to be evolved in all jails to provide separate food with ingredients to take care of the nutritional needs of children who reside in them on a regular basis.

(d) Separate utensils of suitable size and material should also be provided to each mother prisoner for using to feed her child.

(e) Clean drinking water must be provided to the children. This water must be periodically checked.

(f) Children shall be regularly examined by the Lady Medical Officer to monitor their physical growth and shall also receive timely vaccination. Vaccination charts regarding each child shall be kept in the records. Extra clothing, diet and so on may also be provided on the recommendation of the Medical Officer.

(g) In the event of a woman prisoner falling ill, alternative arrangement for looking after any children falling under her care must be made by the jail staff.

(h) Sleeping facilities that are provided to the mother and the child should be adequate, clean and hygienic.

(i) Children of prisoners shall have the right of visitation.

(j) The Prison Superintendent shall be empowered in special cases and where circumstances warrant admitting children of women prisoners to prison

6. Education and recreation for children of female prisoners:

(a) The child of female prisoners living in the jails shall be given proper education and recreational opportunities and while their mothers are at work in jail, the children shall be kept in crèches under the charge of a matron/female warder. This facility will also be extended to children of warders and other female prison staff.

(b) There shall be a creche and a nursery attached to the prison for women where the children of women prisoners will be looked after. Children below three years of age shall be allowed in the creche and those between three and six years shall be looked after in the nursery. The prison authorities shall preferably run the said creche and nursery outside the prison premises.

7. In many States, small children are living in sub-jails that are not at all equipped to keep small children. Women prisoners with children should not be kept in such sub-jails, unless proper facilities can be ensured which would make for a conducive environment here for proper biological, psychological and social growth.
8. The stay of children in crowed barracks amidst women convicts, undertails, offenders relating to all types of crimes including violent crimes is certainly harmful for the development of their personality. Therefore, children deserve to be separated from such environments on a priority basis.
9. Diet: Dietary scale for institutionalized infants/children prepared by Dr. A.M. Dwarkadas Motiwala, MD (Paediatricds) and Fellowship in Neonatology (USA) has been submitted by Mr. Sanjay Parikh to Supreme Court. The document submitted recommends exclusive breastfeeding on the demand of the baby day and night. If for some reason the mother cannot feed the baby, undiluted fresh milk can be given to the baby. It is emphasized that "dilution is not recommended; especially for low socio-economic groups who are also illiterate, ignorant, their children are already malnourished and are prone to gastroenteritis and other infections due to poor living conditions and unhygienic food habits. Also, where the drinking water is a question mark. Over-dilution will provide more water than milk to the child and hence will lead to malnutrition and infections. This in turn will lead to growth retardation and developmentally delay both physically and mentally." It is noted that since an average Indian mother produces approximately 600-800 ml. milk per day (depending on her own nutritional state), the child should be provided at least 600 ml. of undiluted fresh milk over 24 hours if the breast milk is not available. The report also refers to the "Dietary Guidelines for Indians–A Manual", published in 1998 by the National Institute of Nutrition, Council of Medical Research, Hyderabad, for a balanced diet for infants and children ranging from 6 months to 6 years of age. It recommends the following portions for children from the ages 6-12 months, 1-3 years and 4-6 years, respectively: Creals and Millets 45, 60-120 and 150-210 grams respectively; Pulses 15, 30 and 45 grams respectively; Milk 500 ml (unless breast fed, in which case 200ml); Roots and Tubers 50, 50 and 100 grams respectively; Green Leafy Vegetables 25, 50 and 50 grams respectively Fruits 100 grams; Sugar 25, 25, and 30 grams respectively; and Fats/Oils (Visible) 10, 20, and 25 grams respectively. One portion of pulse may be exchanged. With one portion (50 grams) of egg/meat/chicken/fish. It is essential that

the above food groups to be provided in the portions mentioned in order to ensure that both macronutrients and micronutrients are available to the child in adequate quantities.

10. Jail Manual and/or other relevant Rules, Regulations, instruction etc. should be suitably amended within three months so as to comply with the above directions. If in some jails, better facilities are being provided, same shall continue.
11. Schemes and laws relating to welfare and development of such children shall be implemented in letter and spirit. State Legislatures may consider passing of necessary legislations, wherever necessary. Having regard to what is notice in this judgment.
12. The State Legal Services Authorities shall take necessary measures to periodically inspect jails to monitor that the directions regarding children and mother are complied with in letter and spirit.
13. The courts dealing with cases of women prisoners whose children are in prison with their mothers to give priority to such cases and decide their cases.

National Expert Committee on Women prisoners (1986-87) headed by justice V.R. Krishan Iyer farmed a draft Model Prison Manual. Chapter XXIII of this manual makes special provisions for children of women prisoners. This manual was circulated to the States and Union Territories for incorporation into existing jail manuals. This committee made important suggestions regarding rights of women prisoners who are pregnant and regarding child birth in prison. It also made suggestions regarding age upto which children of women prisoners can reside in prisons, their welfare through a creche and nursery, provisions of adequate cloth suiting the climate conditions, regular medical examination, education and recreation, nutrition for children and pregnant and nursing mothers. Unfortunately, these recommendations were never implemented.

The Prison Management Bill, 1998 was prepared which deals with plight of women prisoners, under chapter XIV and XVI. This Bill was prepared with laudable aim of bringing uniformity to jail management across the country. Chapter II of Bill delineates various rights and duties of prisoners. The rights include right to live with human dignity, adequate diet, health and medical care, clean hygenic living conditions, proper clothing and right to communication. It is important to note the Bill provides a Fair Price Shop in all prisons accommodating more than 200 prisoners. This shop should also offer essential items for children of prisoner. This Bill also provides for temporary or special leave being granted to a prisoner, who shows sufficient cause to State Government or concerned authority. This can be utilized to grant Parole to pregnant women. Chapter IV relates to release and after care and chapter XVI deals with special categories of prisoners. Both of these chapters have special significance when considering the rights of children of women prisoners. Unfortunately this proposed Bill has not yet been passed and enforced.

CONCLUSION AND SUGGESTIONS

It is quite clear that living condition of female prisoners in jails is pitiable. The children living with mothers in jails are being deprived of their basic rights, entitlements and amenities. Though jails Manual contains some provisions for such children e.g. in regard with their diet, education, recreation etc. The diet being provided to such children is insufficient and non-nutritional. Children are provided with same food as to adults. No care of nutritional needs of children is taken. Sufficient quantity of milk & boiled water is not provided to children in jails. Health services are very poor. There are no facilities for pre-natal and post-natal care of mothers. Immunization is not provided on regular basis. There is no arrangement for Paediatrician and nurse. Medicines for such children are not available in jails. Although Jail Manual provides that child can stay in jail with mother upto the age of six years, but there is no arrangement for elementary education of such children. Now right to education is a fundamental right, but such children are deprived of this basic right. Recreational facilities is next to nil. No facility of clothing and bedding is available to such children. Directions on Supreme Court to amend jail Manual, and other relevant Rules and Regulations has still not complied with even after six months of judgment, when this time permitted by Supreme Court was three months.

SUGGESTIONS

Following suggestions can prove helpful to improve the living standard and conditions of children of female prisoners:

1. Proper implementation of present Jail Manual and provisions of Constitution and other statues, which cast an obligation on State to look after the welfare of children and for proper development of such children must be made.
2. Such children must be provided with special diet as per requirement of every child. This diet should be standardized according to age of

the child. Special need of the child should be kept in mind. Toned milk may be provided to such children. For satisfying such needs and providing satisfactory diet to such children a separate kitchen unit should be created in jails.

3. The minimum facility of Balwadi for such children and a crèche for those under the age of two years should be provided in jails. The Balwadi should be manned by a trained teacher and should have facilities of a visiting psychiatrist and Paediatrician.
4. Primary health facility should be available to such children. There should be proper arrangement for pre-natal and post natal care for mothers. Facility of immunization against preventive diseases should be provided by the State to such children.
5. Before sending a woman in stage of pregnancy, to jail, the concerned authorities must ensure that particular jail has got minimum facility for child delivery and providing pre-natal and post natal care to mother and child.
6. Such children should be separated from over crowed barracks, where offenders relating to all crimes, including violent crimes, are detained. It may be harmful for such children in their personality development.
7. Children of women prisons should be provided with multiple sets of clothes, bed sheet etc. Separate utensils should be provided to each mother according to feeding need of each child.
8. Proper and adequate arrangement should be available in all jails to impart formal and informal education to every child of the women inmates.
9. Diversified recreational facilities should be made available to the children of different age groups.
10. Arrest of women suspects should be made only by lady police. As such arrests made sparingly adverse affect on innocent children who are taken into custody with their mother. To avoid arrest of innocent children the care and custody of such children should be handed over to voluntary organizations which can assist in the growth of children in congenial & healthy atmosphere.
11. Directions of Supreme Court should immediately be implemented.

NOTES AND REFERENCES

1. Justice P.N. Bhagwait and R.N. Pathak in Sheela Barse V. Secretary, Children Aid Society. AIR 1987 SC 656.

2. As per Hansaria, J. in M.C. Mehta V. State of Tamil Nadu. AIR 1997 SC 701.
3. Inserted by Constitution (Amendment) Act, 2002.
4. Again amended by Act No. 33 of 2006.
5. Paras Diwan and Peeyushi Diwan : Child and Legal Protection, p. 9, 1991.
6. Published in Extra-ordinary Gazette of India, Part-I, Section-I, Government of India, Ministry of Human Resources Development, Department of Women and Child Development, New Delhi 9th February 2004.
7. Act No. 4 of 2006.
8. Ibid, Section 3.
9. Ibid, Section 17.
10. Ibid, Section 25.
11. This Act came into force on October 10, 2006.
12. Referred in R.D. Upadhyay V. State of A.P., AIR 2006 SC 1946 at page 1949.
13. Ibid, at page 1954.
14. AIR 2006 SC 1946.
15. Ibid, at page 1953.

HUMAN RIGHTS OF CHILDREN

*S.N. Yogish**

INTRODUCTION

Human rights are essentially a product of democracy. Man's struggle against tyranny has been long and sustained. Tyranny has from time to time, surfaced in different forms and modes. Human being has always tried to assert their right, more often than not successfully. Sometime there has been a dismal failure, onslaught on human rights continues. So does man's struggle against tyranny.

Human rights are the basic and absolute rights that every person has because he or she is a human being. They recognize the vulnerability of the human being in civil, political, economical, social and cultural processes and provide protection.

Every human being has these rights although the extent to which they can be enforced in practice varied from country to country. Having rights comes with having duties and responsibilities. In preserving the freedom, rights and justice for all, everyone has a responsibility to abide by the law and everyone has duties in the community. In exercising freedoms and rights, everyone must also respect the rights and freedoms of others.

At the international level most of these basic human rights have been described in the Untied Nations (UN). Universal declaration of Human Rights (1948). Some of the basic human rights include;

- The right to equal treatment and non-discrimination.
- The right to nationality
- The right to own property.
- The right to education.
- The right to work and to just and favourable conditions of works.

---

* Reader, DOS in Economics, Kuvempu University, Jnana Sahyadri, Shankaraghatta- 577451.

- The right to freedom from slavery and forced labour.
- The right to freedom of movement.
- The right to equal assess to public service in the country.
- The right to freedom of through, opinion and expression.
- The right to freedom of association.

The fundamental human rights are often described in each country's contribution which guarantees the fundamental rights of its citizens, regardless of their sex, race, ethnicity, class or caste, religion or other statuses. National legal rights are those rights which are defined by national laws in each county, usually consisting of constitutional rights and specific rights laid down in national legislation such as the penal code, the labour code and the civil code and rules such as government regulations.

While there is considerable variations in national legislation between countries most constitutions world wide state that everyone is equal before the law and that each person us entitled to equal protection under the law without discrimination. If person is entitled to seek justice and to just and fair judicial process.

In 1998 ILO member states adopted the declaration of fundamental principles and rights at work which sets out the core labour principles that are fundamental to the rights of the human beings at work, irrespective of the level of development of countries. The core labour principles endorsed by the international community over four main areas:

- The elimination of all forms of forced and compulsory labour.
- The abolition of child labour.
- The elimination of description on respect of employment and occupation.
- Freedom of association and the recognition of the right to collective bargaining.

ABOUT CHILD RIGHTS

A century that began with children having virtually no rights in ending with children having the most powerful legal instrument that not only recognizes but protects their human rights. Carol Bellany-UNICEF Executive Director.

Since, child rights adoption in 1989 after more than 60 years of advocacy, the conversion on the right of child has been ratified more quickly and by more governments than any other human rights instrument. Its basic premise is that children with fundamental freedom and inherit rights of all human beings.

Many governments have even further enacting legislation, creating mechanism and putting into place a range of creative measures to ensure protection and realization of the rights of those under the age of 18.

Nevertheless, as UN Secretary General Koji Anan said "The Principle of all children, all rights is still much too far from being a reality".

The rights of the child as defined by the convention on the right of child include four core principles as follows.

EQUALITY

Like adults, children can be just to discrimination which has a negative impact on a child's opportunities and conditions in life. Therefore all children are entitled to equal rights and governments have an obligation to uphold these. For example:

- Right to birth registration.
- Right to protection from all forms of abuse, neglect, discrimination and exploitation.

RIGHT TO SURVIVAL AND HEALTHY DEVELOPMENT

Every child has a right to develop to develop his/her fullest potential and is entitled to:

- Right to basic needs, including food, shelter and access to health care.
- Right to free primary education.
- Right to childhood-to rest and play and to have friends.
- Right to protection from economic exploitation or any work that interferes with education or that is hazardous and harmful to health, physical, mental and social development.
- Right to assistance for children with special needs: for example: child refugees displaced children, child victims for abuse and disabled children.

PARTICIPATION

All boys and girls, according to their age and maturity, have the right to affect them. Boys and girls should be encouraged to take part in decision making at home, in school and in their own community. Key participation rights are:

- Right to express views and opinions.
- Right to receive and give information in an accessible and understandable form
- Right to be an active member of community to enjoy own culture, to practice own religion and to use own language
- Right to be a member of a group.

BEST INTEREST OF THE CHILD

The two notions of children as competent human beings on the one hand and as children who are vulnerable and need protection on the other hand may confliction deciding what is best for the child. This principle provides the solution to this problem: all decisions that affect boys and girls must give primary consideration to them. In determining what is best for them, it is important to seek the views of the affected girls and boys.

CHILD LABOUR

Work is not always bad for children and can be healthy but it can also seriously hamper children's development. In order to decide whether children's economic activities are healthy or harmful the international community has set the following yard sticks.

CHILD WORK

- Light work (less than 14 hours/week) for 12-17 year olds.
- Not harmful to child's health and development.
- Not obstructing schooling or vocational training
- Not hazardous in nature.

CHILD LABOUR

- Regular work (14-43 hours/week)
- Causes physical or psychological damage

- Hinders educational and mental and or physical development.
- Child under minimum age set by ILO Convention No-138.
- Hazardous was defined by provisions of ILO Convention No.-182.

THE WORST FORMS OF CHILD LABOUR

- All forms of slavery or practices similar to slavery, such as sale and trafficking of children, debt bondage and seldom and forced or compulsory recruitment of children for use in armed conflict.
- The use, procuring or offering of a child for prostitution of pornography and for pornographic performances.
- The use, procuring or offering of a child for illicit activities, in particular for the production and trafficking of drugs.

CHILD LABOUR STATISTICS

Age group and sex	*Economically active children*	*Child labour*	*Children hazardous*	*Definitions of child labour based on ILO conventions Nos. 138 and 182*
5-11	109.7	109.7	60.5	In ages 5-11= all children economically active activities.
Boys	56.3	56.3	30.7	
Girls	53.4	53.4	29.8	
12-14	101.1	76.6	50.8	In ages 12-14= all children in economically activities excepts those in light work.
Boys	52.7	41.5	30.6	
Girls	48.4	35.1	20.2	
15-17	140.9	59.2	59.2	In ages 15-17= all children in hazardous work and other work forms of child labour.
Boys	75.7	34.4	34.4	
Girls	65.8	24.8	24.8	
Total (5-17)	351.7	245.5	170.5	Statistics does not include children engaged in work that is not considered economic activities such as domestic work where girls are after found.
Boys	184.1	132.2	95.7	
Girls	167.6	113.3	74.8	

CHILDREN IN THE WORST FORMS OF CHILD LABOUR

Worst forms of Child Labour	*Global Estimates*	*Estimates in Asia-Pacific*
Forced and bonded labour	5.7	5.5
Forced recruitment into armed conflict	0.3	0.12
Prostitution and pornography	1.8	0.59
Helicit activities	0.6	0.22
Trafficked children	1.2	0.25
Subtotal	8.4	6.43
Children in hazardous work	170.5	104
Total	178.9	110.5

According to ILO report every child counts new global estimates on child labour;

- 70% of child workers are in agriculture, fishing , hunting and forestry.
- 9% of child workers are in manufacturing.
- 9% of child workers are in whole sale, retail trade, restaurants and hotels.
- 6% of child workers are in community, social and personal services.
- 4% of child workers are in transport, storage and communication.
- 4% of child workers are in construction, mining and quarrying.

At the start of the new millennium about 18% boys and girls up to the age of 14 were economically active, in other words, were working for money and other compensation. In 2002, 211 million children aged 5-1 years are economically active. Sixty per cent (127 million) were found in Asia, and the Pacific. One of every five children in this age grow-up was working in this region.

In sub-saharan Africa there were 48 million children working. One of every three children in this age group was working in this region. Just over 6% (13.4 million) were found in North Africa and the middle east and 8% (17.4 million) in Latin America and the Caribbean.

Following the ILO definitions of child labour, as many as 246 million children aged from 5-17 are in child labour. Of this group, 110 million are younger than 12. of all child labour as many as 170.5million are found in hazardous work and 6.05 million in this category are younger than 12.

Statistically should be considered critically because by nature child labour exploitation is hidden and getting accurate information is difficult. The number of working girls is underestimated by statistical surveys which do not generally account for unpaid economic activities such as domestic work or hidden activities such as prostitution, the type of work in which more girls are involved.

One of the most wide spread forms of labour exploitation of children is domestic work. Traditionally, domestic work is seen as an easy and safe work for children especially for girls. However, it has been proven recently that domestic work can be among the dangerous work for children and has been recognized as a worst form of child labour. While, domestic work with good employers can offer children in poverty chance to develop, a good education and earn a living, domestic work in most countries has a very low status and is among the lowest paid and many CDW's end up being exploited. Because most CDWs live in and have little freedom, their life and safety after depends on the mercy of the employers. An overwhelming majority of CDWs are girls and many face phsycial, emotional or sexual abuses.

There are an estimated 1.2 million children being trafficking for labour and sexual exploitation worldwide, about 250000 in Asia and Pacific. However, estimates of the number of children being trafficked often vary widely, depending on the source. For example, numbers of children trafficked for prostitution in India range between 25,000 and 50,000 respectively. Therefore estimates should be considered with caution. Despite difficulty in determining the exact number of trafficked children, there is a clear trend that it is rising worldwide particularly for sexual exploitation. In South and South east Asia, the overwhelming number of child victims of trafficking are girls with the exception of Sri Lanka and to a lesser extent Pakistan, where boys are also found to be trafficked for commercial sexual exploitation.

TRAFFICKING AND PROSTITUTION

Human trafficking affects a considerable number of indigenous peoples. This has been particularly documented in South and South east Asia. In Nepal, an IPEC Rapid Assessment of trafficking in girls, with specific reference to prostitution, shows the presence of several different ethnic groups. Trafficking of indigenous girls is also being documented in Thailand, Burma, Indonesia and Cambodia.

In India, abduction, trafficking of Adivasi girls linked to brothers, forced concubinage and the overall inadequacy of legal protection available to Adivasi women at risk of rape or trafficking requires urgent action. B. Janardhan quoting M. Devi from 1984, notes that traffickers still continue to purchase Adivasi children and women openly, often at a price cheaper than that paid to purchase animals. A whole network of slaves exists stretching from the Adivasi villages to centers as far away as Ludhiana, Jalandar, Amritsar and Hoshiarpur districts in Punjab. A large proportion of migrant workers are women and face sexual exploitation at all stops in that belt. A group do contractors recruit these Adivasi women through older women who themselves have been victims of these practices. After receiving the recruits the contractors transport the human cargo to states such as Punjab. The recipients of the Human cargo auction the Adivasi girls in the open market. These slaves are paid roughly Rs. 15 a day or Rs. 1000 on an average.

Similar processes have been described in Taiwan, China where high numbers of indigenous girls have been trafficked top work in the sex industry. While indigenous peoples account for only 1.6 per cent of the Taiwanese population estimates of the percentage of indigenous women involved in the sex industry range from 20% to 60%. Moreover, the presence of minor and debt bondage is considerable.

Known as sold daughter prostitution girls are contracted for a period of years or even for life against an initial payment to her parents, with or without her informed consent. The girls are usually minors and find themselves in the low price brothels, where conditions are worst.

There is little information regarding trafficking and prostitution among indigenous peoples in Africa. However, abduction raids taking place in Sudan during the last 15 years of civil war are known to have particularly focused on one conflict zone. Bahr and Ghazal, and have mainly affected Dinka children. Often put to work to look after cattle for Arab Baggara pastoralist groups from North Sudan.

The total number of children involved ranges from 5000 to 14000. In many cases children who have been forced into labour have also been forced to forget their own language and identity.

As noted in a recent IPEC rapid assessment on trafficking in children in the Thailand, Laos and Myanmar border areas, surveys may not necessarily succeed in identifying trafficking among indigenous communities. It may exist but he hidden away by already stigmatized communities.

CONVENTION ON THE RIGHT OF CHILD

The human rights of children and the standards to which all government must aspire in realizing these rights for all children are most concisely and fully articulated in one international human right treaty, the convention on the right of the child. The convention is the moist universally accepted human rights instrument in history it has been ratified by every country in the world except two and therefore uniquely places children center stage in the quest for universal application of human rights. By ratifying this instrument national government have committed themselves to protecting and ensuring children rights and they have agreed to hold themselves accountable for the commitment before the international community.

The optional protocol on the involvement of children in armed conflict entered into force in February 12th 2002. On that date becoming a binding instruments for states having ratified it.

To date 117 countries have signed and 88 have ratified this protocol.

Optical protocol on the sale of children and child prostitution and pornography.

1. It entered into force on 18th January 2002. On that date becoming a binding instrument for states having ratified it.
2. To date 110 countries have signed and 87 have ratified this protocol.

But, on varied legal systems and cultural traditions, the conventions of the right on the child is a universally agreed set on non-negotiable standards and obligations. It spells out the basic human rights that children every where without discrimination have the right to survival to develop the fullest to protect from harmful influence, abuse and exploitation and to participate fully in family, cultural and social life. Every right spelled out in conversion is inherent to the human dignity and harmonious development of every child. The conversion protects children rights by setting standards in health care, educational and legal civil and social services. The standards are bench marks against which progress can be accessed.

States that are partly to the convention are obliged to develop and undertake all actions and policies in the light of the best interests of the child.

The conversion on the right of the child is first legally binding instrument to incorporate the full range of human rights and 4 civil, political and economical, social, cultural and 4 rights. Two optional protocols on the involvement of children in armed conflict and on the sale of children, child prostitution, pornography we adopted to strengthen the provision of the conversion in these areas. They entered into force respectively on 12th January and 18th January 2002.

PROVIDING QUALITY EDUCATION

Education is a human right and key factor to reducing poverty and child labour and promoting democracy, peace and tolerance and development. Yet more than 100 million children of primary school age, the majority of the girls are not enrolled in school. Millions more are taught by untrained and underpaid teachers in over crowded, unhealthy and poorly equipped classrooms and 1/3rd of children do not complete five years of schooling, the minimum required for basic literacy.

As agreed at the world education forum in Dakar which reconfirmed the mandated role of the United Nations Educational Scientific and Cultural Organization in coordinating education for all partners and maintaining their collective momentum within the process of securing education we will accord high priority to ensuring by 2015 that all children have access to and complete primary education that is free, compulsory and of good quality. We will also aim at progressive of secondary education.

As a step towards these goals, we resolve to achieve the following targets.

1. Expand and improve comprehensive early childhood, care and education, for girls and boys especially for the most vulnerable and disadvantaged children.
2. Reduce the number of primary school age children who are out of school by 50% and increase net primary school enrollment or participation in alternative, good quality primary education programmes to at least 90% by 2010.
3. Eliminate gender disparities in primary and secondary education and achieve gender equality in education by 2015, with a focus on ensuring girls full and equal access to and achievement in basic education of good quality.
4. Improve all aspects of the quality of education so that children and young people achieve recognized and measurable learning outcomes especially innumeracy, literacy and essential life skills.
5. Ensure that the learning needs of all young people are met through access to appropriate learning and life skill programmes.
6. Achieve a 50% improvement in levels of adult literacy by 2015, especially for women.

To achieve these goals and targets we will implement the following strategies and actions.

1. Develop and implement special strategies to ensure that schooling is readily accessible to all children and adolescent and that basic education is affordable for all families.
2. Promote innovative programmes that encourage schools and communities to search more actively for children who have dropped out or are excluded from school and from learning, especially girls and working children, children with special needs and children with disabilities and help them enroll, attend and successfully complete their education, involving governments as well as families, communities and non governmental organizations as partners in the

educational process. Special measures should be put into place top prevent and reducc drop out due to inter alia, entry into employment.

3. Ensure that all basic education programmes are accessible, inclusive and responsive to children with special learning needs and for children with various forms of disabilities.

4. Develop and implement special strategies for improving the quality of education and meeting the learning needs of all.

5. Provide education and training opportunities to adolescent to help them acquire sustainable livelihood.

6. Develop strategies to mitigate the impact of HIV/AIDS on education systems and schools students and learning.

ARMED CONFLICT

Two million children have been killed in armed conflict in the last decade. Three times as many have been seriously injured or permanently disabled. Millions of others have been forced to take part in or witness horrifying acts of violence. Increasingly children are targets not identical casualties, a devasting carriage that reflect a wide trend in recent decade, a rise in proportion of war victims who are civilians from 5% over 90%.

In countless cases, the impact of armed conflict in children themselves may be removed form the public in institutions, prostitution. Those who have lost parents often experience humiliation, rejection and discrimination, suffering in silence as their self esteem crumbled. Their insecurity and fear cannot be measured.

CONCLUSION

Human rights are the basic and absolute rights that every person has because he or she is human being. All human rights apply to all boys and girls. While, societies may vary in their ideas on childhood and child development. One thing that all can agree on, is the importance of the well being of the children.

However, over the past few years, the stories of child abuse has grabbed the attention of the international community, provoking world wide discussion of this issue child labour remains a major cause of child exploitation and abuse in the world depriving millions of children world wide of adequate education and good health. Many of these children are the victims of the worst forms of child labour, which include slavery, bonded labour drug trafficking, commercial, sexual exploitation, domestic labour, armed conflict and all other physically and morally hazardous types of the work.

Today, it is well recognized everywhere that children need special care and protection for healthy development b'coz of their special needs and vulnerability. Numerous international organizations, government in both developing and industrialized countries and advocacy groups are creating and implementing strategies and initiatives the address the issues of child rights violations. Special instruments have been drawn up to safeguard and enforce child rights. The recognized standard is the UN convention on the right of the child (CRC), which was drawn up in 1989 and has been ratified by all most all countries in the world. The convention gives guiding principles to protect child rights. It is intended to make people aware of the importance of protecting human rights of children.

We make this solemn pledge secure in the knowledge that in giving high priority to the rights of the children to their protection and development and ensure the well being all children in all societies.

BIBLIOGRAPHY

Van. G. Bueren. *The International Law on the Rights of the Child.* Martinus Nijhoff Publishers. pp. 22-30.

Parker. S. *The Best Interests of the Child.* International Journal of Law. pp. 1-10.

Jyotsna Tiwari. *Child Abuse and Human Rights.* pp. 1-25.

Paras Diwan and Peeyushi Diwan. *Human Rights and the Law.* pp. 18-22.

David Son. S. *Human Rights.* pp. 5-10.

Chiranjeevi. S. *Human Rights in India.* pp. 4-50.

IMPLEMENTATION OF THE CONVENTION ON THE RIGHTS OF THE CHILD, 1989 IN BANGLADESH: A CRITICAL REVIEW

M. Abdul Hannan, M. Shahidul Islam***
*& M. Sahal Uddin****

INTRODUCTION

Convention on the Rights of the Child[1] has adopted by the United Nations Organization (UN) in 1989 upon the spirit of segment upon the weaker by the stronger. Stronger segment is much more active in establishing its influence and dominance upon the weaker by any means. Particularly, children being the vital part of this weaker segment have been the target of this stronger segment. Situation of the children in many parts of the world remains critical as a result of inadequate social conditions, natural disasters, armed conflicts, social exploitation, illiteracy, hunger and disability.[2] Right to life, liberty, security, and justice including some other basic rights is being jeopardized alarmingly. However, efforts, both in national and international levels, have been taken to give remedy to it from time immemorial. Meetings, seminars and programmes of this kinds are being undergone frequently to generate the sense of understanding that children of today is the citizens of tomorrow and future development of a country largely depends upon the all-round development of the children. Independent states of the world have, as part of their constitutional obligation, arranged and adopted measures for the implementation of rights of the children. The UN has been found very much active in implementing Childs rights soon after the its establishment. The Universal Declaration of Human Rights 1948,[3] the Convention on the Elimination of All Forms Racial Discrimination 1965, International Covenant on Economic, Social and Cultural Rights 1966 and Optional Protocol there to; Convention on the Elimination of All

* Associate Professor Department of Law & Justice Rajshahi University Rajshahi-6205 Bangladesh.

** Lecturer Department of Law IIUC, Kumira Chittagong, Bangladesh

*** Lecturer Department of Law & Justice Rajshahi University Rajshahi-6205 Bangladesh.

Forms of Discrimination Against Women 1989; Convention on the Rights of the Child 1989 etc can be cited among some of the efforts undertaken by the UN. Since 1971 after the independence, Bangladesh has taken different initiatives to ensure and implement the human rights of the children in the light of international documents in line with the Constitution of Bangladesh. Accordingly Bangladesh has ratified the Convention with a view of ensuring and establishing maximum rights of the children. Objective of this paper is to examine the existing rights of the children and implementation of the Convention in Bangladesh.

DEFINITION OF THE CHILD

As per the Convention any one who is below the age of eighteen years is a child, unless the law applicable to the child, majority is attained earlier.[4] However, in Bangladesh, according to the *Factories Act* 1965, any one who is sixteen years of age is a child[5] while whether an offence constitutes rape, age of the raped has been fixed fourteen years if she is not the wife of the rapist, below thirteen years, if she is the wife of the rapist.[6] Furthermore, another peculiar feature of this law is, punishment of the rapist also varies if the raped is not twelve years and she is the wife of the rapist.[7] Meanwhile, according to the National Policy of the Children of Bangladesh, any one who is seventeen years of age is a child.[8] So in Bangladesh there remains vagueness as to the age of childhood.

RIGHTS GUARANTEED IN THE CONVENTION

The Convention could easily be termed as the legacy of the efforts enshrined in the principles which have been the guiding factors behind the establishment of the UN in 1945. It is superfluous to mention that one of the key purposes behind the establishment of the UN is to achieve international cooperation in solving international problems of economic, social, cultural, or humanitarian character and in promoting and encouraging respect for human rights and fundamental freedoms for all without discrimination as to race, sex, colour, language or religion.[9] With a view to protect and promote human rights in every aspects of human understanding, ceaseless efforts have been exerting by the UN and its affiliated agencies by undertaking and adopting various international conventions. The Convention can be taken as one of the most drastic initiatives taken by the UN for the children. Rights guaranteed in the said convention for the promotion and protection of the children over the world can be summed up in this article.

As per the provisions of Article 2 of the Convention there shall not be discrimination of any kind irrespective of the child or his/her parents or legal guardians, race, colour, sex, language, religion, political or other opinion, national, ethnic or social origin, property, disability, birth or other status perpetrated by the State parties. In ensuring the rights set forth in Articles 3 and 4 of the Convention for serving the best interest of the child either by public or private social welfare institutions, courts of law, administrative authorities or legislative bodies. Article 5 recognizes the duties and responsibilities of the parents or the members of the extended family or community for the development of the children. Right to life has been recognized as the most fundamental human right through Articles 6, 7 and 8 conjointly.

As parents naturally, the best persons to nourish and nurture their children, they should not be separated from their parents unless it is determined that such a separation is necessary for the best interest of the child and article 9 guarantees it while article 10 points out the provisions for the maintenance of communication between the parents and children in appropriate cases. Freedom of opinion as one of the most significant fundamental human rights, fundamental rights has been given due emphasis in this convention through article 9 in the sense that every child who is capable of forming his or her own views can express these views freely in all matters affecting the child.

Freedom of opinion that includes freedom to seek, receive and impart information and ideas of all kinds, regardless of frontiers, either orally, in writing or in print, in the form of art or through any other media of the child's choice has been guaranteed to the children through article 13 while article 17 ensures the right to access to information and material from diversity of national and international sources, especially those aimed at the promotion of his or her social, spiritual and moral well-being and physical and mental health. The convention also directs the state parties to encourage the mass media to disseminate information and material of social and cultural benefit to the child and encourage international cooperation in the production, exchange and dissemination of such information and material from a diversity of cultural, national and international sources.

Article 18 ensures that both parents have common responsibilities for upbringing and development of the child while article 19 guides the state parties to take all appropriate legislative, administrative, social and educational measures to protect the child from all forms of physical or mental violence, injury or abuse, neglect or negligent treatment, maltreatment or exploitation including sexual abuse. Articles 20 and 21 speak of especially about the deprived of parental love or family environment. Article 23 stresses the need to recognize the rights of the disabled child. It points out that state parties should adopt measures so that a mentally or physically disabled child can enjoy effective access to education, training, heath care services, rehabilitation services, preparation for employment and recreation opportunities in a manner conducive to their possible social integration and individual development including his or her cultural and spiritual development. Article 25 and 27 are *volatile* in ensuring environment conducive to them.

Right to benefit from social security including social insurance has been ensured through article 26 while right to education, which is the key factor in achieving development of any kind, either mental or physical has been guaranteed through 28 of the convention. Compulsory free primary education has to be made for the entire child. This ideas to be made available and accessible to them with a view to eliminating ignorance and illiteracy throughout the world and facilitating access to scientific and technical knowledge. In article 30 rights of the minority child has been guaranteed stating 'the state parties should protect that child belonging to any *ethnic*, *religious* or *linguistic minorities* or of *indigenous origin'*. Article 32 brings safeguard for the protection from economic exploitation and from performing any work that is likely to be hazardous or to interfere with the child s education, or to be harmful to the child's health or physical, mental, spiritual, moral or social development while article 34 provides protection from sexual exploitation that includes protection of the children from prostitution or other unlawful sexual practices. The convention speaks of the measures for protection of child from illicit use of narcotic drugs and psychotropic substances. With that end in view, the states parties are advised to take all appropriate measures including legislative, social and educational measures.

As per the principle of natural justice the convention says that no child shall be subjected to torture or other cruel, inhuman or degrading treatment or punishment. Though Capital punishment has been allowed, there should be possibility of release. These are, after all, the rights guaranteed to the child in the Convention on the Rights of the Child 1989.

Bangladesh and the Convention on the Rights of the Child 1989

The Peoples Republic of Bangladesh became a signatory to the convention on 26 January, 1990[10] and ratified it on 3 August, 1990[11] with a reservation to article 14, paragraph 1 along with another preservation on article 21 in the sense that provisions of this article would be applicable to the extent of its consistency with the existing laws and practices of Bangladesh.[12]

CONSTITUTIONAL AND STATUTORY RECOGNITION OF THE RIGHTS MENTIONED IN THE CONVENTION ON THE RIGHTS OF THE CHILD 1989 IN BANGLADESH

Since independence on 16 December 1971, Bangladesh has always been vocal against oppression, suppression of all kind with a view to implementing the basic human rights of all of her citizens particularly the backward segment of population that includes the child and the women.[13] On 4 November 1972, Bangladesh adopted a Constitution that guarantees a bundle of rights, which resemble the rights set forth in the CRC 1989. The Constitution of Bangladesh declares that the Republic shall be in democratic nature where fundamental human rights and freedoms and respect for the dignity and worth of human person shall be guaranteed.[14] As per the Constitution, equality before the law,[15] non-discrimination on any ground,[16] protection of law,[17] right to freedom and personal liberty,[18] protection from unlawful arrest and detention,[19] protection in respect of trial and punishment,[20] freedom of movement,[21] assembly,[22] association,[23] thought and conscience and speech,[24] religion,[25] right to property[26] and protection of home and correspondence[27] have been given the status of fundamental rights. The Constitution also directs that food, clothing, shelter, education and medical care should be treated as basic human necessities by the Republic[28] and the Republic should adopt effective measures for the purpose of establishing a uniform, mass-oriented and universal system of education and extending free and compulsory education for all the children to such stage as determined by law.[29] Besides these the Government of Bangladesh also has passed the Children Act, 1974, the Children and Women Oppression Act, 2003 etc for the maximum benefit of the child of Bangladesh.

IMPLEMENTATION OF THE CHILD RIGHTS IN BANGLADESH

Now an effort is being made to examine the conditions as to how far the rights of the child have been or are being implemented in Bangladesh.

Right to Life

Despite constitutional and other statutory guarantees, life of the child of Bangladesh is not secure in the complete sense of the term. In each moment they are undergoing death threats from various factors. A simple analysis of the dailies of Bangladesh is enough to have the actual scenario of it. They are facing death either by killing, suicide or accident. A domestic help of three years of age was beaten to death by her employee on 22 June, 2006,[30] a dead body of one Mahmud Hasan Saad, a school boy of 12 years of age was recovered by the police from the Burigonga

River on 19 June, 2006,[31] Sharmin, a four year old girl was killed for her witnessing an extra-marital sexual contact on 20 August, 2006,[32] a dead body of an unidentified girl was recovered,[33] a dead body of a teenage girl of fifteen years of age was found with different marks of injuries in her body on 7 August, 2006,[34] one Zillur of ten years of age was strangulated to death in Natore on 23 Agust, 2006,[35] while a father killed his kid Yasmin by strangulation.[36] The child of Bangladesh is also loosing their life by being victim of wrong treatment by the doctors. One Nawshin, a girl of two years, was alleged to have been killed due to the wrong treatment of the doctors.[37] Besides road accidents, suicide and other incidents are also taking away the life of the child of Bangladesh every day.

Protection from Rape, Sexual Harassment etc.

Besides vulnerability to life, children are going to be the victim of rape, sexual harassment and other forms of torture in Bangladesh. Almost 4 crore 24 lakh child are growing here with different types of psycho-social, insecurity, economic, political and other forms of exploitation.[38] This includes rape, sexual harassment teasing of school going girls, torture by the employees of the domestic help etc. Generally daughter of the domestic help day labourer, garment workers, orphanage child are the widely vulnerable to rape, torture or sexual harassment in Bangladesh.[39] The following diagram shows the gravity of this type of torture in the year 2005.[40]

Month	*Number of Dailies*	*Victim*	*Nature of torture*		*Case*	*Arrest*	*Judgement*
			Injured	*Killed*			
January	71	61	48	6	25	20	10
February	110	101	70	8	41	23	14
March	115	117	89	9	40	28	8
April	188	178	131	11	73	50	20
May	164	150	121	7	58	64	18
June	133	145	122	6	46	31	8
July	130	150	116	9	56	37	13
August	138	166	155	9	59	36	10
September	127	125	108	14	52	36	5
October	93	98	90	5	42	46	3
November	97	92	85	7	38	31	5
December	46	44	38	5	20	6	2
Total	1412	1427	1173	96	551	407	116

One Bijlee Akhter Swapna committed suicide after sustaining continuous teasing by the hooligans[41] while a schoolgirl was raped on 26 July 2006 in Mymensingh.[42]

Protection from Torture

Children of Bangladesh are being vulnerable to many kinds of torture. This includes physical and mental torture, torture leading to death, death due to family violence, death by enmity etc.[43] The following diagram shows some of the pictures of child torture in Bangladesh in 2005.[44]

Month	*News*	*Victim*	*Injured*	*killed*	*Others*	*Cases*	*Arrest*	*Judgement*
January	53	54	7	38	7	14	14	3
February	91	99	27	60	10	27	30	2
March	85	182	100	58	22	23	22	3
April	65	76	32	35	7	14	13	5
May	76	93	48	42	1	23	18	3
June	65	116	59	52	3	12	8	11
July	90	115	64	47	2	14	17	9
August	76	103	60	39	2	13	12	1
September	64	69	24	42	1	19	7	2
October	65	77	33	41	5	13	7	1
November	69	79	26	47	4	13	2	3
December	53	64	27	35	5	8	12	1
Total	852	1102	507	536	69	194	162	44

In July 2006, one Palash, a student of class four, became perhaps the worst victim of familial conflict generating from the desire of satisfying materialistic end. All five fingers of his hand have been cut off with a sharp knife by his own nephew following a conflict between his mother and uncle and his sons. At one point of the conflict, his nephews cut off all the fingers of Palash with a sharp knife.[45] In the same month, Arifur Rahman, an orphan of 11 years, was strangulated to death following a conflict on landed property.[46] In the next month, August 2006, one Shaheda of 9 years age, returned to her mother after a long period of four years after sustaining continuous brutal torture by the housewife.[47]

Right to a Fair Trial

It is reported that the children are not getting proper legal protection in their way of development either as an inmate in the prison cells or else where. They are even seen in languishing in the prison cells for unknown reason. Shahnewaz, as per a report of a daily in July, an eleven years old boy who is mentally and physically challenged, have been languishing in Bagherhat Jail since January, 2006, for unknown reason though the police reports that he has been arrested under section 54 of the Code of Criminal Procedure1898.[48] Another report released by a daily in July says that 57 juveniles have been languishing in the Kashimpur Jail due to the acute influx of negligence shown by the authority concerned.[49] In a Round Table discussion entitled In Search of Justice for Children on July 19, 2006, the speakers pilled up allegations and stressed the need of immediate implementation of the Children Act, 1974. In that meeting it has been observed that regular intervention on the correction centres by the authority is a must to prevent abuse and drug addiction.[50] This is enough to show that children of Bangladesh are being denied of justice frequently.

Child Trafficking

Child trafficking or kidnapping is one of the most heinous crimes that are happening alarmingly in Bangladesh. At every moment the child of Bangladesh is being undergoing a serious risk of being kidnapped and trafficked in many parts of the world by the trafficking syndicate working actively in Bangladesh. The kidnappers are using various techniques in doing this crime. For example, promise to give job, marriage, by making love affair, tempting to give something to eat etc.[51] The following diagram may be considered in this regard.[52]

Month	*Number of dailies*	*Victim*	*Rescued*	*Arrest*	*Case*	*Judge-ment*	*Injured*	*Killed*
January	16	18	15	8	1	2	–	3
February	24	23	20	7	4	9	–	–
March	27	69	69	7	6	3	1	–
April	17	28	24	10	4	1	–	–
May	24	37	23	15	11	3	–	–
June	25	75	62	19	7	2	1	–
July	25	51	48	9	4	4	–	1
August	24	28	25	14	4	–	–	–
September	10	17	10	7	–	–	–	–
October	12	50	46	11	2	–	–	–
November	13	23	20	13	2	–	–	–
December	–	–	–	–	–	–	–	–4
Total	217	419	362	120	45	25	2	

On 11 June, 2006, two school girls identified as Khuku Moni, 13, and Shumi,12, student of class six of National Junior High School at Sonardanga area of Khulna were abducted.[53] Police rescued 11 people from traffickers on Bhorma border of whom three were child namely Mou, 16, Rozina Khatun, 18, and Munni, 10 years of age on 15 August, 2006.[54] In Hobigong, three kidnappers were captured while kidnapping Saiful, boy of 10 years of age, by the villager on 1 September, 2006.[55]

Child Labour

Though both national and international arena, laws provide ample provisions on prohibition of child labour in Bangladesh, child are getting themselves involved in numerous rigorous labour. A survey conducted by the Bangladesh Statistical Bureau reveals the following conditions of child labour in Bangladesh.[56]

- There are around 4 crore and 24 lakh child between 5-17 years of age that constitutes 32% of the total population of Bangladesh.
- Around 75% child go to school and the remaining 25% not.
- Around 74 lakh child is involved in earning money.
- Around 59% children are involved in family work.
- Only 33% of the children who are involved in familial work go to school.
- Around 13 lakh children work 43 hours in a week each.

Besides in a conference on the rights of the child it is has been reported that around 12 lakh 91 thousands children are involved in risky work and the male children earn taka 1000 per capita while the female taka 800 per capita.[57]

Involvement of Child in Smuggling, Drugs and Arms Trafficking

As per a report served by the police and Rab that as many as 7 lakh child have been engaged in carrying, throwing and making bombs, picketing during hartals and in many other crimes in the capital city, Dhaka.[58] A report recently released by the police head quarters says that 35 thousands child who are between 8-18 years of age have been involved in many criminal offences all over the country.[59]

Juvenile delinquency

At the childhood mind of the child remains soft and pure and is easily vulnerable to the target of the criminal groups of the society. The criminal groups are very prompt in using our child commit different heinous crimes. In a confessional statement to the police a teenager, Jahan, a student of class seven of Mirpur Cadet School of Dhaka, said that on 15 June, 2006, he along with his two other friends, Rajib and Masud, made an attack on his three classmates Kazi Naimul Islam Badhon,Wahidul Kabir Tonmoy and Kazi Nibrush Niluv and got their throats slit with a sharp razor, subsequently, they tied them with scarves and left the spot looting a cheque of taka 50,000, gold bangles and cash.[60] This horrific incident proves that child of Bangladesh are going to be involved in serious crimes day by day. In recent June, 2006, a report released by the Khulna Metropolitan police reveals that 70 teenagers who are between 16-18 years of age have been recruited afresh by the outlawed Purba Bangla Communist Party and trained on how to make and explode bomb successfully.[61] So it is clear that day-by-day our child are getting involved in many gravies offences unconsciously.

Right to Education

Unless and until a nation is properly educated, it cannot attain the maximum benefit from the modern inventions of science. Childhood is the golden age of learning education. However, child of Bangladesh are not getting proper education or in many cases they are being deprived of the light of education due to lack of schools, developed communication system, lack of teachers and educational instruments, library, corruption in appointing teacher, irregularities in distributing stipend and specially poverty in the countryside area are some of the mentionable grounds. However the Government of Bangladesh is determined to ensure education for all in line with the Millennium Development Goal in 2015.[62] In Bangladesh the government has arranged compulsory free primary education for all the children of her from 1 January 1993. However the frustrating information for us is that as per a report released by a daily unveils the fact that there are as many as around 2 corer and 24 lakh children aged between5-17 in Bangladesh but 91,00,000 of them do not got to school.[63]This is of course frustrating news for us.

Child as Camel Jockey

The gulf region particularly United Arab Emirate is a playground of camel race, which still continues as means of enjoyment by the people of residing therein.[64] In this race a child is usually used to set on the back of the camel which runs faster and faster competing with other camel in the race as the child on its back cries loudly. This child is known as camel jockey. This very often throws the jockey to death. The Arab

Emirate government imposed a restriction on this system saying that no child below 15 years of age could used as camel jockey but no punishment has yet been inflicted for its deliberate violation.[65] These children are not of UAE origin rather trafficked from different parts of the world especially from the third world countries. So Bangladeshi children are going to be victim to this death trapping use of camel jockey as they are being trafficked by the trafficking syndicate. In this regard the case of Faruque, a boy of 13 or 14 years of age could be picked up as an example.[66] He was trafficked to the UAE to be used as a camel jockey and returned to his mother in Bangladesh after 7 years.

Besides, there are also other forms of incidents, which form the grounds of violation of child rights in Bangladesh.

CONCLUSION

Children are the future of any nation. With a view to producing efficient citizen, social reformer, politician the children of this day should be provided with adequate environment, habitation and other essentials appropriately. With this end in view, the government should take more steps and initiatives in all its sectors including executive, legislative and judicial sectors. Besides social awareness should be strengthened to protect and nurture our children from all kinds social, economic and other forms of exploitation. Otherwise the nation will be unable to reach its goal.

NOTES

1. Hereinafter referred to as *the Convention* or *the CRC.*
2. Preamble to the *Convention on the Rights of the Child,* 1989.
3. Hereinafter referred to as *the UDHR.*
4. *Convention on the Rights of the Child* 1989, Article 1.
5. *The Factories Act* 1965, Section 2(e).
6. *The Penal Code* 1860, Section 375.
7. *Ibid.*
8. Shahabuddin Nipu and M. Rabiul Alam Khan (ed), *Sangdad Paribĭxman* 2005, (Mass-line Printers, 1/15, Humayun Road, Dhaka, 2006), 115.
9. *United Nations Charter,* Article 1 (3).
10. www. Google.com
11. Ibid.
12. Ibid.

13. Preamble to the Constitution of the Peoples Republic of Bangladesh.
14. Art-11 of the Constitution of the Peoples Republic of Bangladesh.
15. Art-27 of the Constitution of the Peoples Republic of Bangladesh.
16. Ibid, Art-28.
17. Ibid, Art-31.
18. Ibid, Art-32.
19. Ibid, Art-33.
20. Ibid, Art-35.
21. Ibid, Art-36.
22. Ibid, Art-37.
23. Ibid, Art-38.
24. Ibid, Art-39.
25. Ibid, Art-41.
26. Ibid, Art-42.
27. Ibid, Art-43.
28. Ibid, Art-15(A).
29. Ibid, Art-17(A).
30. The Daily Star, 22, June '06, P. 16, C-1.
31. The Daily Star, 20, June '06, P. 2, C-1.
32. The Daily Star, 21, August '06, P. 2, C-8.
33. The Daily Star, 15, August '06, P. 3, C-3.
34. The Daily Star, 8, August '06, P. 2, C-5.
35. Dainik Jaijaidin, 24, August '06, P. 4, C-7, 8.
36. Ibid.
37. Dainik Jaijaidin, 5, August '06, P. 1, C-2, 3.
38. Sangbad Paribixman 2005, ed by Shahabuddin Nipu and Khan Md. Rabiul Alam, *op. cit*, P. 118.
39. Ibid.
40. Ibid.
41. The Daily Star, 25 July, 2006, P. 3, c- 5.
42. The Daily Jaijaidin, 27 July, 2006, P. 12, C- 4.
43. Sangbad Paribixman 2005, Edited by Shahabuddin Nipu and Khan Md. Rabiul Alam, *op. cit*, P. 130.
44. Ibid.
45. The Daily Jaijaidin, 26 July, 2006, P. 1, C- 7, 8.

46. The Daily Jaijaidin, 31 August, 2006, P. 12, C-1.
47. The Daily Star, 16 July, 2006, P. 6, C-7.
48. The Daily Star, 12 July, 2006, P. 6, C-7.
49. The Daily Star, 12 July, 2006, P. 3, C-1, 2, 3, 4.
50. The Daily Star, 20 July, 2006, P. 3, C-4-8.
51. Sangbad Paribixman 2005, Edited by Shahabuddin Nipu and Khan Md. Rabiul Alam, *op. cit*, P. 133.
52. Ibid.
53. The Daily Star, 12 June, 2006, P. 2, C- 1.
54. The Daily Star, 16 August, 2006, P. 1, C- 5.
55. The Daily Jaijaidin, 2 September, 2006, P. 11, C- 8.
56. Sangbad Paribixman 2005, Edited by Shahabuddin Nipu and Khan Md. Rabiul Alam , *op. cit*, P. 143.
57. Sangbad Paribixman 2005, Edited by Shahabuddin Nipu and Khan Md. Rabiul Alam, *op. cit*, P. 144.
58. Ibid, P. 153
59. Ibid.
60. The Daily Star, 19 June, P. 16, C- 8.
61. The Daily Star, 25 June, P. 6, C- 8.
62. Sangbad Paribixman 2005, Edited by Shahabuddin Nipu and Khan Md. Rabiul Alam, *op. cit*, P. 162.
63. The Daily Star, 13 August, 2006, P. 12, C- 4.
64. Sangbad Paribixman 2005, Edited by Shahabuddin Nipu and Khan Md. Rabiul Alam, *op. cit*, P. 150.
65. Ibid.
66. Sangbad Paribixman 2005, Edited by Shahabuddin Nipu and Khan Md. Rabiul Alam, *op. cit*, P. 152.

EDUCATIONAL STATUS OF SCHEUDLED CASTE CHILDREN AND THEIR DEVELOPMENT IN PUDUCHERRY REGION

K. Sasicoumar Brumot & T. Subramanyam Naidu***

INTRODUCTION

Scheduled Castes (SCs) is the most backward sections of Indian society in terms of educational development. They constitute the statutorily recognized weaker sections of society and form a distinct target group under the existing pattern of planning. Due to the affirmative policies followed since independence, India has made significant progress in the educational development of Scheduled Castes. The enrolment of SC has increased considerably at the primary stage and their participation in primary education is now more or less in proportion to their share in population. But dropouts are still significantly large. There are glaring gender and regional disparities. The efforts of the government are directed towards bridging these gaps. In all the programmes in education there is a well-conceived edge in favour of SCs.

As per the Census 2001, the total population of the SC's in India is 166,635,700, which is 16.3 per cent of the total population (Registrar General, 2005), form the lowest rung of the social and economic ladder. The Scheduled Castes had been the bugbear of social apathy and discrimination before independence and cut off from the mainstream for centuries.

Since independence, the Government has taken a number of initiatives to strengthen the educational base of Scheduled Castes. Provision of educational institutions in the areas predominantly inhabited by these communities on priority basis, provision of incentives like scholarships, free ships, mid-day meals, uniforms, books and

* Research Scholar, Department of Antropology, Pondicherry Central University, Pondicherry-605014.

** Dean SSSIS & Head of the Department, Department of Antropology, Pondicherry Central University, Pondicherry-605014.

stationery, reservation of scats in educational institutions, relaxation of standards for admission to institutes of higher learning, provision of coaching, provision of hostels, etc., are some of the steps which have contributed a great deal in raising their educational attainments.

The government followed the policy of protective discrimination for the welfare of SC populations. To mention some of them, in the field of education certain number of seats 15 per cent for SC and 3 per cent for Scheduled Tribes (ST) therefore totally 18 percentages of seats based on SC/ST population are reserved in institutions of higher education. Similarly, as job and education are interlinked, reservations in job opportunities are extended to SC population. Further, to promote education among them scholarships and hostel facilities are provided. Right from the primary level financial assistance along with free distribution of books, uniforms and so forth are given to the students of SC population.

In the first two five-year plans, not much emphasis was laid on education. The government policy then emphasized on providing the immediate basic necessities like food and shelter to the people. It was only during the third five-year plan the Government were allotted good amount of money towards education of SC population. Accordingly, state governments were directed to implement all the schemes connected with the education of SC children. In order to fulfill the constitutional guarantees for the amelioration of the downtrodden, various measures have been taken. While stressing the importance of education, Gosal (1979) opined that 'a certain minimum level of literacy is a basic requirement for the people to get out of ignorance and backwardness.

The Indian Education Commission, 1882, was the first to recognize the need for the education of the Harijans, Backward castes, Aboriginals and the Hill Tribes.

The Hartog Committee, 1929, too suggested that Harijans should study along with other people.

The Present study attempts to analyze the educational problems among the SC population in Puducherry state, the welfare measures undertaken by the state government. Attempts also made to know the reasons for dropout.

AREA OF STUDY

For the present study, five rural villages i.e. *Nonankuppam, Seliamedu, Sooramangalam, Sorapet, and Thondamanatham* and three urban villages *Thiruvalluvar Nagar, Uppalam,* and *Vinobah Nagar* of Puducherry region were selected. Purposive sample methodology was adopted in selecting the villages.

From each village 50 households were selected with the total selected sample of 400 households with the total population of 1,822, out of which 921 are male and 901 female.

Table 1
shows the study villages and the sample household

Sl. No.	*Village Names*	*Sample Households*
1.	Nonankuppam	50
2.	Seliamedu	50
3.	Sooramangalam	50
4.	Sorapet	50
5.	Thondamantham	50
6.	Thiruvalluvar Nagar	50
7.	Uppalam	50
8.	Vinobah Nagar	50
	Total	400

OBJECTIVES OF THE MSTUDY

The main objective of the study is to examine the literacy rate among scheduled castes children in Puducherry region. Keeping in view, a large number of objectives may be set for this study, but few of them are:

- To probe the scheduled castes children literacy and educational levels in Puducherry.
- To know the literacy status of Scheduled Castes children in rural and urban villages of Puducherry region.
- To examine the supportive measures of government for the benefit of scheduled castes children in the study area.
- To examine at micro-level the low level of literacy and educational development among scheduled castes in Puducherry.

METHODOLOGY

The study is based on exploratory research design. The study is confined to educational development of the SC children of rural and urban areas of Puducherry region. For the present study, Anthropological techniques and methods are used in association with what is called the 'holistic approach', a methodological entity is adopted. The intensive techniques are participant observation, group discussion, informal conversation and frequent visits of the school going children to assess the Educational facilities of the Scheduled Castes children in Puducherry region. All the school going children from age group of 5 -18 were interviewed with the prepared formal schedules.

LITERACY LEVEL OF SCHEDULED CASTE POPULATION IN THE STUDY AREA

Education is a key factor for the socio-economic development of any community. It is a dynamic force in the life of every individual, which influences the physical, mental, emotional, ethical and social development. It helps to stimulate and accelerate the process of change by cultivating knowledge, skills and values appropriate to the changing socio-economic and political structure. Literacy is considered the life-blood of development.

Analysis of data in Table 2 reveals that the literacy level of SC in the study area is 75.84 per cent, out of which male literacy is 43.49 per cent and female literacy is 33.35 per cent. Out of 1822 total persons, 386 (27.83) are illiterates among which male constitutes of 130 (8.14) in number and female constitutes 256 (16.02) in number.

Table 2
Literacy level of Scheduled Caste Population in the study area

Sl. No.	*Literacy Level*	*Male*	*Female*	*Total*
I.	Illiterates	130 (8.14)	256 (16.02)	386 (24.16)
II.	Literates	679 (42.49)	533 (33.35)	1212 (75.84)
	Total	809 (50.63)	789 (49.37)	1598 (42.32)
Educational Status				
1.	Primary (1-5)	120 (9.74)	133 (36.24)	253 (20.54)
2.	Middle (6-8)	188 (15.26)	183 (14.85)	371 (30.11)
3.	High School (9-10)	210 (17.05)	157 (12.74)	367 (29.79)
4.	Higher Secondary (11-12)	84 (6.82)	44 (3.57)	128 (10.39)
5.	Diploma	17 (1.38)	5 (0.41)	22 (1.79)
6.	I.T.I	13 (1.06)	0 (0.00)	13 (1.06)
7.	Graduation	38 (3.08)	27 (2.19)	65 (5.28)
8.	Post Graduation and above	9 (0.73)	4 (0.32)	13 (1.06)
	Total	679 (55.11)	553 (44.89)	1232 (30.13)

Table 3 analyzes the sex-wise literacy status in rural and urban villages. The literacy percentage in urban area is higher than in rural villages. It is 87.52 per cent and 68.03 per cents respectively. The table clearly shows that the literacy rate for better in the urban villages when comparing to the rural villages.

Table 3
Educational Status of Male and Female Scheduled Caste in Rural and Urban areas

Sl. No.	*Educational Status*	*Rural villages*			*Urban Villages*		
		Male	*Female*	*Total*	*Male*	*Female*	*Total*
I.	Illiterates	111 (11.60)	195 (20.38)	306 (31.97)	19 (2.96)	61 (9.52)	80 (12.48)
II.	Literates	397 (41.48)	254 (26.54)	651 (68.03)	282 (43.99)	279 (43.53)	561 (87.52)
	Total	508 (53.08)	449 (46.92)	957 (52.52)	301 (46.96)	340 (53.04)	641 (35.18)
Educational level							
1.	Primary (1-5)	74 (11.03)	66 (9.84)	140 (20.86)	46 (8.20)	67 (37.22)	113 (20.14)
2.	Middle (6-8)	96 (14.31)	93 (13.86)	189 (28.17)	92 (16.40)	90 (16.04)	182 (32.44)
3.	High School (9-10)	113 (16.84)	74 (11.03)	187 (27.87)	97 (17.29)	83 (14.80)	180 (32.09)
4.	Higher Secondary (11-12)	62 (9.24)	20 (2.98)	82 (12.22)	22 (3.92)	24 (4.28)	46 (8.20)
5.	Diploma	13 (1.94)	2 (0.30)	15 (2.24)	4 (0.71)	3 (0.53)	7 (1.25)
6.	I.T.I	11 (1.64)	0 (0.00)	11 (1.64)	2 (0.36)	0 (0.00)	2 (0.36)
7.	Graduation	23 (3.43)	16 (2.38)	39 (5.81)	15 (2.67)	11 (1.96)	26 (4.63)
8.	Post Graduation and above	5 (0.75)	3 (0.45)	8 (1.19)	4 (0.71)	1 (0.18)	5 (0.89)
	Grand Total	397 (59.17)	274 (40.83)	671 (36.83)	282 (50.27)	279 (49.73)	571 (100.00)

LITERACY LEVEL OF SCHEDULED CASTE CHILDREN IN THE STUDY AREA

The table 4 Shows that the number of students studying in the selected eight villages. In the study area out of 1822 total population 538 (42.19 per cent) students are going to Schools. Out of which 282 (52.42 per cent) are boys and 256 (47.58 per cent) are girl students. This persists 29.5 per cent children are in Primary School. When it comes to Middle School education 28.25 per cent children are there. About 20.45 per cent children are in high schools in the sample. In the Higher Secondary 11.34 per cent of children are studying. In Technical courses only 3.34 per cent it is very less when compared to the general population in studying technical courses.

Table 4
Total Numbers of Students Studying in the Study Area

Sl. No.	*Educational Status*	*No. of Students Studying in the Study Area*		
		Boys	*Girls*	*Total*
1.	Primary	75 (13.94)	84 (15.61)	159 (29.55)
2.	Middle	76 (14.13)	76 (14.13)	152 (28.25)
3.	High School	59 (10.97)	51 (9.48)	110 (20.45)
4.	Hr.secondary	38 (7.06)	23 (4.28)	61 (11.34)
5.	Diploma	7 (1.30)	4 (0.74)	11 (2.04)
6.	I.T.I	5 (0.93)	2 (0.37)	7 (1.30)
7.	Graduate	18 (3.35)	15 (2.79)	33 (6.13)
8.	Post Graduate	4 (0.74)	1 (0.19)	5 (0.93)
	Total	282 (52.42)	256 (47.58)	538 (42.19)

STUDENTS STUDYING IN THE GOVERNMENT AND PRIVATE SCHOOL IN THE STUDY AREA

The table 5 highlights the number of students studying in the Government schools in the study areas. Out of 538 students 458 (43.67 per cent) are studying in the Government Schools, Which constitutes 245 (53.49 per cent) boys and 213 (46.51 per cent) girls. The highest number of boys and girls are studying in the government school where in the primary level, the number is 131 (28.60 Per cent) which persists of 59 (12.88 per cent) boys and 72 (15.72 per cent) girl students. Whereas in the primary school level of education, the number of girl students are more in number than the boys. This clearly shows the numbers of girls are more in the age groups of 5-16 years than the boys.

In rest of the classes the number of students is more or less same in number. This table clearly upshot that their economic status has generally restricted their children's to enter into private educational institution and also the impact of incentives which is given by Government as a scheme were attracted them to not send their children to private institution.

The table 6 reveals that the numbers of students studying in private schools, out of 538 students' only 76 (25.00 per cent) students are studying in the private schools. Mostly the parents of these children are working in the government sectors are sending their children to private schools and very few from agricultural sector are sending their children to the private schools. This too the numbers of students from urban areas are more in private schools. For elicit this, the number of private school going children are good in number when compared to rural area students. Availability of private schools, mode of education, and the literacy level of parents are some of the major causes for their children to the private schools in urban areas.

Table 5
Total Numbers of Students Studying in the Government School in the Study Area

Sl. No.	*Educational Status*	*No. of Students Studying in the Government Schools*		
		Boys	*Girls*	*Total*
1.	Primary	59 (12.88)	72 (15.72)	131 (28.60)
2.	Middle	64 (13.97)	63 (13.76)	127 (27.73)
3.	High School	53 (11.57)	44 (9.61)	97 (21.18)
4.	Hr.secondary	37 (8.08)	16 (3.49)	53 (11.57)
5.	Diploma	7 (1.53)	1 (0.22)	8 (1.75)
6.	I.T.I	5 (1.09)	1 (0.22)	6 (1.31)
7.	Graduate	16 (3.49)	15 (3.28)	31 (6.77)
8.	Post Graduate	4 (0.87)	1 (0.22)	5 (1.09)
	Total	245 (53.49)	213 (46.51)	458 (43.67)

Table 6
Total Numbers of Students Studying in the Private Schools in the Study Area

Sl. No.	*Educational Status*	*No. of Students Studying in the Private Schools*		
		Boys	*Girls*	*Total*
1.	Primary	23 (30.26)	13 (17.11)	36 (47.37)
2.	Middle	14 (18.42)	7 (9.21)	21 (27.63)
3.	High School	6 (7.89)	7 (9.21)	13 (17.11)
4.	Hr.secondary	3 (3.95)	2 (2.63)	5 (6.58)
5.	Diploma	0 (0.00)	1 (1.32)	1 (1.32)
6.	I.t.i	0 (0.00)	0 (0.00)	0 (0.00)
7.	Graduate	0 (0.00)	0 (0.00)	0 (0.00)
8.	Post Graduate	0 (0.00)	0 (0.00)	0 (0.00)
	Total	46 (60.53)	30 (39.47)	76 (25.00)

GOVERNMENT SCHEMES FOR THE EDUCATIONAL IMPROVEMENT

To combat with the rise in literacy rate the U.T, Adi Dravidar Welfare Department is implementing a number of schemes to improve the educational standard of the SC students. The table 7 shows increase in the enrolment of the SC students, free supply of text books, uniforms upto primary classes are being given. Supply of free text books have also been extended upto Xth standard to XIIth standard. Free lodging and boarding facilities are being given to SC students so as to continue their studies without any drop out. These facilities are being given from Vth standard to college level. Under the scheme of Post Matric Scholarship, financial assistance to SC students studying upto post matric level are being given so as to enable them to complete their education. Reimbursement of full fees charged by the institution and award of maintenance allowances for meeting their educational expenses and boarding, lodging expenses are given to the day scholars at the rate of Rs. 90/- and Rs. 50/- for student per month.

Table 7
Status of benefiting educational enlistment Schemes by the School going children

Sl. No.	*Items Received*	*Male Students benefiting the Schemes*			*Female students benefiting the schemes*		
		Benefited	*Non-Benefited*	*Total*	*Benefited*	*Non-Benefited*	*Total*
1.	Shirts & Trousers	109 (35.50)	198 (64.50)	307	N.A	N.A	N.A
2.	Shirt & Skirts	N.A	N.A	N.A	117 (43.66)	151 (56.34)	268
3.	Bicycle	121 (39.41)	186 (60.59)	307	76 (28.36)	192 (71.64)	268
4.	Chapels	72 (23.45)	235 (76.55)	307	73 (27.24)	195 (72.76)	268
5.	Break Fast	120 (39.09)	187 (60.91)	307	132 (49.25)	136 (50.75)	268
6.	Mid-day Meals	116 (37.79)	191 (62.21)	307	127 (47.39)	141 (52.61)	268
7.	Note Books	148 (48.21)	159 (51.79)	307	144 (53.73)	124 (46.27)	268
8.	Text Books	116 (37.79)	191 (62.21)	307	133 (49.63)	135 (50.37)	268

Opportunity cost at the rate of Rs. 2000/- per annum to the parents of SC girl students in middle and secondary level classes are also given in order to compensate the loss of income by the parents in the event of sending their daughters to school. The number of students benefited under this scheme during the years 2000-2001, 2001-2002 and 2002-2003 are 4758, 5250 and 6599 respectively. With a view to complete the education upto secondary level, pre-matric scholar ships are also given to the SC students from sixth standards to tenth standard. Students studying fifth, sixth and eighth standard are getting the scholarship at the rate of Rs.1000/- per annum and the student studying tenth standard are given Rs. 2000/- per annum.

To promote talent and imbibe the spirit of competition among SC students, an award of Rs. 10,000/- each to top scoring one SC boys and one SC girls students in higher secondary level is being given. Apart from this, special incentive of Rs. 1000/- each to SC student who secure not less than 65% marks in SSLC/matric/Other equivalent examination is being given in order to encourage them to undergo the post matric education. To encourage SC girl students to under take primary education and to pursue their education continuously without any hardship, a retention scholarship of Rs. 2000/- per student is being given every year, it is clearly given in the table 8.

Table 8
Numbers of Students Receiving the Scholarships in the Study Area

Sl. No.	*Scholarships*	*No. of Students benefiting the scholarships*		
		Boys	*Girls*	*Total*
1.	Pre-Matric Scholarship	76 (20.77)	83 (22.68)	159 (43.44)
2.	Post Matric Scholarship	82 (22.40)	47 (12.84)	129 (35.24)
3.	Retenship Scholarship	N.A	66 (18.03)	66 (18.04)
4.	Stipend to I.T.I Students	9 (2.46)	3 (0.82)	12 (3.28)
	Total	167 (45.63)	199 (54.37)	366 (100.00)

TOTAL NUMBER OF STUDENTS STAYING IN THE HOSTELS

The table 9 explains the total number of students staying in the hostel among the selected samples in the study area. The research was carried out among the five rural villages and three semi or urban areas where the SC population is more or less in prominent. For description of the table overall in the entire eight village out of 1822 total sampled population 575(31.56 per cent) of students are studying in the study area. Out of which 62 (10.78) are staying in the hostels among them 42 (67.74 per cents) of them are boys and 20 (32.26 per cent) of them are girls.

The number of students staying in the hostel is very low in number. In the study area out of 62 students in the hostel, 58 students are from rural villages and only 4 students are from urban areas. This shows that in the rural areas there is no facilities for education so that most of the students comes out from their village to urban areas for their studies.

Table 9
Total Numbers of Students Staying in the Hostel in the Study Area

Sl. No.	*Name of the Villages*	*No. of Students Staying in the Hostels*		
		Boys	*Girls*	*Total*
1.	Nonankuppam	5 (8.06)	2 (3.23)	7 (11.29)
2.	Seliamedu	10 (16.13)	3 (4.84)	13 (20.97)
3.	Sooramangalam	14 (22.58)	6 (9.68)	20 (32.26)
4.	Sorapet	4 (6.45)	5 (8.06)	9 (14.52)
5.	Thondamantham	6 (9.68)	3 (4.84)	9 (14.52)
6.	Thiruvalluvar Nagar	1 (1.61)	0 (0.00)	1 (1.61)
7.	Uppalam	2 (3.23)	1 (1.61)	3 (4.84)
8.	Vinobah Nagar	0 (0.00)	0 (0.00)	0 (0.00)
	Total	42 (67.74)	20 (32.26)	62 (100.00)

When we wondered about the hostel students we found that their staying in the hostel has be giving unambiguous result, for education as well as changing their life style. The only thing is the hygienic condition of hostels are very poor for that the Government has to appoint a counselor for the improvement of SC student's education and life style the hostel will be changed like a residential school. There was a complaint among the student that previously the medical team comes over to the hostel for medical check up of the students for twice in a year. But this is not occurrence presently.

DISCUSSIONS

From Primary to College level education shows that many SC students drop-out between secondary and college level. This is mainly due to the distant location of the schools and higher educational institutions. Secondly, all cannot afford to seek college education. Though government provides subsidy in the form of hostel facilities, books, incidentals, and other expenses, which are connected with their maintenance, the expenses of the students presently invariably very high and not within their reach. Courses like medicine and engineering require better financial support, poor SC parents cannot afford such a costly education for their wards. 20.54 per cent, 30.11 per cent, 10.39 per cent, 1.79 per cent, 1.06 per cent, 5.28 per cent and 1.06 per cent of SC are educated upto primary, middle, high, Higher Secondary, Diploma, Industrial Training Institute (I.T.I.), graduation and post- graduation levels respectively.

The study reveals the percentages of levels of education among the male, is higher than the females, except in the case of primary education. This is because, with the limited resources at their disposal, the impoverished SC families both in rural and urban villages prefer to invest only for their male child. The impoverished SC children do not have proper clothes and also unable to afford school uniform. Lack of books, pens and pencils also enforces many school children to drop the idea of pursuing higher education. Of course government is providing free school education but some of the parents only even the parents cannot afford small expenditure occasionally charged by the school. The non-formal education centers are utterly lacking in these villages. Although, houses have electricity connections, yet the supply is all free one light service in the rural areas. The children belonging to poor SC families do not get light and environment to read and write. Further, as most of the houses belonging to these communities are single room, Children also do not get proper study atmosphere.

Therefore, it is observed that many students became stagnant and dropout even at the primary level of education. Moreover, after the onset of puberty, the traditional and conservative families prefer to retain their daughters at home and arrange marriage rather than sending them to school. Many SC girls do not prefer to receive higher education due to their fear towards the course curriculum.

Even government has taken all measures for the SC education through financing and implementing the schemes. The educational status of SC population in Puducherry region is some what good upto the high school level. It is also seen that SC Parents spend more money in consumption of alcohol in the study area. Therefore, they do not have adequate money to spend for the education of their children. The economic impoverishment pushed many SC children to child labour activities rather than pursuing education in the last decades. But now there are no cases transversely by us while conducted our survey. Although untouchability has been removed through constitutional measures, yet the acceptability of SC children is meager in classes with the upper caste children in the schools.

Barring primary education, as observed already, very few are in institutions of higher learning. The girl student's number is more in Primary schools. But beyond this as usual and common with others, only boys rather than girls are found in large numbers in educational institutions. If these figures are indices of education among SC population, it is clear that the efforts made by the Union Territory in popularizing education by means of introducing incentives to the children of the downtrodden, has not made any marked impact. Primary education has been expanded manifold since the country attained independence but the figures above show that people from SC communities are not utilizing the benefits of education or not reaching the benefits the SC students.

The overall literacy status of SC is 75.84 per cent for females it is only 33.35 per cent. These target were achieved only the schemes which are implemented by the government for this people. Despite the scholarships and education facilities at different stages of education for SC children, their educational level has not improved sufficiently to measure of incentives provided by government for their higher education. Further, the incentive scheme has only improved enrollment status, but not the educational achievement and interest of the patrons.

It has been generally observed that the level of higher education among the SC has not been motivated by the aspiration for government jobs after high school education. Socio-economic and environmental conditions and nutritional intakes have affected their educational achievements. Many of them even fail to secure minimum pass marks for promotion to higher levels of education. These conditions are responsible for the drop-out and stagnation in education among SC in general and girls in particular, It is observed that almost 80 per cent of the SC student's dropout even before they could complete their class X study. It is logically assumed that those children who are out of schools constitute the labour force.

Literacy of SC in rural villages is lower than in the urban areas. This is because of the parents literacy is more in urban areas and very less in rural villages. In Rural villages poverty seems to be the basic obstacle in educating the children for pursuing higher education. Parents are obliged to withdraw their children from the school to earn some additional money for the living of the family.

Female literacy is low both in rural and urban areas. Rural SC families attach the least importance to the education of the girl child. Their large family size and preference for son's education have restricted the prospect of the girl child's education. Moreover, the practice of early marriage also hinders education of the girl child. The middle and high schools are three to five kilometers away from many SC villages.

Therefore, many parents do not like to send their girl child to distance places for education because of security reasons. Thus the chance of higher education, particularly among the girls, is restricted.

SUGGESTIONS FOR THE EDUCATIONAL DEVELOPMENT

1. Education should be made the 'lever of social change' by opening adequate number middle and high schools with hostel facilities in different strategic rural areas.
2. Vocation-oriented education and diversification of the same should be considered as a general proposition also applicable to SCs. Disengagement of education and white collar jobs, job oriented education based on aptitude should be devised to check unemployment, underemployment and wastage.
3. Rise in scholarship amount and its timely disbursement are of urgent need. Inadequate amount and undue delay have adversely affected the cause of education among these students.
4. Proper awareness campaign should be organized to create the awareness and the importance of education.
5. All Schools should be provided with the necessary teaching aids, like black boards, globe, maps, models etc.,
6. The examination results among the SC is very poor, extra-coaching, enhancing the students interest towards education may help to get good results.
7. Administration of incentives needs to be streamlined do that the students may avail all the facilities at proper time.
8. Transport facilities should be improved in the interior villages, So as to increase the school admission and teachers regularity.
9. The attitude of SC parents towards education should be improved through proper counseling and guidance.
10. Proper awareness should be created among the SC students who are staying in the hostels.

REFERENCES

Gosal, G.S. (1979), 'Spatial Perspective of Literacy in India', Population Geography, Vol. I, June–Dec. Pp. 41.

Report of the Indian Education Commission, 1882-83, Government of India, New Delhi, Pp. 595–602.

Kaur, Kuldip (1985), Education in India 1781–1985: Policies, Planning and Implementation; Centre for Research in Rural and Industrial Development, Chandigarh, 1985, pp. 343.

Registrar General and Census Commissioner (2005) *Census and You*, Government of India, New Delhi.

Naidu. T.S. (1999), "Strategic Planning for the Future Development of the Tribes in India", Pondicherry University, Pondicherry.

EDUCATIONAL PROBLEMS OF TRIBAL CHILDREN IN INDIA–A FUTURISTIC STUDY

G. Palanisamy & T. Subramanyam Naidu***

INTRODUCTION

Educating the tribal communities is still remains very crucial due to the fact that the tribals in India are out number the tribal population of any country. There are 574 recognised tribal communities in India with different languages and way of living. The need now is to move away to new knowledge and skills to a new place in a social order. Education is now not for the maintenance of the old, but for coping up with the change (Mead:1955). To develop the tribals, proper knowledge about their cultural traits and their felt needs require specific consideration (Vidyarthi: 1984).

Several research studies on tribal education considered socio-economic and cultural background of family is a very important variable, that affects the education of children. Therefore, the studies tried to examine the relationship between various aspects of family background and educational participation and continuing in the school. These studies examined the economic status of parents (interms of household income, parental occupation, size of land holding, size of the family). Vis-à-vis educational participation and continuing in the school for social aspects the studies considered parental education as an important one. Individual tribal status, exposure to modernity, parental awareness, attitude towards education, perception about teachers, parental expectations from education and aspiration for education of children are some of the factors that were investigated.

According to Steere, (1967) a class of 30, 40 or 50 pupils were treated as a group and a single teacher at a time imparted lessons to the group.

* Research Associate, Department of Anthropology, Pondicherry Central University, Pondicherry-605 014.

** Dean SSSIS & Head of the Department, Department of Antropology, Pondicherry Central University, Pondicherry-605014.

It was economical and information was information was uniformly given to all the students. This system had to be a graded approach, since the students were classified into different grades to theie age and achievement. It is administratively convenient for the schools to have graded classes.

Haimendorf (1982) in his work "Tribes in India" the struggle for survival", studied the problem of tribal education and their exploitation by minor government officials, as well as money lenders, land lords and other agents of vested interests, can largely be traced to their illiteracy and general ignorance of the world outside the narrow confines of their traditional environment in Andhra Pradesh and he carried out the language problems in educational institutions and the number of schools and the infra-structural facilities of the tribal schools and the reasons given by parents for not sending their children to school, that is most of them are economically backward and dwelling in remote hill villages, had until recently no access to any kind of schools and a further obstacle to the spread of eduation was the fact that such tribes as Saoras and Gadabas speak Munda languages, whereas teaching was available only in Telugu even where schools had been opened in the vicinity of tribal settlements.

The present study was conducted in four Southern states of India namely Tamilnadu, Karnataka, Kerala and Andhra Pradesh. In total 44 tribal villages was taken for the study comprising of 1200 households. By using census method of data collection it was identified that about 652 drop-out school students, and further the study examines their issues and problems to continue their studies. Based on these empirical evidences the present study suggests policy measures for the future development of the tribal education.

DROP-OUT DIFFERENTIALS

For the purpose of the study 652 drop-out children from forty-one villages of the four tribal area viz. Yelagiri hills, Attapadi, Araku valley and B.R. hills were personally interviewed. The Table 1 gives the details of the drop-out children in the study areas.

In Tamil Nadu, one hundred and four drop-out students were interviewed in the Yelagiri tribal area. Among them, sixty-three were female drop-outs. Athanavur has the highest (male11; female 16) drop-outs, followed by Kottaiyur (male 18; female 12). Male drop-outs are comparatively higher than female drop-outs. Puthur (male 6; female 4), Pallakaniyur (male 6; female 4) and Kottur (male 3; female 7) have a less number of drop-outs.

Table 1
Drop-out Differential among the Tribes in Different Areas

Sl. No.	*Village Name*	*Male*		*Female*		*Total*		*MFDR*
		No.	*P.C*	*No.*	*P.C*	*No*	*P.C*	
Tamil Nadu (Yelagiri hills)								
1.	Athanavur	11	40.74	16	59.26	27	100.00	1454.55
2.	Mangalam	3	20.00	2	80.00	15	100.00	4000.00
3.	Kottaiyur	8	40.00	12	60.00	20	100.00	1500.00
4.	Puthur	6	60.00	4	40.00	10	100.00	666.67
5.	Mettukaniyur	4	33.33	8	66.67	12	100.00	2000.00
6.	Pallakaniyur	6	60.00	4	40.00	10	100.00	666.67
7.	Kottur	3	30.00	7	70.00	10	100.00	2333.33
	Sub-total	41		53		104		1536.59
Kerala (Attapadi)								
8.	Mellamullai	3	17.65	14	82.35	17	100.00	4666.67
9.	Budhuvazhi	12	40.00	18	60.00	30	100.00	1500.00
10.	Chemanur	5	62.50	3	37.50	8	100.00	600.00
11.	Agali	4	57.14	3	42.86	7	100.00	750.00
12.	Mamanur	10	52.63	9	47.37	19	100.00	900.00
13.	Nellupathi	12	57.14	9	42.86	21	100.00	750.00
14.	Thadikindu	16	57.14	12	42.86	28	100.00	750.00
15.	Annavai	6	46.15	7	53.85	13	100.00	1166.67
16.	Mulli	1	33.33	2	66.67	3	100.00	2000.00
17.	Mukkali	11	91.67	1	8.33	12	100.00	90.90
18.	Mellakakupadi	1	20.00	4	80.00	5	100.00	4000.00
19.	Thallakakupadi	8	61.54	5	38.46	13	100.00	625.00
20.	Pottikal	10	41.67	14	58.33	24	100.00	1400.00
	Sub-total	99		101		200		1020.20
Andhra Pradesh (Araku Valley)								
21.	Sowa	24	51.06	23	48.94	47	100.00	958.33
22.	Madagada	6	50.00	6	50.00	12	100.00	1000.00
23.	Thevaduvalasa	7	53.85	6	46.15	13	100.00	857.14
24.	Kothapalakuda	9	33.33	18	66.67	27	100.00	2000.00
25.	Pathapalakuda	5	41.67	7	58.33	12	100.00	1400.00
26.	Ganjakuda	2	66.67	1	33.33	3	100.00	500.00
27.	Sunkarametta	7	38.89	11	61.11	18	100.00	1571.42
28.	Simbulikuda	6	50.00	6	50.00	12	100.00	1000.00
29.	Nandhivalasa	2	40.00	3	60.00	5	100.00	1500.00
30.	Cannela	25	44.64	31	55.36	56	100.00	1240.00
31.	Araku	9	37.50	15	62.50	24	100.00	1666.67
32.	Shompi	8	72.73	3	27.27	11	100.00	375.00
	Sub-total	110		130		240		1181.82

Contd....

Sl. No.	Village Name	Male		Female		Total		MFDR
		No.	P.C	No.	P.C	No	P.C	
Karnataka (B.R. Hills)								
33.	Hosapodu	4	36.36	7	63.64	11	100.00	1750.00
34.	Banglipodu	8	80.00	2	20.00	10	100.00	250.00
35.	Muthugadagadda	2	50.00	2	50.00	4	100.00	1000.00
36.	Erakanagada	4	44.44	5	55.56	9	100.00	1250.00
37.	Seegabetta	4	57.14	3	42.86	7	100.00	750.00
38.	Kannericolony	9	45.00	11	55.00	20	100.00	1222.22
39.	K.Gudi	1	20.00	4	80.00	5	100.00	4000.00
40.	Puranipodu	15	60.00	10	40.00	25	100.00	6666.67
41.	K.Devarahalli	11	64.71	6	35.29	17	100.00	545.45
	Sub-total	58		50		108		862.02
	All States	309		343		652		1116.88

Male-Female drop-out ratio is calculated to identify the number of female drop-outs per male drop-outs. Highest MFDR is observed in the Mangalam village (4000.00), i.e. for every 1000 male drop-outs, 4000 female drop-outs takes places. Kottur accounts for a MFDR of 2333.33 and Mettukaniyur (2000.00) Palla Kaniyur (666.67) and Puthur (666.67) are engaged by only very few female drop-outs. In addition to that, in these villages male drop-outs are exceeding female drop-outs. An average MFDR of 1536.59 is observed among the Malayali tribes. Compare to the other states, MFDR is high in Tamil Nadu, which indicates a high female drop-out.

Two hundred tribal drop-out students were interviewed in Attapadi tribal agency of Kerala, among them one hundred and one were female. Unlike, Tamil Nadu, male drop-outs are equal in number to the female drop-outs. In Kerala, the tribal villages, Budhavazhi (30), Thadikundu (28) and Pottikal (24) were having large number of drop-outs. Drop-outs were very less in villages like Mulli (3), Mellakakupadi (5), Agali (7) and Chemanur (8). Variation between male and female drop-outs is marked in the above said villages. The numbers of male and female drop-outs of the Kerala villages are as follows, Budhuvazhi (male 12, female 18), Thadikundu (male 16, female 12) and Pottikal (male 10, female 14) and Thzhakakupadi (male 8, female 5).

Male-Female drop-out ratio of the Attapadi tribal agency is 1020.20. i.e. in Attapadi 1020 female students are dropped out from the schools per every 1000 boys, Highest MFDR is observed in Mellamullai (4666.67), Mulli (2000.00), Mellakakupadi (4000.00), Pottikal (1400.00), Budhuvazhi (1500.00) and Annavai (1166.67). Lowest MFDR is found in

Chemanur (600), Agali (750), Nellupathi (750) and Thadikundu (750) villages.

The above result shows that, the MFDR and the general drop-out number is very less in the villages nearer to the tribal schools. The village Thadikundu is 8 Kms away from the Primary school and 19 Kms away from the High school. Children of Thadikundu village have to cross a rivulet, which is located in between their home hamlet and the school town. In rainy season, it is very difficult for the students to cross the rivulet. In rainy season, they use cultivated land as their path, if any peasant sees them in their land, they use to beat them, parents are usually afraid about these incidents. So, they never allow their children to go for schools during rainy seasons. In addition to that, lack of mid-day meals and unavailability of schools in their native nearby villages are the main reasons for the drop-outs.

Two hundred and forty drop-out students were interviewed in Araku valley of Andhra Pradesh. Among them one hundred and thirty were female students. Large number of drop-out students was found in the village Sovva (47), Gannela (56), Kothapalakuda (27) and Aruku (24).

Like the surrounding states, male and female drop-outs vary from village to village. Male drop-outs are high in the villages of Sovva (24) and Gannela (25), on the other hand female drop-outs are high in villages like Sovva (23), Kothapalakuda (18), Gannela (31), Araku (15) and Sunkarametta (11), Low male and female drop-outs are found in Ganjakuda (male 2, female1), Nandhivalaso (male 2; female 3) and Madakada (male 6; female 6).

An average MFDR ratio of 1981.82 is observed in Andhra Pradesh. MFDR is high in Kothapalakuda (2000), Araku (1666.67), Sungkarametta (1571), Pathapalakuda (1400) and Gannela (1240). Lowest is observed in Shampi (375), and Ganjakuda (500). Gannela and Sovva villages are the High school towns, students from the surrounding villages like Devudolara, Ganjaguda and Sunkarametta are came to Gannela for their High school education. These villages are located at a distance of 6-15 Kms away from the school town Gannela. Distance of the school makes fear among the parents as well as students to continue their education.

Female education has not received the required attention in tribal areas of Araku valley. Illiteracy and ignorance gripping the female folk distort the female role models and perpetuate ignorance and suppression. And moreover shyness is a characteristic feature of the primitive tribes. Particularly girls are extremely shy. Submissiveness of their nature hinders their inquisitiveness. For any clarification in the course of study they hesitate to approach their teachers. Apart from this improper school administration also sometimes reduce the enthusiasm of both students and parents.

One hundred and eight students from ten villages of B.R.Hills in Karnataka were selected for the present study. Among them fifty were female students. In B.R. hills tribal hamlets, Kanneri colony (20), Puranipodu (35), K. Devarahalli (17), and Hosapodu (11) were noted for large number of drop-outs. An interesting point noted in Karnataka tribal schools is that, unlike the other states, male drop-outs are higher in number than the female drop-outs in some villages. Large numbers of female drop-outs are found in villages like Kanneri (11) and Puranipodu (10) villages.

An average MFDR of 862.20 was observed in Karnataka tribal villages. Puranipodu has the highest MFDR of 6666.67, followed by K.Gudi (4000.00) and Hosapodu (1750.00). The villages like Banglipodu (250.00) and Segabetta (750.00) are noted for very low drop-outs. Puranipode and Kanneri are located 10-16 Kms away from their school town B.R. hills. Only one tribal school is functioning for the above said villages. Parents fear about sending their children to such a long distance and it is the only major reason prevailing largescale drop-outs in Karnataka.

Drop-outs are more in the interior villages of Puranipodu and K.Devarahalli. A male student who completes the Primary school education in the interior villages are not interested to join in the V.G.K.K. school, because of its long distance from their home town. And there is a general tendency among the tribal parents to withdraw their children from the school and to make them work along with them in their economic pursuits.

Geographical and communication factors play an important role in education of the ST. For example in the interior villages of Puranipodu and K.Devarahalli the drop-out rate is more, and enrolment is low. Importance of transportation from the interior villages to school plays a major role for the decrease in drop-out rate. More over, easy communications of the tribes with the outsiders expose them to outside influences, and make them to change easily.

TRIBAL DIFFERENTIALS AMONG DROP-OUT STUDENTS

Table 2 explains the tribal variations existing in tribal students. Among the selected ten tribes, large number of drop-outs were found in Soliga's (108) of Karnataka. Irular (101) of Kerala and Malayali (104) of Tamil

Nadu. Drop-out is very less among the Nukadora (18) and Valmiki (43) of Andhra Pradesh, and Mudugar (45) of Kerala.

Table 2
Drop-out Differences among Various Tribes

Sl. No.	*Village Name*	*Male*		*Female*		*Total*		*MFDR*
		No.	*P.C*	*No.*	*P.C*	*No*	*P.C*	
Tamil Nadu (Yelagiri hills)								
1.	Malayali Kerala (Attapadi)	41	39.42	63	60.58	104	100.00	1536.59
2.	Irular	46	46.46	55	54.46	101	50.50	1195.65
3.	Mudugar	23	23.23	22	21.78	45	22.50	956.52
4.	Kurumbar	30	30.30	24	23.76	54	27.00	800.00
	Sub-total	99	49.50	101	50.50	200	100.00	1020.20
Andhra Pradesh (Araku Valley)								
5.	Valmiki	19	17.27	24	18.46	43	17.91	1263.61
6.	Kondadora	40	36.36	29	22.31	69	28.75	725.00
7.	Nukadora	7	6.36	11	8.46	18	7.50	1571.43
8.	Bagatha	19	17.27	33	25.38	52	21.67	1736.84
9.	P.Porja	25	22.73	33	25.38	58	24.17	1320.00
	Sub-total	110	45.83	130	54.17	240	100.00	1181.82
Karnataka (B.R. Hills)								
10.	Soliga	58	53.70	50	46.30	108	100.00	862.07
	All States	308	47.24	344	52.76	652	100.00	1116.68

Influence of tribe in female education is very high in tribal societies like the non-tribal. Variations in drop-outs exist between various tribes. Large number of male drop-outs were identified in Malayali (41), Irular (46), Soliga (58), and Kondadora (40), Male drop-outs were very less in Nukadora (7), Bagatha (19) and Mudugar (23) tribes. Like the male drop-outs female drop-outs are also high among Malayali (63), Soliga (50), and Bagatha (33) and P. Porja (33). Male-female drop-out is very high among the Malayali (1536.59), P.Porja (1320.00), Bagatha (1736.84), Nukadora (1571.43), and Valmiki (263.16), Kurubar (300.00) and Soliga (862.07) are noted for their very low male-female drop-out ratio. It is very interesting to note that total drop-outs are very less among Nukadora and Bagatha tribes of Andhra Pradesh, but female drop-outs are very high compare to the other. Child marriages, particularly pre-pubertal marriages and a long distance of schools from these interior villages is the main reason for very high female drop-outs in these villages.

Muduga and Kurumba are living in isolated hill tops of Kerala. They are dwelling far away from the school of Agali and Anavai. But Irula are inhibiting nearer to the school and are having regular contact with the plain people and other tribal groups. The Muduga and Kurumba depend mainly on shifting cultivation. During agricultural seasons the Muduga and Kurumba children are also engaged in collecting and food gathering minor forests products like roots, tubers, adda leaves (useful for making leaf plates) honey, tamaind, medicinal herbs etc. The children's involvement in economic activities is also one of the reasons for irregularity to the school.

The Soliga who are living in the hilly and forest areas of B.R hills in Karnataka are depending only on the Ashram school which was established in 1953 by the V.G.K.K. a voluntary agency funded by IRDP for their High school education. The V.G.K.K. school is located at a distance of nearly 8 to 16 Kms away from the interior villages. Students inhibiting within 3 Kms range are not allowed in the hostels. This also increases the drop-out rate to certain extent. In addition to this, parents fear about sending their children to long distance. Drop-outs are more in the interior villages of Puranipodu and K. Devarahalli. Male students who completes the Primary School education in the interior villages are not ready to come and join in the V.G.K.K. school, because of its long distance to their home town, and there is a general tendency among the tribal parents to withdraw their children from the school to make them to work along with them in their economic pursuits.

DEMOGRAPHIC VARIATION AMONG THE DROP-OUT STUDENTS

Along with the socio-economic factors, demographic factors also extend their influence in education. Age is the main factor, which effects school enrolments, and drop-outs. Table 3 explains the variations in drop-out among various age-groups.

In Yelagiri hills of Tamil Nadu, drop-outs are high in the age group of 5-0 (42) years, and 11-15 years (46). Female drop-outs are exceeding male drop-outs in these age groups, male and female drop-outs are 15 and 27 in the age group of 5-10, and 14 and 32 in 11-15 years age groups. Male-female drop-out ratio shows that the ratio is high in the age group of 11-15 years. Pubertal attainment of the girl students are the main reasons for the high MFDR in 10-15 years age group and care of the younger siblings in the absence of their parents.

Like Tamil Nadu in Kerala also large number of drop-outs are found in the age groups of 5-10 years (80) and 11-15 years (94). But the MFDR is higher among the Primary schools, 5-10 years, when compared to 11-15 years. In Kerala, the non-availability of High schools in the nearby villages leads to large number of drop-outs in the age of 11-15 years.

Table 3
Age Distribution of Drop-out Students

Sl. No.	*Village Name*	*Male*		*Female*		*Total*		*MFDR*
		No.	P.C	No.	P.C	No	P.C	
Tamil Nadu (Yelagiri hills)								
1.	5-10	15	35.71	27	64.29	42	100.00	1800.00
2.	11-15	14	30.43	32	69.57	46	100.00	2285.71
3.	16-20	12	75.00	4	25.00	16	100.00	333.33
	Sub-total	41	39.42	63	60.58	104	100.00	1536.59
Kerala (Attapadi)								
4.	5-10	33	41.25	47	58.75	80	100.00	1424.24
5.	11-15	50	53.19	44	46.81	94	100.00	880.00
6.	16-20	16	61.54	10	38.46	26	100.00	625.00
	Sub-total	99	49.50	101	50.50	200	100.00	980.19
Andhra Pradesh (Araku Valley)								
7.	5-10	61	46.56	70	53.44	131	100.00	1147.54
8.	11-15	46	47.42	51	52.58	97	100.00	1108.69
9.	16-20	3	25.00	9	75.00	12	100.00	3000.00
	Sub-total	110	45.83	130	54.17	240	100.00	1200.00
Karnataka (B.R. Hills)								
10.	5-10	10	45.45	12	54.55	22	100.00	1200.00
11.	11-15	30	52.63	27	47.37	57	100.00	900.00
12.	16 20	18	62.07	11	37.93	29	100.00	611.11
Sub-total		58	53.70	50	46.30	108	100.00	862.07
All States		308	47.24	344	52.76	652	100.00	1116.88

Like Kerala, Andra Pradesh is also experiencing large number of drop-outs in the age-group of 5-10 years (131) and 1-15 years (97). Female drop-outs are higher than male drop-outs in all the age group, particularly in the age group of 5-10 years. The MFDR is high among thc 16-20 years age group. It is interesting to note that, Andhra Pradesh is experiencing a high MFDR ratio in 16-20 years age group.

In Karnataka, drop-outs are high in 11-15 years (57) followed by 16-20 years (29) and 5-10 years (22). Female drop-outs are high in the age group of 11-15 years. The MFDR is high among the 5-10 years age group and in the age group of 11-15 years.

CLASS DIFFERENTIALS IN DROP-OUT

Drop-out of students from different classes (Table 4), shows that in Tamil Nadu, large number of students are dropped out from first (7) and second (9) standards. Female drop-outs are high in first (14), second (9), third (8) and fifth classes (10). On the other hand male drop-outs are high in number in Primary and late High school classes.

Table 4

Class Differential in Drop-out Rate among the Tribal Students

Sl. No.	*Village Name*	*Male*		*Female*		*Total*		*MFDR*
		No.	*P.C*	*No.*	*P.C*	*No*	*P.C*	
Tamil Nadu (Yelagiri hills)								
1.	First	7	33.33	14	66.67	21	100.00	2000.00
2.	Second	9	50.00	9	50.00	18	100.00	1000.00
3.	Third	3	27	278	72.73	11	100.00	2666.67
4.	Fourth	4	40.00	6	60.00	10	100.00	1500.00
5.	Fifth	2	16.67	10	83.33	12	100.00	5000.00
6.	Sixth	3	33.37	6	66.67	9	100.00	2000.00
7.	Seventh	2	28.57	5	71.43	7	100.00	2500.00
8.	Eighth	-	-	-	-	-	-	-
9.	Nineth	3	100.00	-	3		100.00	-
10.	Tenth	8	61.54	5	38.46	13	100.00	625.00
	Sub-total	41	39.42	63	60.58	104	100.00	1536.59
Kerala (Attapadi)								
12.	First	11	42.31	15	57.69	26	100.00	1363.64
13.	Second	11	42.31	15	57.69	26	100.00	1363.64
14.	Third	14	60.87	9	39.13	23	100.00	642.86
15.	Fourth	22	91.67	24	52.17	46	100.00	1090.91
16.	Fifth	11	47.83	12	52.17	23	100.00	1090.91
17.	Sixth	15	60.00	10	40.00	25	100.00	666.67
18.	Seventh	6	54.55	5	45.45	11	100.00	833.33
19.	Eighth	5	55.56	4	44.44	9	100.00	800.00
20.	Nineth	-	3	100.00	3	100.00	-	
21.	Tenth	4	50.00	4	50.00	8	100.00	1000.00
	Sub-total	9	49.50	101	50.50	200	100.00	1020.20
Andhra Pradesh (Araku Valley)								
23.	First	21	50.00	21	50.00	42	100.00	1000.00
24.	Second	12	44.44	15	55.56	27	100.00	1250.00
25.	Third	16	42.71	19	54.29	35	100.00	1187.50
26.	Fourth	16	48.48	17	54.29	35	100.00	1187.50
27.	Fifth	7	35.00	13	51.52	33	100.00	1062.50
28.	Sixth	7	35.00	13	65.00	20	100.00	1857.14

Sl. No.	*Village Name*	*Male*		*Female*		*Total*		*MFDR*
		No.	*P.C*	*No.*	*P.C*	*No*	*P.C*	
29.	Seventh	8	38.10	13	61.90	21	100.00	1625.00
30.	Eighth	8	100.00	-	8	100.00	-	
31.	Nineth	6	100.00	-	6	100.00	-	
32.	Tenth	-	13	100.00	13	100.00	-	
	Sub-total	110	15.83	130	54.57	240	100.00	1181.82
Karnataka (B.R. Hills)								
34.	First	1	25.00	3	75.00	4	100.00	3000.00
35.	Second	4	57.14	3	42.86	7	100.00	750.00
36.	Third	5	71.43	2	28.57	7	100.00	400.00
37.	Fourth	5	53.57	13	46.43	28	100.00	866.67
38.	Fifth	15	52.63	9	47.37	19	100.00	900.00
39.	Sixth	10	41.18	10	58.82	17	100.00	1428.57
40.	Seventh	2	40.00	3	60.00	5	100.00	1500.00
41.	Eighth	6	60.00	4	40.00	10	100.00	666.67
42.	Nineth	6	100.00	-	6	100.00	-	
43.	Tenth	2	40.00	3	60.00	5	100.00	1500.00
	Sub-total	58	53.70	50	46.30	108	100.00	862.07
	All States	308	47.24	344	52.76	652	100.00	1116.88

The reason for the large number of drop-outs in the late Primary classes is that, the students are not interested to continue their education after their Primary schooling, and in addition to that their poor economic situation leads them to engage in economic activities. Distance of High schools from the native places, along with the parent's compulsion and fear are also account to some extent.

The figure 1 explains in Kerala, large number of drop-outs are found in fourth (male 22, female 24), sixth (male 15, female 10), and first and second standards (male 11, female 15). Distance of the schools from the native villages is the main reason for large number of drop-outs at Primary school level.

In Andhra Pradesh also large number of drop-outs was seen in Primary classes first standard 42, second standard 27, third standard 35, fourth standard 35. Male and female drop-outs show the same trend. Distance of the schools from the native villages, poor economic condition, fear about teachers, unsuitable curriculum and medium of instruction are the main reasons for drop-outs in Andhra Pradesh.

In Karnataka large number of drop-outs are in the Primary classes, forth (28), fifth (19) and sixth (17) classes. In Karnataka, hostel accommodation are the major reasons for drop-outs at Primary level.

REASONS FOR DROP-OUT

Education is an acquired character, which influenced by various economic, cultural and political factors. Drop-out of children from a school is mainly because of economic necessities. Various views are held among different personalities, as some argue that economy of the family is the main reason for drop-out, and some argue that, society and culture are the main hindrance for higher education. To clarify the above reasons, the data was collected from the drop-out students. Table 5 explains the reasons for drop-out among the tribal students.

In Tamil Nadu, economic needs of the family (85) are the predominant factor lead to drop-out. Student disinterest (20) distance of the school from the native village (18), parent compulsion, (24) and care of younger siblings (18) are also took important place in trial children school drop-out, in which parent compulsion (19), to care younger siblings (6) and distance of the school (18). Student disinterests in education (18) are the main reasons for higher male drop-outs.

In Kerala economic necessity (63), absence of mid-day meals scheme (57), distance of schools from the native places (46), parents compulsion (41) are the reason for large scale drop-outs.

The reasons explained by male students are the economy of the family (30), distance of the school from the native place (26), absence of mid-day meals scheme (20), hatred to school (14), environment (14), detained from previous class (10), and parents compulsion (14). For the girls, in addition to economic necessity (33), and absence of mid-day meals (37) parents compulsion (27) and to take care of younger siblings (13) are the main reasons for the drop-out.

Table 5
Reasons for Drop-outs among the Tribal Students

Sl. No.	*Village Name*	*Male*		*Female*		*Total*	
		No.	*P.C*	*No.*	*P.C*	*No*	*P.C*
Tamil Nadu (Yelagiri hills)							
1.	Parents/Head of the family compulsion	5	20.83	9	79.17	24	100.00
2.	To take care of their sibilings	6	33.33	12	66.67	18	100.00
3.	They felt the need of the family	32	37.65	53	62.35	85	100.00
4.	Puberty		-	3	100.00	3	100.00
5.	Marriage		-	1	100.00	1	100.00
6.	Health problem of students/ parents	3	42.86	4	57.14	7	100.00
7.	Distance from native place	8	44.44	10	55.56	18	100.00
8.	Less interest in Education	13	65.00	7	35.00	20	100.00

Sl. No.	Village Name	Male		Female		Total	
		No.	P.C	No.	P.C	No	P.C
9.	Fear of teachers	7	50.00	7	50.00	14	100.00
10.	Customary norms		-	1	100.00	1	100.00
11.	Detain in the previous class	8	61.54	5	38.46	13	100.00
12.	Lack of free books and dresses	-	-	-			
13.	Lack of mid-day meals	-	-	-			
14.	Lack of scholarships	-	-	-			
15.	Lack of hostel facility			1	100.00	1	100.00
16.	Unsatisfied school environment			1	100.00	1	100.00
	Kerala (Attapadi)						
17.	Parents/Head of the family compulsion	14	34.15	27	65.85	41	100.00
18.	To take care of their sibilings	4	23.53	13	76.47	17	100.00
19.	They felt the need of the family	30.	47.62	33	52.38	63	100.00
20.	Puberty	-	-	-			
21.	Marriage	-	-	-			
22.	Health problem of students/parents	4	50.00	4	50.00	8	100.00
23.	Distance from native place	26	56.52	20	43.48	46	100.00
24.	Less interest in Education	8	57.14	6	42.86	14	100.00
25.	Fear of teachers	8	57.14	6	42.86	14	100.00
26.	Customary norms	1	33.33	2	66.67	3	100.00
27.	Detain in the previous class	10	50.00	10	50.00	20	100.00
28.	Lack of free books and dresses		-	1	100.00	1	100.00
29.	Lack of mid-day meals	20	35.09	37	64.91	57	100.00
30.	Lack of scholarships	1	33.33	2	66.67	3	100.00
31.	Lack of hostel facility	4	36.36	7	63.64	11	100.00
32.	Unsatisfied school environment	10	71.43	4	28.57	14	100.00
	Andhra Pradesh (Araku Valley)						
33.	Parents/Head of the family compulsion	68	44.44	85	55.56	153	100.00
34.	To take care of their sibilings	25	32.47	52	67.53	77	100.00
35.	They felt the need of the family	73	52.52	66	47.48	139	100.00
36.	Puberty	1	100.00	-	-	1	100.00
37.	Marriage	1	100.00	-	-	1	100.00
38.	Health problem of students/parents	6	50.00	6	50.00	12	100.00
39.	Distance from native place	20	57.14	15	42.86	35	100.00
40.	Less interest in Education	44	49.44	45	50.56	89	100.00
41.	Fear of teachers	11	100.00	-		11	100.00
42.	Customary norms	5	83.33	1	16.67	6	100.00
43.	Detain in the previous class	11	55.00	9	45.00	20	100.00
44.	Lack of free books and dresses	28	53.85	24	46.15	52	100.00
45.	Lack of mid-day meals	30	51.72	28	48.28	58	100.00
46.	Lack of scholarships	22	48.89	23	51.11	45	100.00
47.	Lack of hostel facility	3	50.00	3	50.00	6	100.00
48.	Unsatisfied school environment	3	75.00	1	25.00	4	100.00

Contd...

Sl. No.	Village Name	Male		Female		Total	
		No.	P.C	No.	P.C	No	P.C
	Karnataka (B.R. Hills)						
49.	Parents/Head of the family compulsion	23	50.00	23	50.00	46	100.00
50.	To take care of their sibilings	1	33.33	2	66.67	3	100.00
51.	They felt the need of the family	32	61.54	50	38.46	52	100.00
52.	Puberty		-	2	100.00	2	100.00
53.	Marriage	-	-	-			
54.	Health problem of students/parents	2	50.00	2	50.00	4	100.00
55.	Distance from native place	9	60.00	6	40.00	15	100.00
56.	Less interest in Education	31	58.49	22	41.51	53	100.00
57.	Fear of teachers	1	50.00	1	50.00	2	100.00
58.	Customary norms	-	-	-			
59.	Detain in the previous class	4	50.00	4	50.00	8	100.00
60.	Lack of free books and dresses	-	-	-			
61.	Lack of mid-day meals	-	-	-			
62.	Lack of scholarships	-	-	-			
63.	Lack of hostel facility	-	-	-			
64.	Unsatisfied school environment		-	1	100.00	1	100.00

Unlike other States, in Andhra Pradesh economic needs (139), and parents compulsion (153) lead to large number of drop-outs, students disinterest (89) and care of younger siblings (77) are also the main reasons. In Andhra Pradesh large number of female drop-out are because of parents compulsion (85), economic need (66), care of siblings (52), disinterest in education (45), unavailability of free books and dress (24), absence of mid-day meals (28), and scholar ships (23). A considerable number of students are dropped out from schools, because of the fear about teachers, lack of books, uniform and scholarships, distance of the school, and health problem of the students.

In Karnataka, students disinterest in education (53), leads to large number of drop-out in addition with economic need of the family (52) and parents compulsion (46). Large number of students are dropped-out from schools because of parents compulsion (male 23, female 23), economic necessity (male 23, female 20), and disinterest and deviation of the students from education (male 31: female 22) to economic activity.

DISCUSSION

Results of the above analysis shows that, provision of education facilities in the tribal areas are very meager. Drop-out students are very high in the interior and distant villages. Female drop-outs are more in number than the male drop-outs.

In Tamil Nadu female drop-out are high compare to other states. It was noted that parents never allow their female children to school after their puberty. In Attapadi tribal area the percentage of drop-out children are more, among the Irula, Kurmaba and Muduga. In Araku valley majority of the drop-out children belongs to Kondadora, Bagatha and P. Porja. In B.R. hills the female drop-outs are less in number than male drop-outs.

The percentage of drop-out is more in the age group of 5-10 years. In Yelagiri hills, drop-out children are more in the age group of below 15 years. In Attapadi, Araku valley and B.R. hills more than 50 per cent of the drop-out students are in the age group of 5-10 years and in the age group of 11-15 years. More than fifty per cent of the students in all the states were dropped out in the primary sections of the school.

Economic necessity of the parents lead the students to engage in labour force, the non-availability of high school education in their native and nearby villages, in addition with their parents fear about sending their children to long distance lead them to stop their children's education after primary school. Students disinterest in education, parents compulsion, economic contribution of the children are the major reasons leading to large scale drop-outs. In addition with this in some state like Kerala, Andhra Pradesh and Karnataka, absence of mid-day meals and non-availability of text books and scholarships are also the important reasons for the drop-out of students. Apart form this social customs attitude of parents about female education, and early marriage of female children are also the contributing factors for the drop-out of tribal children.

The drop-out children are giving suggestions to improve their education. In Yelagiri hills, Attapadi and Araku valley more than 50 per cent of the female children need more number of schools in their and nearby villages. They need financial assistance to continue their education. And also, students stressed, a good school environment and to create educational awareness among their parents.

The drop-out students are interested to continue their education. In all the states more than forty per cent of the children like to continue their studies through informal education. Male drop-out children are interested to continue technical education, i.e weaving, printing work, industrial trainings, manufacturing etc. It was observed in all the four areas, the female drop-out children like to do tailoring, handicraft works, etc.

The nature and extent of the drop-outs varies not only between various states and societies, and with in a society it differs between groups. Geographical and communication factors play an important role in education of the ST. The above discussion shows that the MFDR and the general drop-out number is very less in the villages nearer to the tribal schools, and the MFDR is very high in the interior villages. Along with the socio-economic factors demographic factors also extend their influence in education. Age is the main factor, particularly among the females which effects school enrolment and drop-out. MFDR increase from 5-10 years to 16-20 years. Puberty attainment of the girls, early marriage and economic utility of the male children leads to large scale drop-outs in 16-20 years age group.

Economic necessity and parent's compulsion, absence of mid-day meals schemes, improper provision of uniforms and text books leads to large scale drop-outs in all the states. Proper councelling and guidance to the children and parents regarding the importance of education should be given. Free note-books and uniforms should be distributed at the beginning of every academic year. Above all the school environment should be changed to attract the students in terms of providing sports facilities, encouraging tribal art and culture etc.

SUGGESTIONS

Based on the empirical findings, the following suggestions are made for the future development of tribal education:

1. Education should not be limited only the attainment of literacy and should include different levels. Literacy is only means to education and not an end in itself. In many tribal areas, though the percentage of literacy is high, the educational level is by and large low. So, more number of high schools and junior colleges should be opened in the tribal areas.
2. Proper awareness campaign should be organized to create the awareness and the importance of education.
3. Educational institutions should be attached with the hostels upto the primary level and should be available within a walkable distance (2 to 3 kms), and high schools should be provided within 5 kms distance from the tribal villages.
4. All schools, old as well as new, should have proper buildings. Repairs of the existing school buildings should be carried out at regular intervals.
5. All schools should be provided with the necessary teaching aids, like black boards, globe, maps, models etc.,

6. Every school must design programmes which gives a lot of scope for tribal talents and put them to proper use, agriculture, horticulture, wood work, pet rearing, plant identification, herbal medicine and gardening are some of the extra curricular programmes which should be introduced in every tribal school.
7. To bring the tribal children to the mainstream the school curriculum should be modified according to their culture, dialect and local environment.
8. The examination results among the tribals are very poor, extra-coaching, enhancing the student interest towards education may help to get good result.
9. Higher level officials should check the functioning of the schools frequently, not only the attendance registers but also the teaching methods, working hours and days of the schools, particularly the schools that are situated in remote places.
10. Number of teachers and official staff should be increased in the tribal schools.
11. Residential quarters with all amenities like water, electricity and transport should be provided to teachers and other staff in the school premises.
12. Educated tribal youth should be recruited as teachers and posted in tribal areas.
13. Merit scholarship and attendance scholarships should be provided.
14. Administration of incentives needs to be streamlined so that the students may avail all the facilities at proper time.
15. There is a need to have more incentives in the form of grants allocated to uniform, books, learning materials, mid-day meals, supply of sports equipment etc., to meet the needs of the tribal children.
16. Hostels and Ashram schools need considerable improvement. The hostels and schools should be housed separately; each hostel should be provided with water, electricity, clean kitchen and toilets.
17. The system of giving admission to the non-local students should be changed, and admission must be given to the local students also. It may help to enhance the local student enrolment at a considerable level.
18. Grants to Ashram school must be enhanced keeping the present day need and costs in mind.

19. Transport facilities should be improved in the interior villages. So as to increase the school admission and teachers regularity.
20. Students have many health problems due to polluted water and unhealthy atmosphere. Frequent visit of the doctors for medical check up of the children may help in reducing the drop-out rate.
21. Vocational institute should be for the tribal students for creation of new avenues of employment. Community participation in education has to be stepped up by the teachers establishing close relationship with the people.
22. The attitude of tribal parents towards education should be improved through proper counseling and guidance.
23. Non-formal education and evening schools should be opened in the tribal villages, which may help the tribal students to continue their education without affecting their economic activities.
24. More number of tribal schools and hostels should be opened in the interior tribal village schools.

REFERENCES

Joshi, N.D. "Adult Education and Development". Tribal Education in India, Vol. 1782.

Khan.Q.U. (1972), "Wastage in India School Education" (a review and Further Analysis). Institute of Applied Man Power, New Delhi.

Naidu. T.S. (1998), "The Future of Endangered Aborigines and Environment of Andaman and Nicobar Islands", Pondicherry University, Pondicherry.

Naidu. T.S. (1999), "Strategic Planning for the Future Development of the Tribes in India", Pondicherry University, Pondicherry.

Steere B.F. (1967), "A comparative Study of a Non-graded and Graded Secondary School as to Achievement, Attitude and Critical Thinking Ability", USOE Project No.7-P80 Unpublished Doctoral Dissertation, Department of Educational Administration Utah State University.

Haimendorf. C.F. (1982), Tribes of India Oxford University Press Bombay, Calcutta, Madras.

Mead Marget (1955), Culture and Commitment: A study of the Generation Gap, New York, Doubleday.

Vidyarthi L.P. (1984), "Education in Tribal Bihar", Ram in India, Vol.35, No.1.

TRAFFICKING AND SEXUAL EXPLOITATION OF CHILDREN: NATIONAL AND INTERNATIONAL PERSPECTIVES

*Subhash Chandra Singh**

INTRODUCTION

Any issue relating to children attracts the attention of the media and quickly turned into an international issue. In the 1970s, it was the malnourished and starving children in Africa. During the early 1980s, it was child labour in Asia, which was followed by street children in South Asia and South America. Now it is child prostitution and trafficking in children for other illegal activities. It is often seen as a global problem leading to new laws being passed in some countries enabling that country to prosecute its own citizens for abuses committed against children abroad.[1] The increase in awareness about incest and child abuse in India has sensitised people to create a climate of absolute intolerance to child sexual exploitation in all circumstances.[2]

Asia has recently seen a rapid growth in the sector of the sex industry directed at tourists and has gained much international attention because of the emergence of young female sex workers. Thailand in Asia is a country which earned its income through the prostitution of the children that lived there. There is a stereotype of child prostitution that claims that they are tricked into leaving home, or sold by impoverished parents into a brothel where they are repeatedly raped and terrorised into servicing up to twenty clients a night. For this purpose, children have been kidnapped from neighbouring countries, especially China and Burma, and kept in appalling conditions.[3] Others have been sold or debt-bonded by their parents.[4] There have also been horrific cases of young girls and women imprisoned in brothels and unable to escape when the brothel has caught fire.[5]

Trafficking in children is a global problem affecting large numbers of children. Children are sold, rented out, sexually abused by adults and

* Head and Dean, Faculty of Law, M.G. Kashi Vidyapith, Varanasi – 221002 (U.P.)

trafficked for other illegal activities everywhere. While it is almost impossible to obtain accurate figures, it is a fact that millions of girls and boys worldwide are being used in sex industry, pornography and other forms of sexual abuse and exploitation. Every year more than one million girls in the industrialised and developing worlds are brought into the sex industry by deception or find themselves forced to stay within it against their will. Children and their families are often unaware of the dangers of trafficking, believing that better employment and lives lie in other countries.

THE GRIM SCENARIO

It is estimated that roughly 100,000 to 160,000 Nepalese girls and women are working as sex workers in India. Roughly 20 per cent of them are estimated to be less than twenty years of age, with 35 per cent abducted under the pretext of marriage or jobs.[6] Studies on trafficking from Nepal to India have specifically mentioned the open border between the two countries as a major factor facilitating trafficking of Nepalese girls.[7] Nepalese and Indians do not have visas to cross the border between the two countries. The Bangladesh border is not open but quite easy to cross even without the correct papers.[8]

The trafficking of children touches nearly every part of Asia. But Thailand and India in particular serve as hubs of the flesh trade: exporter and importers of children on a massive scale. An estimated 7,000 Nepalese girls are smuggled into India each year to join sex industry. In the age of AIDS, children increasingly earn the biggest profits. With a girl's virginity selling for as much as higher price, recurring recessions have ensured a ready supply of daughters sold by poverty stricken families.[9]

Sexual abuse and exploitation can cause permanent physical and psychological harm. In some cases police can demand sexual services from trafficked and street children, threatening them with arrest if they do not comply. In detection and correctional facilities children may be sexually abused by staff or are not protected from sexual abuse by other inmates. In refugee camps many children are exploited by adults or sometimes forced to sell their bodies for food and other necessaries. In conflict areas children are kidnapped to serve as child soldiers and also sexual servants for adult soldiers. Children working as domestic workers may be assaulted or raped or detained by employers.[10]

(The) End Child Prostitution in Asian Tourism (ECPAT) brochure says, "On a global scale millions of children have been forced into prostitution and tourists create a demand for more than one million 'fresh' child prostitutes every year." It is estimated that as many as 1.2 million children are trafficked every year. There is a demand for trafficked children as cheap labour or for sexual exploitation. Trafficking always violates the child's right to grow up in a family environment.

Child trafficking is a lucrative and linked with criminal activity and corruption. Trafficking always violates the child's rights to grow up in a family environment. In addition, children who have been trafficked face a range of damages including violence and sexual abuse. Trafficked children are even arrested and detained as illegal aliens.[11] The grim picture of trafficking is compounded by the use of children as prostitutes in countries throughout the World. An unknown but very large number of children are used for commercial sexual purposes every year, often ending up with victims of HIV/AIDS and other sexually transmitted diseases. Prostituted children can be raped, beaten, sodomised, emotionally abused, tortured, and even killed by pimps, brothel owners and customers. Child prostitutes are frequently treated as criminals by law enforcement and judicial authorities, rather than as children who are victims of sexual exploitation.[12]

DEFINING 'TRAFFICKING' AND 'COMMERCIAL SEXUAL EXPLOITATION'

The word trafficking can be applied to any kind of commodities being traded or bartered; however it also has sinister and illicit, implications. In the context of sex, the term is being used with the implicit assumption that it is women and girls who are being transacted as non-consenting prostitutes to fulfill mail sexual desires. The international conference on Traffic in Persons in Utrecht, the Netherlands (on November 15-19, 1994) produced a definition emphasising force rather than the nature of work to be the dominant factor in trafficking. In its final statement the Utrecht Conference stated: "The traffic in persons is not only for purposes of prostitution, but for a range of other activities as well.... It is important to emphasise that the element that defines traffic is force and not the nature of the labour to be performed... the trafficker cannot use as a defence the fact that the person is or was at any time, for example, a prostitute or a domestic worker...."

Trafficking has been defined by the UN General Assembly in 1991 as: "the illicit and clandestine movement of persons across national and international borders, largely from developing countries, with the end goal of forcing women and girl children into economically oppressive exploitative situations for the profit of recruiters, traffickers, and crime syndicates as well as other illegal activities such as forced domestic labour, false marriage, clandestine employment, and forced adoption."[13]

Trafficking in children is the systematic buying and selling of girls and boys, and it continues so despite being illegal under the Immoral Traffic in Persons (Prevention) Act and the Indian Penal Code (IPC). Trafficking also operates internationally within an expanding network of supply-demand and transit of girls for commercial sex. The buying and selling aspect of trafficking is a system of payment for the procurer's work of finding, cajoling, perhaps marrying, and then transporting the girl. Some say that it is her income but in fact the girl does become a commodity, and the amounts that change hands depend on the girl's capacity to earn money for others. The prices depend upon the age, complexion, looks, and physique, and where she is sold to. According to a study by Rozario (1988) the highest amounts change hands in Delhi and Bombay.[14]

The 'commercial sexual exploitation' of children commonly refers to using a child for sexual purposes in exchange for cash or favours in kind between the client/customers and the intermediary or agent who profits from such trade in children. Those who profit may be from a wide range of persons, including parents, family members, procurers, agents, community members—largely men, but also women.[15]

Child sexual exploitation involves practices by which a person, usually an adult, achieves sexual gratification, financial gain or advancement through the abuse or exploitation of a child's sexuality by abrogating that child's human rights to dignity, equality, autonomy, and physical and mental well-being, i.e. trafficking, prostitution, sex tourism, mail-order bride trade, pornography, stripping, battering, incest, rape and sexual harassment. The sexual exploitation of children may be of commercial or non-commercial nature. The commercial sexual exploitation of children may be either monetary or non-monetary (i.e., for food, shelter, drugs) in nature. But in every case the commercial sexual exploitation involves maximum benefits to the exploiter and an abrogation of the basic rights and dignity of the children.[16]

For campaigners against prostitution, there has been much debate on what to call children who sell sex. Kevin Ireland for example writes here: "Child prostitution is where the persons selling or hiring their sexuality is under eighteen years of age, although, wherever possible the terms "child prostitute" and "child prostitution" have been avoided, as they imply a sense of decision and control on behalf of the child. All children under the age of eighteen who are in prostitution are considered, *de facto*, to be sexually exploited."[17]

INTERNATIONAL TRAFFICKING AND MIGRATION

International trafficking seems to be on the rise. Children of young age are traded from one country to another, and customers even come from abroad to use them. Asian women and girls abroad are confined against their will and have their passports confiscated. Forms of international trafficking range from mail-order bride syndicates, forced marriages, abuse of entertainment workers, to contract work as domestic helpers, all of which can result in sexual exploitation and yet occur under the legal cover of 'labour migration'.[18] To understand the international scenario clearly, countries have been categorised as sending, transit or receiving centers for the trafficking of children. India is mainly a receiving country, a reception center for women from Bangladesh and Nepal. It also acts as a transit country and, being so large, have its own internal sending, transit and receiving areas. Kolkata itself is an important receiver. It also functions as a transit place where Indian, Bangladeshi and Nepalese girls who come to the city, either independently or through agents, are taken to red-light areas in the other cities such as Mumbai, or even to other countries in the Middle East.[19]

The victims of this international trafficking network routinely suffered serious physical abuse, including rape, beating, arbitrary confinement and exposure to HIV/AIDS. Held in debt-bondage for years at a time, girls worked under constant surveillance. Escape was virtually impossible. Both the Indian and Nepali governments were complicit in the abuses. Police and officials in India protected brothel owners and traffickers in return for bribes; Nepali border police accepted bribes to allow trafficking. Even when traffickers were identified, few arrests and even lower prosecutions resulted.[20]

Human Rights Watch has investigated the trafficking of women and girls from Burma to Thailand and from Nepal to India, where they worked in conditions tantamount to slavery. The victims of this international trafficking network routinely suffered serious physical abuse, including rape, beating, arbitrary confinement and exposure to HIV/AIDS in brothels.[21]

According to a United Nations report on trafficking in Burma "with the growth of sex tourism and the commercial sex trade in neighbouring countries of the region, child abuse and exploitation has assumed a new form : sexual trafficking of children across international borders...... the number of Myanmar (Burma) girls working in Thai brothels has been conservatively estimated at between 20,000 to 30,000, with approximately

10,000 new recruits brought in yearly. The majorities are between 12 and 25 years old.[22]

THE UNDERLYING CAUSES

Although the source of the problem is differently located for child prostitutes abroad and child prostitutes at home, the image of children selling their bodies for profit arouses indignation and outrage. It is a powerful metaphor for many things, societal decay, moral degeneracy, capitalism and patriarchy in its extreme forms of both business and tourism. The children do not have a choice as to whether they were exploited or not or between prostitution and work free childhood. If they were not prostitutes, they still would have been impoverished and probably forced into the illegal labour market. The prostituted children are basically neglected by the parents and the state and are given few viable options by their society.

It is said that the children in general, do not enter in the commercial sex industry, on their own. Persuasion or deception from adults; threats, exploitation, and acts of violence are committed mostly by adults seeking advantage from children. Children are victimised and such acts are damaging to children's physical, intellectual, emotional and mental well-being.[23] Bringing children into and using them in the commercial sex industry is a lucrative business for offenders. The target groups are children below 18 years, who are in the commercial sex business.

Sexual activity is often seen as a private matter, making communities reluctant to act and intervene in cases of sexual exploitation. These attitudes make children more vulnerable to sexual exploitation. Myths such as the belief that HIV/AIDS can be cured through sex with a virgin, technological advancement such as the Internet which has facilitated child pornography and sex tourism targeting children all add to their vulnerability.[24] The conditions under which the prostituted children live in are found to be extremely difficult. Their lack of education, their poverty and ill health all made them vulnerable to abuse and exploitation by those with more power. Yet, child prostitution is always seen as the ultimate indignity and one, which is far beyond all others. It is always seen as one, which they passively accept. In all the accounts of child prostitution the children's passivity is always emphasised. They are weak, helpless, and have no control at all over their own lives. But what is seen, as passivity by outsiders may in fact be a form of protest.[25]

Children are forced by men into prostitution in all situations where men use a variety of means ranging from deceptive promises of jobs or marriage or the invisible enslavement of love and loyalty for pimp to physical kidnapping and imprisonment. Rightly has remarked K. Barry: "Female sexual slavery is present in all situations where women or girls cannot change the immediate conditions of their existence, where regardless of how they got into those conditions they cannot get out and where they are subject to sexual violence and exploitation."[26]

Barry's definition thus brings out a very important dimension of prostitution, which other authors have ignored, namely coercion.[27] While defining prostitution, it demands to say a few words regarding juvenile prostitution or child prostitution. Juvenile or child prostitution is one of the forms of prostitution where the possibilities of taking an option are minimum and most times non-existent. The preference for social scientists is to use the term prostituted minor or prostituted girl than to say girl prostitute to emphasise the fact that minor girls are forced into prostitution with no options open to them. When we refer to child prostitutes we cannot speak of free prostitution as juvenile prostitution refers to the phenomenon of sexual exploitation to which minors are practically forced to submit. There are various factors, which force the children to prostitution. Abuse and family violence, sexual violence, abandonment of the home, misery, exploitation and sexual trade are such prominent factors. In general, for juvenile prostitution, directly or indirectly, family plays an essential role in the process, which leads minors to prostitute themselves. One study shows that majority of juvenile prostitutes had experiences of sexual violence during infancy, particularly on the part of family members like father, step-father, uncles, brothers, step-brothers and grand-fathers. Many times it is the family itself that decides to trade with its daughters as the item of trade. Besides physical and sexual violence, the lack of affection, the needs to supplement the family income are the important cause behind child prostitution. Once outside the home the minor girls satisfied their survival needs by participating in marginal activities for income or in labour activities that demand little or no training.[28]

Poverty is an often-cited cause of child prostitution. However, poverty and prostitution should not be linked too simplistically. Most children from poor families are not prostitutes and poverty is not necessarily the root cause of all child prostitution. The most powerful mitigating circumstances for many children was not that they were earning money because they were poor but that they were earning money to help their parents.[29] It was their money that supported their parents and kept the families together. Even though they were socially and economically very marginal, by most definitions they were dutiful children whose respect and difference towards their parents was honorable and admirable. For people who are poor and powerless, prostitution does not seem to be a unique and ultimate horror or something they have to be forced into but one difficult choice among. They can be forced into many forms of work that they dislike such as scavenging or collecting garbage, neither of which pay nearly as well as prostitution. The children would earn more money in any given month from prostitution compared to what if they sorted garbage every day for around ten hours a day. It is unlikely that given a full range of choices and options, many of the children would choose prostitution, but these options, have never been open to them. Their choices are limited because once made the victims of trafficking, their power and ability to change their situation are extremely constrained.[30]

There is trafficking, often combined with debt-bondage, which transport women and girls across national boundaries for various purposes, of which domestic work, 'mail-order' marriage and prostitution are most common. Agents in the sex industry bring women and girls from Nepal to India, where they are completely dependent upon their traffickers. They have little knowledge of the local language, customs or law. At the mercy of the traffickers, they are forced to work long hours in inhumane surroundings.[31]

CHILD PROSTITUTION AND INTERNATIONAL INITIATIVES

Trafficking is viewed as a global conspiracy, which can be dismantled through international cooperation and the paternalistic rehabilitation of victims. It is worthwhile at this juncture to refer to the major international conventions relating to prostitution and traffic in women and girls. Efforts to restrain traffic in women and children stem back to the nineteenth century in Europe. In 1877, an international Convention was held in Geneva to discuss problems concerning legalised prostitution and traffic in women and children. Subsequent meeting of major European countries led to the conclusion of the International Agreement for the Suppression of the White Slave Traffic singed at Paris in 1904, and the International Convention for the Suppression of the White Slave Traffic signed at Paris in 1910. There had the efforts of requiring State Parties to cooperate and punish those involved in the requirement of women and children for prostitution. Due to the spread of venereal diseases after World War I, the League of Nations set up an Advisory Committee for prostitution. An international conference was held in Geneva in 1921. The outcome was an international convention to suppress the Traffic in Women and Children, 1921, signed by thirty three states.

The Convention requires State Parties to punish any person who procures, entices or leads away another person for the purpose of prostitution with the consent of that person. Protection is extended to persons including boys and girls under the age of twenty-one.[32] Despite all these international measures, the problem of traffic in women and children continued to persist. This gave rise to another convention called the International Convention for The Suppression of the Traffic in Women of Full Age in 1933. This extends protection to all women even those who attain the age of majority.[33]

The work of the Advisory Committee on the Traffic in Women and Children under the League of Nations has been continued by the United Nations until the present day. On 10 December 1948, the General Assembly of the United Nations adopted a Universal Declaration of Human Rights. Articles 3 and 4 of the Declaration specifically state that, "everyone has the right to life, liberty and security of person and no one shall be held in slavery or servitude; slavery and the slave trade shall be prohibited in all their forms." In the following year, a Convention for the Suppression of the Traffic in Persons and of the Exploitation of the Prostitution of Others was approved by the General Assembly on 2nd December, 1949. The 1949 Convention has consolidated all the previous Conventions relating to immoral trafficking in women and children. This Convention requires that State Parties shall punish various acts related to traffic in persons and exploitation of the prostitution of others even with the consent of that person (Article 1), to keep or manage or finance a brothel or to let or rent building or other place or any part thereof for the purpose of the prostitution of others (Article 2). These offences are extraditable offences (Article 8). In states where the extradition of nationals is not permitted by law, nationals who have returned to their own state after the commission abroad of any of the offences referred to in Articles 1 and 2 shall be prosecuted and punished by the courts of their own states. State Parties are to adopt preventive measures in connection with immigration and emigration to check the traffic in persons (Article 14). They shall also take necessary measures for the supervision of employment agencies in order to prevent persons seeking employment, in particular women and children, from being exposed to the danger of prostitution (Article 20). The Convention on the Elimination of All Forms of Discrimination Against Women (CEDAW) 1979 is one of the four basic United Nations human rights treaties. Article 6 of the Convention provides that State Parties shall take appropriate measures, including legislation to combat all forms of traffic in women and exploitation of prostitution of women.

(The) UN Declaration in 1959 emphasised to protect child against all forms of neglect, cruelty and exploitation. He/she shall not be subject of traffic in any form, the Declaration stated. Articles 34 and 35 of the Convention on the Rights of the Child (1989) forbid sexual exploitation or trafficking of children and the Committee on the Rights of the Child has devoted time and efforts to the issue urging governments to crack down on the practice. Other international instruments on human rights, humanitarian law, refugee law, and labour standards protect children against sexual exploitation.[34] International attention was also focussed on the issue at the World Congress on the Commercial Sexual Exploitation of Children in Stockholm in 1996, and at a follow-up conference in Yokohama, Japan, in December 2001. In Yokohama, governments and NGOs assessed progress achieved since the Stockholm Congress; exchanged information on lessons learned and addressed ongoing challenges.[35]

INDIA'S APPROACH

In respect of India, it is worthy to discuss the national policy and plan of action for the prevention and eradication of the commercial exploitation of children are the total elimination of entry into the commercial sex business by children of both sexes under 18. At the same time government prohibits of luring, threats, exploitation and acts of violence in the operation of the commercial sex business and finally the government decides imposition of punishment to all persons. The government's policy at all times gives priority to the prevention.

The Constitution of India, which came into effect on 26th January 1950, provides a protective umbrella for the rights of children. In addition to basic fundamental rights which are available to both adults and minors. There are certain fundamental rights especially for children. These rights are necessary because of their physical and mental immaturity, as the children are especially vulnerable and need special protection. Article 15 of the Constitution prohibits discrimination of citizens on the grounds only of religion, race, castes, sex, place of birth, or any of them. But sub clause 3 adds: "Nothing in this Article shall prevent the State from making any special provisions for women and children. Therefore, laws can be made giving special protection to children. Some protective rights of children are included in Part III and Part IV of the Constitution. Under the Constitution, it is the duty of the State to secure that children of tender age are not abused and forced by economic necessity to enter vocations unsuited to their age and strength [Article 39(e)] and to secure that children are given opportunities and facilities to develop in a healthy manner and in conditions of freedom and dignity [Article 39(f)]. According to Article 23 of the Constitution, trafficking in human beings is prohibited. The Constitution directs the State to enact special legislations and policies for protecting children and youth against exploitation of moral and material abandonment. Because of judicial interpretations, many of the directive principles have now become enforceable through legal actions brought before the courts (for example, the right to education, which has now become a part of fundamental right). There are certain aspects relating to children that are dealt with in the State and Concurrent list of the Constitution.

Presently, the legal intervention in India is in the form of criminal investigation, punishment and rehabilitation. Sections 366-A and 366-B of the Indian Penal Code relate to export and import of girls for prostitution.[36] Under these sections the girl should be below eighteen years and she should be intentionally induced by the accused to go from any place or to any act that is likely to force her into prostitution. As a result of India being a signatory to the UN Convention on the Suppression of the Traffic in Persons and of the Exploitation of the Prostitution of Others 1949, the Suppression of Immoral Traffic in Women and Girls Act 1956 was passed. This was later amended in 1978 and 1986 to the now Immoral Traffic (Prevention) Act.[37] Both intended to abolish organised prostitution by criminalising pimps, landlords and brothel-keepers. The present Act has treated prostitutes as victims of poverty, social problems and organised crimes. The heavier penalty is for procurers, brothel-owners, pimps, managers and madams, customers and even parents who send their children into prostitution. Moreover, customers who buy sex from minors under the age of 18 years are to be imprisoned. Parents are also liable to imprisonment and their guardianship may be revoked by a court order. The Amending Act has created certain presumptions in favour of child victims. These are:

1. If a child is found in a brothel or under suspicious circumstances in the custody of a person, other than the parent or lawful guardian who is unable to explain satisfactorily the presence of such a child, that person shall be presumed to have procured the child for the purposes of prostitution.

2. A report in a newspaper on the use of certain premises as a brothel is deemed to be sufficient proof of the landlord, occupier, or tenant knowingly allowing such use.

3. If a child is found accompanying in suspicious circumstances,[38] a person who is neither its parent nor lawful guardian and who is

leaving the country, that person is committing the offence of immoral trafficking.

The Immoral Traffic (Prevention) Act 1956 (amended in 1986) does not make prostitution *per se* a criminal offence or punish a person because the person prostituted himself/herself. The purpose of the Act is to inhibit or abolish commercialised sexual abuse and exploitation and the traffic in persons as an organised means of living. The object is attempted to be achieved by two major strategies, namely, by punishing those who are guilty of such conduct and by rescuing and rehabilitating the victims of such exploitation.[39] The Act has introduced the concept of child victims as against minors and majors and imposes higher degree of criminality to sexual exploiters of children. Under Section 67 of the Information Technology Act, 2000, publication and transmission of pornography is also made an offence.

The government is bound to provide rehabilitation in a protective institution, or under the supervision of a person appointed by the magistrate, for girls rescued from prostitution. A minor or a child rescued under the ITPA, 1986 is treated as a neglected child [Section 2 (l)] under the Juvenile Justice (Care and Protection of Children) Act, 2000, and has to be produced before the Juvenile Welfare Board [Section 4(1)] now the Child Welfare Committee for reception and rehabilitation, and placing in safe custody. There is a provision for providing for intermediate custody in a shelter home or corrective institution [Section 2 (b)] after rescue pending detailed inquiry.

CONCLUSIONS AND SUGGESTIONS

India is committed to ending the commercial sexual exploitation of children. India has ratified many international conventions, which strengthens international cooperation towards the prevention of the abduction, sale or trafficking of children. The Indian Penal Code (IPC), the Immoral Traffic (Prevention) Act, 1956 (amended in 1986), and the Juvenile Justice (Care and Protection of Children) Act, 2000 attack the roots of sexual exploitation by promoting children's rights, providing protection and education, and assisting the victims of the sex trade. Apart from legal mechanisms, many non-governmental organisations (NGOs) are also actively involved in efforts to end child prostitution. In recent years some NGOs have played a significant role and have been in the forefront position in providing services to children. There has been a shift from the welfare approach to thrust on development and empowerment in the intervention for children.

In spite of all such concern, the children are facing inhuman and degrading situation. Instead of protecting their rights for their well-being, they are being even sexually abused at their tender age. Even those who are supposed to protect their female relatives (such as fathers, brothers, social workers, police and others) turn out to be their abusers/exploiters. Even in jails, observation and protective homes, sexual exploitation of children is taking place. In *Devdasi* system and *Jogin* tradition as prevailing in the society, minor girls are subjected to sexual abuse. According to International Labour Organisation, at least one million children are prostitutes in Asia, with the greatest numbers in Thailand, India, Taiwan and Philippines. Child sexual exploitation is a growing problem, fueled by the Asian economic boom and the subsequent bust, which has fostered an increasingly yawning gap between rich and poor. Because of extreme poverty and unemployment thousands of girls are being sold into brothels every year.

Legal reform alone cannot bring justice to the sexually abused and prostituted children. Inter-agency structures and systems need to be worked out laying great emphasis on prevention. Undoubtedly, the most effective prevention measure is awareness of such possible abuse and how to deal with it amongst the various service providers—the doctors, teachers, lawyers, judges, police, volunteers and social workers—so that they can significantly reduce the risks of abuse, if it does occur, by responding appropriately.

India has ratified many international conventions, which strengthens international cooperation towards the prevention of the abduction, sale or trafficking of children. India supports a variety of local initiatives in the neighbouring countries to attack the roots of sexual exploitation by promoting children's rights, providing protection and education, and assisting the victims of the sex trade. Many non-governmental organisations are also actively involved in efforts to end child sexual exploitation.

Government must implement the international conventions to which it has agreed, and prosecute those who abuse and sexually exploit children, or profit from the practice. Children engaged in prostitution must be treated as victims of sexual exploitation, violence, and forced labour, and not as criminals. Government and NGOs should support quality rehabilitation and recovery programmes for children who leave the sex trade, which include psychological counselling, health care, education and vocational training, and shelter, as appropriate. The government must develop prevention programmes that will raise public awareness and encourage actions that protect children. As commercial sexual exploitation of children is a global problem, the international community, must make every effort to end these abuses. In some cases new laws are required; in others the political will must be mobilised to implement existing legislation and prosecute those involved in sexual abuse and exploitation of vulnerable children.

NOTES

1. Australia has passed a law which would imprison its citizens for up to seventeen years if they are found guilty of sexual offences against children abroad. Norway, Germany, France, Belgium, New Zealand, Britain and Sweden have passed similar laws allowing for if they cannot be convicted abroad.
2. Montgomery, H., Children, Prostitution and Identity : A Case Study from a Tourist Resort in Thailand, in Kamala Kempadoo and Jo Doezema (eds.), *Global Sex Workers: Rights, Resistance, and Redefinition* (New York: Routledge, 1998), p. 139.
3. Asia Watch Women's Rights Project, *A Modern Form of Slavery : Trafficking of Burmese Women and Girls into Brothel in Thailand*, Human Rights Watch, 1993, 16.
4. Muecke, M., Mother Sold Food, Daughter Sells Her Body: The Cultural Continuity of Prostitution, *Social Science and Medicine* 35 (1992): 891-901.
5. In the most notorious incident, a brothel in the seaside town of Phuket (Thailand) caught fire in 1995, killing five young prostitutes who were chained to their beds and unable to escape. In a similar fire in 1994 two women died.
6. A study by Thapa 1989; Quoted in B.C. Jyoti, and M. Poudel, *Trafficking of Women in Nepal : An Overview*, Paper presented at the International Workshop on Migration and Traffic in Women, Thailand, 1994, p. 8.
7. *Ibid.*
8. Sleightholme, C. and Indrani Sinha, *Guilty Without Trial : Women in the Sex Trade in Calcutta*, (Kolkata : Stree, 1996), p. 4.
9. Perry, A., Slavery: Indentured for Life, *The Times* (February 4, 2002/Vol. 159 No. 4), p. 22.
10. Available at http://www.hrw.org/campaigns/crp/promises/abuse.html (visited on 16th December, 2005).
11. Available at http://www.unicef.org/protection/index_exploitation.html (visited on 16th December, 2005).
12. *Supra* note 10.
13. The definition of trafficking by the UN General Assembly clearly indicates that trafficking has the distinct components of recruitment, movement

through transportation, forced or slavery like labour, and third-party profit. Children are usually trafficked for prostitution, begging, organ transplant, pornographic and other unlawful activities, child brides, camel races and domestic labour.

14. Rozario, R., *Trafficking in Women and Children in India* (New Delhi: Uppal Publishing House, 1988).
15. UNICEF (2001), *The State of the World's Children* (New York, USA).
16. Available at http://caster.ssw.upenn.edu/~restes/CSEC.htm (visited on 16th December, 2005).
17. Ireland, K., *Wish You Weren't Here*, London : Save the Children Fund, 1993, p. 3.
18. Sancho, N., *Trafficking in Women as Human Rights Violations*, AWHRC, Philippines, Paper presented on behalf of AWHRC at the International Workshop on Migration and Trafficking in Women, Thailand, 1994.
19. Sleightholme and Indrani Sinha, Guilty Without Trial, *supra* note 8 at 40.
20. *Supra* note 10.
21. *Ibid.*
22. *Children and Women in Myanmar: A Situation Analysis*, UNICEF, 1995, 38.
23. Ghosh, Lipi, *Prostitution in Thailand: Myth and Reality* (New Delhi: Munshiram Manoharlal Publishers, 2002), p. 271.
24. *Supra* note 11.
25. Kamala Kempadoo, Global Sex Workers, *supra* note 2 at 148.
26. Barry, K., *Female Sexual Slavery* (New York, 1981), p. 40.
27. *Ibid.*
28. Ghosh, Prostitution in Thailand, *supra* note 23.
29. Kamala Kempadoo, Global Sex Workers, *supra* note 2 at 143.
30. *Ibid* at 149.
31. Bindman, Jo, An International Perspective on Slavery in the Sex Industry, in Global Sex Workers, *supra* note 2 at 67.
32. Ghosh, Prostitution in Thailand, *supra* note 23 at 179.
33. *Ibid.*
34. *Supra* note 10.
35. Available at http://www.dfait-maeci.gc.ca/foreign_policy/human-rights/hr6a-exploit-en.asp (visited on 16th December, 2005).
36. Section 366 A. Procuration of minor girl—Whoever, by any means whatsoever, induces any minor girl under the age of eighteen years to go from any place or to do any act with intent that such girl may be, or knowing that it is likely that she will be, forced or seduced to illicit intercourse with

another person shall be punishable with imprisonment which may extend to ten years, and shall also be liable to fine.

Section 366-B. Importation of girl from foreign country—Whoever imports into India from any county outside India or from the State of Jammu and Kashmir any girl under the age of twenty-one years with intent that she may be, or knowing it to be likely that she will be, forced or seduced to illicit intercourse with another person, shall be punishable with imprisonment which may extend to ten years, and shall also be liable to fine.

37. Prostitution under this Act means the sexual exploitation or abuse of persons for commercial purposes and the expression 'prostitute' should be construed accordingly. See the Immoral Traffic (Prevention) Act, 1986, Section 2 (f).

38. Suspicious circumstances in this section includes situation in which (i) the mother tongue of the accused is different from that of the child or the language is different from the generally spoken in the society, (ii) where the child is wrongfully confined without access to others, and (iii) where the child is married to foreigner.

39. Menon, N.R.M., *Prevention of Immoral Traffic and Restoration of Human Dignity*, Select Materials on Public Legal Education, Legal Services Clinic, National Law School of India University, Bangalore, 1991.

HUMAN RIGHTS PROMOTION AND IMPACT OF WAR ON CHILDREN

*Md. Reyaz Ahmad**

INTRODUCTION

Despite increased international attention to and awareness of children's rights, children are largely overlooked in the peacemaking and peacekeeping process. Rules of engagement for peacekeepers disregard children, and reconstruction and reconciliation programs that emerge from negotiations ignore the differential impact on and particular needs of children. The effect is to marginalize persistent problems like the rehabilitation and reintegration of child soldiers and, more broadly, to miss the opportunity to address widespread systemic problems common to war-torn societies.

Children suffer disproportionately in war, and they benefit disproportionately less in peace. The international community has recognized the deficiency of the international bill of rights in addressing specific classes of injustice or the status of entire groups of persons, and it has acknowledged the need for programmatic tools to address the special needs of vulnerable communities. The United Nations Convention on the Rights of the Child (CRC). to which I refer throughout as a guidepost for children-oriented initiatives. is the most widely ratified human rights treaty and obliges States to take positive measure the protection of children's rights both in peace and in war. A similar approach is both warranted and reasonable in peace processes. Peacemakers must buffer children from the potentially negative consequences of the peace process while respecting their evolving capacities and their right to guided participation.

In addition to the CRC, international humanitarian law, which has long provided special protection for vulnerable children, reflects these concerns. Many other declarations, resolutions, and regional instruments,

* Academic Councillor of Maulna Azad National Urdu University, Patna

applicable in distinct circumstances and binding to different degrees on different actors, also urge greater protection for children in war. The law relevant to children's rights may vary depending on circumstances but a child's moral claim to special care does not.

The general thrust behind national and international action on behalf of children is the moral and legal recognition of their emotional, physical and psychological vulnerability, their need for special care, and recognition of the obligation to respect and ensure respect for their rights. These concerns reflect the value that society places on childhood for its own sake, not as a training ground for adulthood. Simultaneously, we must recognize that events in childhood will affect the individual as an adult and consequently, society as a whole.

PURPOSE OF THIS PAPER

This study examines the nature of war's impact on children, point out patterns common to children across conflict-types and cultures, and stress the psychosocial implications of war-related experiences.

ANALYSIS OF THIS STUDY

War affects children differently depending on the region and nature of the conflict[1] Any one child's experience might include direct participation in, witnessing of, or victimization during hostilities; displacement; separation from or loss of loved ones; physical injury; restricted freedoms of movement, expression or association. Types of weapons, methods of recruitment, economic insecurity, exposure to chronic violence, the influence of ideology, politics, religion, peer groups and family, a child's developmental processes and her subjective appraisal of the causes and meanings of events and of her own abilities to cope. all play a role in exacerbating or mitigating war's impact.

The experience of children in war varies widely. Land mines remain a particular danger in Afghanistan, Cambodia, and Angola but not in Guatemala. While forced recruitment of children was not a salient concern in the former Yugoslavia, it most certainly was in Mozambique and Liberia and is today in Sierra Leone and Uganda.[2] Ideological commitment and political activity allegedly play an important role in buffering Palestinian children from some deleterious effects of the violence in the Israeli Occupied Territories[3] and the spirit of *jihad* armed Afghan children spiritually and emotionally for battle with Soviet-backed government troops[4] but this was not the case in Mozambique or in Uganda today.[5] Treatment of children also varies widely. Sectors of some societies, in Lebanon or the former Yugoslavia for example, managed to continue their children's education and to retain a certain level of family functioning even under siege; the continuity may do much to mitigate war's negative impact and to bolster resiliency.[6] Children in other places will never have had access to a pre-war educational infrastructure or will suffer the indirect effects of war's destruction of the existing health, education and welfare infrastructure.[7] Unaccompanied children may scarcely exist in regions where extended families can absorb them, but others will become refugees, or internally displaced. Some young children will be forced to become heads of large households after parents have been killed.

How wars are brought to a close can also have varying implications for children. A negotiated partial solution in Bosnia-Herzegovina that leaves many entrenched in hostile environments will have a different impact than a negotiated solution in El Salvador, where post-conflict governmental reform is meant to benefit all citizens and the peace agreements can serve a unifying function. Little data exists on the psychosocial impact of peace processes on youth. but one tentative effort by Palestinian psychologists found that the peace treaty signed between Israel the PLO [on September 13 1993] positively influenced Palestinian children's well-peace treaty than before, those who welcomed the peace treaty by participating in the celebrations suffered less from neuroticism and enjoyed better self-esteem than those who did not.[8]

Despite the varied consequences of specific wars for children, patterns emerge in the experience of children that are distinct from those of adults. The explanation for war's differential impact on children and adults is to be found in the very reasons children require greater protection than adults. Age, physical stature, and developmental factors limit children's and adolescents' capacity to adapt or to respond to war crises.[9] "A mine explosion is likely to cause greater damage to the body of a child than to that of an adult[10] and maimed child survivors require extended medical treatment and psychological support. Displacement is stressful in general, but for a child, separation from family is devastating. A child's reactions to war often reflects those of a parent or caretaker; a child whose parent can provide physical closeness, reassurance and an opportunity to process the experience will cope better than one whose caregiver is anxious, fearful, and resists a child's attempts at questioning or discussion.[11] A child's moral intelligence, more so than an adult's, reflects his war-time experiences and the way in which he is able to make sense of the suffering.

Numerous studies and papers describe the wide-ranging impact of war on children and indicate the psychosocial consequences of exposure to chronic violence.[12] Research on children living in war-torn areas "point(s) to numerous domains of cognitive, social, emotional, and psycho physiological functioning that can be severely affected by exposure to violence, including depression, withdrawal, fear, anxiety, affect deregulation, aggression, dissociative reactions, and intrusive thoughts.[13] There is little evidence to support the view that "children either are resilient in the face of adversity or are too native to fully appreciate events that trouble adults."[14]

CONCLUSIONS

This paper concludes that a child-conscious approach to human rights promotion, peacekeeping, and peace-building will help us promote a stable and sustainable peace settlement. No peace treaty to date has formally considered specific children's rights issues related to the conflict, such as the need to demobilize child combatants, address the health needs of victims of gender-based violence, provide educational opportunities, or pay special attention to mental and physical health concerns. Yet the mandate and moral obligation to do so are clear.

The international community's commitments to children codified in the CRC dictate a comprehensive response. Every article in the Convention remains relevant during armed conflict and, as there is no derogation clause, the entire Convention remains in effect regardless the level of national emergency. Human rights norms and humanitarian law must be employed in tandem to ensure what is often a higher standard of protection for children than for adults. But norms alone are insufficient. Respect for children's rights in war and war's aftermath is more likely to be advanced when the national and international debates over the nature of transitional and peace-time societies include children and when specific peace processes and peace-building agendas design specific programmatic responses and initiatives to redress children's rights violations and implement and protect their rights.

NOTES AND REFERENCES

1. All regions in the 20th century have seen alarming and ever-increasing numbers of civilian war victims, many of them children. "During the Spanish Civil War, World War II, and the Korean and Vietnam Wars, 50%, 48%, 34%, and 48% of the deaths respectively, occurred among civilians. In the 1980s, 85% of war deaths were civilians." Edward Goldson, *The Effect of War on Children,* 20 Child Abuse & Neglect 809, 809 (1996). This century

has been called "mankind's most bloody and hateful century," in which "over 87,000,000 combatants and civilians were lost to war, and another estimated 80,000,000 persons were deliberately killed by their own governments." Walter Gary Sharp. Sr., *Protecting {the Avatars of international piece and Security* 7 Duke J. Compo & Int L. 93. 93 .1996 citing Zbigniew Brzezinski, out of Control: Global Turmoil on the Eye of the Twenty-First Century 4 (1993).

2. The Lord's Resistance Army is abducting children and forcing them to participate in atrocities in Uganda. Human Rights Watch/Africa and Human Rights Watch/Children's Rights Project, The Scars of Death: Children Abducted by the Lord's Resistance Army in Uganda (1997). In most countries, few victimizers are ever detained, and even fewer are ultimately held accountable in domestic or international fora. But hundreds of Rwandan children, some as young as six during the 1994 genocide, are being held in re-education centers and juvenile detention centers, accused of being *genocidaires.* Mary Braid, *Silent Scream of Rwanda's Youth,* The Independent (London), May 23, 1998, at 17.

3. Some research maintains that the role of Palestinian children in the Intifada "was the most dominant feature of Palestinian adolescents' and children's lives. They viewed themselves as freedom fighters, and this ideological commitment functioned as a protective factor and source of resilience." Samir Qouta et al., *The Impact of the Peace Treaty on Psychological Well-Being:*

   A Follow-up Study of Palestinian Children, 19 Child Abuse & Neglect 1197, 1205 (1995), *citing* Garbarino et al., No Place to Be a Child: Growing Up in a War Zone (1991); Y. Nashef, The Psychological Impact of the Intifada on Palestinian Children Living in Refugee Camps in the West Bank, As Reflected in Their Dreams, Drawings, and Behavior (1992). Other "research has shown that active participation in the Intifada increased self-esteem among Palestinian children . . . . " Samir Qouta et al., *supra* at 1206, *citing* A. Baker, *The Psychological Impact of the Intifada on Palestinian Children in the Occupied West Bank and Gaza: An Exploratory Study,* 60 Am. J. Orthopsychiatry 496 (1990). However, at least one other study of Palestinian children showed that "traumatic experiences increased children's active participation in the national struggle, but this activity did not save them from psychological suffering." *Id.* at 1206. Research is lacking on the relationship between exposure to or participation in war-related or political violence and psychological outcomes in children, and on the role of individualistic and society factors in mediating the impact of violence on children's psychological responses.

   But. Patterns have been empirically observed and the need for further research is widely acknowleage<:. Raija-Leena Punamaki-Gitai, Political Violence and Psychological Responses: A Study of Palestinian Women, Children and Ex-Prisoners 9-15, (Tampere, Peace Research Institute, Research Reports No. 41, 1990).

4. Helsinki Watch/Asia Watch, To Win the Children: Afghanistan's Other War 2, 14-16 (1986).
5. *See* Elizabeth Rubin, *Letter from Uganda: Our Children are Killing Us,* New Yorker, Mar. 23, 1998, at 56.
6. *See* Lina Kurdahi Zahr, *Effects of War on the Behavior of Lebanese Preschool Children: Influence of Home Environment and Family Functioning,* 66 Am. J. Orthopsychiatry 401 (1996).
7. For a discussion of the direct and indirect physical effects of war and political violence on children see Goldson, *supra* note.
8. Samir Qouta et al., *supra* ote, at 1204.
9. One author noted:

   It has been assumed that children's stress reactions vary according to their emotional and cognitive maturity. Researchers suggest that the younger the child at the time of exposure to political violence, the more severe the psychological consequences .... Boys have been found to be more vulnerable to stress up until the age of puberty, whereas thereafter females are more vulnerable.

   Raija-Leena Punamaki-Gitai, Political Violence and Psychological Responses: A Study of Palestinian Women, Children and Ex-Prisoners, *supra* note, at 13.
10. *Impact of Armed Conflict on Children, Report of the Expert of the Secretary-General. Ms. Graca Machel,* U.N. Doc. A/51/306, 116 (1996) [hereinafter Machel study]
11. *See* Morris Fraser, Children in Conflict 73-87 (1973).
12. *See, e.g.,* Machel study, *supra* note. at Annex: Research Contribution to the report on the Impact of Armed Conflict on Children. *Ill1-*
13. Richters, *Community Violence and Children's Development Towards a Research Agenda for the 1990s,* 56 Psychiatry 3-6 (1993), *cited in* Stephen L. Buka & Isolde Birdthistle, *Exposure to Violence: Extending the Research Frontier,* The Chicago Project News (The Project on Human Development in Chicago Neighborhoods, Harvard Univ., Boston, Mass.) Vol. 3, No. 1, Winter 1997, at 2.
14. Felton Earls and Leon Eisenberg, *International Perspectives in Child Psychiatry, in* Child and Adolescent Psychiatry: A Comprehensive Textbook 1196, 1202 (M. Lewis ed., 1996).

THE LAW AND THE CHILD ABUSE IN NIGERIA: AN APPRAISAL

*Bashir L. Ijaiya**

INTRODUCTION

It is a notorious fact that child abuse has become so endemic in Nigeria that one then wonder whether same has been legalized and if not what is the government and the people in authority doing to curb the menaces and the dimension the act is taking in our society. Nigerian children have been and are being subjected to various forms of inhuman treatment, servitude, torture, cruelty, deprivation, neglect and all sorts of intimidation.

It is saddening and disheartening to see of recent about a hundred African children brought into Nigeria illegally through child trafficking from Benin Republic. Not only that, one feel unhappy when one see quite number of Nigerian children on our highways hawking petty trade, placing them in danger all in quest for money to earn a living. Also, it has also been observed that, Nigerians especially those residing in the rural area are fond of subjecting their wards to what may be referred to as child labour that is making their children to work as house boy/girl where most of these innocent children are subjected to a lot of inhuman treatment, torture and deprivation.

Against this backdrop therefore, one should have expected the government and people in authority to check the excess abuses on the Nigerian children through the various enactments and legislations but alas, it does appear that, it is either the law has been rendered moribound, toothless, ineffective and unenforceable or that defaulters are allowed to go unpunished turning them to sacred cows and making a mess of the rule of law.

It is therefore, the desire of this paper to describe what a child abuse is? types of child abuse, the causes of child abuse, the various laws of

* Department of Private & Property Law, Faculty of Law, University of Ilorin, Ilorin, Nigeria

child abuse, the prevention of child abuse in the Nigeria perspectives as well as some recommendations that can be used to arrest the endemic child abuse cases in Nigeria.

In the next section that follows, the definition, the types and causes of child abuse are discussed. Section three assesses the existing child abuse law in Nigeria. Section four discusses the likely measures that can be used to prevent child abuse in Nigeria. The conclusion is contained in the last section.

CHILD ABUSE

(a) What is Child Abuse

It should be noted that, in a wider context, child abuse now includes any form of deprivation or neglect to which a child is subjected in the family or the society, There is a false impression that it does not exist in the traditional African Society. This concept has been created by the sociological concept of protection, love and care enjoyed by the child within the extended family system and his cultural milieu. Some aspects of traditional child rearing practices inflict physical and emotional trauma on the child Such practices concern discipline and treatment of diseases as burns and sacrifications.[1]

(b) Types of Child Abuse in Nigeria

It is pertinent to highlight the various types of child abuse for the proper understanding of this concept. Child abuse may be physical, social, emotional, nutritional or sexual. It is physical where the form of injuries affect the musculo–skeletal system, the brain and other internal organs. Such injuries result in bruises, fractures, sudural hacmatoma, or damage of organs such as the spleen, the kidney or the eye. Physical abuse may also occur in the form of burns.

Also, child abuse becomes social where there is neglect and subsequent abandonment and it may be associated with physical abuse. On thc other hand, emotional child abuse arises where the child is deprived of adequate mother–child relationship, and may be ridiculed because of a handicap. There may be also persistent verbal harassment. Such a child is also likely to be abused physically.

There is also a form of child abuse called nutritional child abuse. It is a form of abuse whereby the child is neglected or deprived and undergoes physical emotional and social abuse. These abuses result into a child who is severely malnourished, emotionally upset and probably mentally retarded.

The most common form of child abuse is the sexual abuse–Although not common in the Nigerian society. It occurs particularly where young girls are hired out as childminders to other families. A form of sexual abuse seen in Nigeria is one in which young adolescent girls are introduced by older women to men in important positions. Such older women often do so in expectation of special or financial rewards. Some of the girls became single parents who eventually physically abandon their children. Very few cases of incest have been reported in Nigeria. However sexual abuse it is observed, could be a hidden paediatric problem.[3]

(c) Causes of Child Abuse in Nigeria

It is also pertinent to highlight some of the causes of child abuse in Nigeria some of which are basically societally influenced. A worldwide study reveals that child abuse is being recognized as a social problem which is alarmingly increasing due to rapid urbanization, high birthrate, unemployment, single parenthood, separation, divorce, financial and other social stresses.[4] It has been estimated by the National Centre for Child Abuse and Neglect that one million cases occur annually in the United States of America and that up to 2,000 death occur.[5] Child abuse may be considered as the outcome of abnormal interactions between the child, parents or guardians and society.

Another significant cause of child abuse in Nigeria is the rate at which an average Nigerian is being bitten by poverty. Everyone uses all sort of ways to see that he or she survives not minding the societal values, norms and most particularly the law of the land against the practice of subjecting child to tortures, deprivations and abuses.

The child abuse in Nigeria is presently at the alarming rate that different non-governmental organizations have sprung up launching campaign organist the incessant abuse and to sensitize the society on the serious adverse effect it has on the child in particular and the society of large. One can but commend all the NGOS which have stood firmly to get rid child abuse of the society.

CHILD ABUSE LAW

It is pertinent to know that child abuse has become not only the concern of sovereign states but also that of international community. The United Nations through its numerous regional and subordinate organizations have stood in defence of incessant child abuse and have put machineries on ground in defence of same. One of such organizations is the United Nations Educational Fund (UNICEF) this organization's main object is to ensure that a child attain an appreciable level of education. That is, education and learning must be provided a child by the government. This, it is belief will automatically breathes a air of sense of belonging to a child thereby saving the child from being abused.

In Nigeria on the other hand, apart from the notorious fact that there are legislations on the subject, there are also many organizations that have stood in defense of incessant child abuse which has become an epidemic in our society. Such a body is the Women. Trafficking and Child Labour Eradication Foundation (WOTCLEF).

Interestingly, Nigerian children are protected by law against all forms of abuses, assault, intimidation, torture and deprivation under the Children's and Young Persons Laws.[6] Importantly, the protection of the child is also enshrined in the Constitution of the Federal Republic of Nigeria 1999 which stated that:

> "That the state shall direct its policy towards ensuring that children, young persons and the aged are protected against any exploitation whatsoever, and against moral and material neglect."[7]

Under the law of Children's and Young Persons Laws of Kwara State,[8] juveniles in need of care include an orphan or child deserted by his parents, a child neglected or ill–treated by the person having care and custody, a child found begging and receiving alms, and a child exposed to moral danger. Such a child may be brought before a Juvenile Court and a committal order may be issued:

(i) Sending him to an "approved school;

(ii) Committing him to the care of any fit person, whether a relative or not, who is willing to undertake the care of the child;

(iii) Order his parents or guardian to enter into recognizance to exercise proper care and guardianship and to protect the child from social exploitation.

The law further stated that, it is an offence:

(a) To barter or sell a juvenile

(b) To place the juvenile in moral danger or in a danger of exploitation.

(c) To give a child into the custody, possession, control, or guardianship of any person other than the grand parent of such juvenile whether or not for pecuniary other benefits.

To effectively and efficiently ensure that the child is protected against neglect the Children's and Young Persons Laws also state that any person who has attained the age of seventeen years or who has the custody, charge or care of any child or young person who has not yet attained the age of fourteen years and who:

(i) Willfully assaults, ill-treats, neglects, abandons or exposes the child or causes or procures the child to be assaulted, ill-treated, neglected, abandoned or exposed in a manners likely to cause the child unnecessary suffering or injury to health, including injury to or loss of sight or hearing or limb or organ of the body or any mental derangement, or

(ii) Exposes the child to the risk of burning by allowing him to be in any place near and open fire without any protection or guard against the risk of the child being burnt of scalded or without taking any reasonable precautions against the risk or

(iii)Leaves the child unattended to by any person over the age of seventeen in a motor vehicle–shall be guilty of an offence and liable upon conviction to a fine not exceeding one hundred pounds or to a term of imprisonment not exceeding two years.

Furthermore, the law also stated that any person who causes or allows any juvenile to be used for the purpose of begging or for the purposes of trading or hawking between the hour of 8 P.M. and sunrise shall be guilty of an offence and liable upon conviction to a fine not exceeding one hundred pounds or to a term of imprisonment not exceeding two years.

It is however very saddening and disheartening to observe that inspite of these enactments and legislation on child abuse, our society is yet to be rid of the menaces of child abuse. It has become so endemic that hardly can it be abolished, eradicated or checked by the law. This, it is submitted has made the mess of the law thereby making it impotent to arrest the situation.

It is to be noted that, it is not surprising that, laws put in place to protect the children have not been effective and efficient. The government has not in any way assisted the situation as the economy of the nation continues to dwindle down day in day out resulting to the increasing rate of poverty in the country. People cannot but resort to trading with their children in order to make ends meet.

PREVENTION OF CHILD ABUSE IN NIGERIA

To arrest the incessant abuses on Nigerian children which has become so endemic, the government, the parents as well as the society has a major role to play. The government is commended to ensure effective and efficient enforcement of the laws on child protection against abuses by putting in place monitoring group to identify and prosecute defaulters. It is also recommended that efficient and effective educational policy with more emphasis on health education be adopted. This should be taught especially to young families and the importance of love, care and close parental attachment to the child right from birth should be emphasized. The unique child rearing practice of breast–feeding which enhances maternal-infant bonding is rapidly on the decline in Nigeria especially among urban elite mothers. It has been suggested that early mother – child separation may lead to subsequent battering of the child. Breast – feeding must be encouraged not only for its intensive advantage, but for its psychosocial importance. Infants who require prolonged hospitalization such as those with low birth weight or congenital malformations, should be visited frequently and touched by their mothers.[10]

It has also been observed that the large number of infants abandoned in the urban areas is as a result of influx of young unmarried girls from the rural areas who remain without any gainful and decent employment thereby involving and indulging themselves in the nefarious jobs in the urban.[11] There is also the need for public enlightenment and education of parents of any child affected with any disability not to subject them to public ridicule and torture but to make available adequate health and medical care. At the same time, there should be improvement of health facilities in order to correct and manage the outcome of these abnormalities and the eventual rehabilitation of the children.

It is strongly advocated that parents should play significant roles in the prevention of child abuse. Parents are thus advised to resist inflicting injury on their children or their wards. Guardians or childminder also contribute to child abuse. A mother who is strict and metes out corporal punishment on her child may unwittingly precipitate physical abuse on her child during her absence from home. It is not unusual for a child to have as many as four childminders within the first year of life. This frequent change of the mother substitute does not enhance attachment and distorts the emotional development of the child. This should be discouraged by parents as far as possible.

Most importantly, the society can also play significant roles to arrest the incessant child abuse. This can be achieved where adequate accommodation, recreational facilities, regular water and electricity are supplied. People should be re-oriented to find for themselves self-employed job to do, so as to minimally provide these basic necessities of life. A child born into a large family which lives in an overcrowded one–room accommodation in the peri-urban slum is likely to be abused by an irritable and stressed parent. Lack of provision of adequate educational and recreational facilities in the society contribute to emotional and social neglect of the child. The unemployed single parent is likely to abandon her child to the society.

It may still be relevant, effective and efficient to re-enact specific laws against this malpractice but the lukewarm attitude towards the enforcement of those legislations should be stopped. Children who are at risk in such circumstances could be fostered or adopted in other families outside the community. The survival and success of these children in later years will convince these people about the facility of their inhuman traditional beliefs and practices.

CONCLUSION AND RECOMMENDATIONS

Finally, it is the responsibility of all and sundry, the government, the parents and the society to see to the eradication of the child abuse. The drastic and prompt steps taken by the federal and state governments to the establishment of the Child Welfare Committees to carry on the objectives of the International Year of the Child–namely to uphold the Rights of the Child as embodied in the Declaration adopted by the General Assembly of the United Nations in 1959 is commendable. It is therefore hoped that, these Child Welfare Committees will, in addition to other functions, keep Registers of children of risk especially those who have already been exposed to abuse.

Also commendable is the effort of the Chairperson and founder of Women Trafficking and Child Labour Eradication Foundation (WOTCLEF), in the eradication of child abuse and trafficking which has resulted in a bill been passed to law on the subject by the National Assembly.

More importantly, those who persistently indulge directly or indirectly in any form of child abuse should be made to face the wrath of the law. Not only that, the children too who are grown up should not always be seemed to be victim as punitive measures can also be laid down to discourage perpetration from the child abuser and the victim. This it is advocated would not make our laws and legislation on the subject to exist only in our Statute books thereby making them ineffective, inefficient and unenforceable.

NOTES

1. Ofodile, et.al (1978)
2. Ibid. pp. 27
3. Kempe (1978)
4. Ibid.
5. British Medical Association Editorial (1981)
6. Kwara State Laws of Nigeria (1994) Cap 29
7. Section 17 (3) (f) of the 1999 Constitution
8. Kwara State Laws of Nigeria (1994) Section 11 (a)-(j) Children's' and Young Persons Laws, Cap, 29
9. Klaus, and Kenneli, (1976)
10. Egeland, and Sronfe, (1981)
11. Burustein, (1981)

REFERENCES

Burustein, M.H. (1981), Child Abandonment: Historical, Sociological and Psychological Perspectives–Child Psychiatry. *Human Development* Vol. 11 pp. 213-21.

British Medical Association Editorial (1981), Child Abuse: The Swing of the Pendulum. *British Medical Journal 1981,* Vol. 283 pp. 170-173.

Egeland, B. and Sronfe, L.A. (1981), Attachment And Maltreatment. *Child Development* Vol. 52.

Federal Republic of Nigeria (1999) *Section 17 (3) (f) of the 1999 Constitution.*

Kempe C.H. (1978), Sexual Abuse, Another Hidden Pediatric Problem: The 1977 C. Anderson Aldrich Lecture. *Pediatrics Vol. 62* pp. 382-389.

Klaus, H.H. and Kenneli J.H. (1976), *Material–Infant Bonding: The Impact of Early Separation or Loss on Family Development.* Saint Louis: The C.V. Mosby Co.

Kwara State Government of Nigeria (1994) *Kwara State Laws of Nigeria Section 11 (a)-(j).*

Children's and Young Persons Laws, Cap, 29 1994.

Ofodile, F., Norria, J. and Garnes, A. (1978), Burns and Child Abuse. *East African Medical Journal. Vol. 56,* pp. 26-29.

INFANTICIDE TO FOETICIDE–THE 'HIGH-TECH SEXISM'

*Priti Saxena**

> *"Morality can not be legislated but behaviour can be regulated, judicial decrees may not change the heart, but they can restrain the heartless".*
>
> **Martin Luther King**

Despite the fact that the gentle touch of a daughter and her voice has a soothing effect on parents, it is unfortunate that for various reasons'[1] the practice of female foeticide still prevails in our country. The crime of infanticide is not confined to India alone. Globally, infanticide has from the time immemorial been the accepted procedure for disposing not only of deformed or sickly infants but of all such new born as might strain the resources of the individual family or the larger community.[2] The first Statute to create a crime of infanticide was passed in 1623 in England. It was a sex-specific crime committed by women and confined to bastered children as victims.

In India during British regime, Regulation VI of 1802, prohibited the practice of infanticide by declaring it equivalent to willful murder and on conviction the person responsible was liable to the punishment of death and all abettors and accomplices were also given the same. Even an attempt to commit the crime of infanticide where the victim would escape of death was given adequate punishment.[3] Infanticide is a crime under Indian Penal Code except where it is necessary to save the life of pregnant woman.[4]

Biological reproduction, that most 'natural' of human activities, has been the subject of major scientific and technological changes during the past 35-40 years. In 1964, Shantilal Shah Committee was set up by

* Head, Department of Human Rights, School For Legal Studies, Babasaheb Bhimrao Ambedkar Central University, Lucknow.

Ministry of Health, to look into the matter of legalising abortion. As a result in August 1971, the Medical Termination of Pregnancy Act, 1971 was passed, for medicalisation of crime through medical practitioners.

The treatment of women by medical profession raises important issues for feminism in today's scenario. From a feminist perspective, the right of the individual to determine questions relating to her own body is of fundamental importance. To deny the right to take decision is to treat the individual as unequal and inferior and to deny the rationality of the women's decision making process and her right to autonomy. But the Indian woman is meant to accept the forced decisions of man-though she is the master of her own body-conferred with equality rights under the *Suprema lex.*[5] The fact, that Indian men have failed to realize the woman as an individual with a mind of her own, the birth of a girl child is neglected,[6] it brings a gloom rather than joy in the family, is still prevalent. To solve the grim problem of unwanted *Girl Child* in most of the big cities and metros in our country the crime of Female Foeticide is flourishing. The primary factor responsible this unhealthy phenomenon is of course the low value ascribed to women in Indian society. Consequently, many families prefer not to give birth to girls or do not nurture girls adequately. Inadequate nurturing results from giving girls a subordinate claim over the family's food, educational and medical care resources compared with boys.

The feminist' struggle against this crime of female foeticide, leading up to passing of the Pre-Natal Diagnostic Techniques (Regulation and Prevention of Misuse) Act, 1994, and Pre-Natal Diagnostic Techniques (Regulation and Prevention of Misuse) Rules, 1996, though meant for preventing the crime, but the desired results were not achieved. Therefore, the Centre for enquiry into health and allied themes[7] and others have filed a Writ Petition before the Supreme Court under Article 32 of the Constitution. The Supreme Court once again on May, 4,2001, issued certain directions and orders regarding proper implementation of the P.N.D.T. Act 1994 to Central Government, Central Supervisory Board, State Governments, Union Territories, and to appropriate authorities. Some of the main directions were:

1. The central Government was directed to create public awareness against the practice of prenatal determination of sex and female foeticide through appropriate releases/programmes in the electronic media provided under section 16(iii) of the PNDT Act, 1994.
2. The central Government was directed to implement with all vigour and zeal the PNDT Act, 1994 and the Rules framed in 1996.

3. The Court directed the Central Supervisory Board (CSB) to meet once in six months.[8] The constitution of CSB is provided under section 7. It empowers the central government to appoint ten members under section 7 (2) (e) which includes eminent medical practitioners, including eminent social scientists and representatives of women welfare organizations, so that persons can genuinely spare time for implementation of the Act.

4. CSB shall review and monitor the implementation of the Act.[9]

5. CSB shall issue directions to all States/UT, appropriate authorities to furnish quarterly returns to CSB and all States/UTs were directed to ensure to furnish such returns to CSB by giving a report on the implementation and working of the Act. The information required to be submitted includes:

   (a) Survey and registration of bodies specified in section 3 of the Act;

   (b) Action taken against non-registered bodies operating in violation of section 3, inclusive of search and seizure of records;

   (c) Complaints received by the appropriate authorities and action taken thereto;

   (d) Number and nature of awareness campaigns conducted and results flowing therefrom.

6. CSB shall examine the necessity to amend the Act if, new technologies and difficulties come in way of implementing the Act and to make recommendations to the Central Govemment.[10]

7. Under section 16(iv) of the Act the CSB shall lay down a code of conduct to be observed by persons working in bodies specified therein and to ensure its publication so that the public at large can know about it.

8. CSB will require medical professional bodies/associations to create awareness against the practice of prenatal determination of sex and female foeticide and to ensure implementation of the act.

9. All the state government A and UTs were directed to appoint appropriate authorities at district and sub-district levels and also advisory committee to aid and advise the appropriate authorities in discharge of their functions. (Section 17(5).

10. The list of appropriate authorities be published in print and electronic media in their respective States/UTs.

11. The public awareness be created against the practice of prenatal determination of sex and female foeticide through advertisement in print and electronic media by hoardings and other appropriate means.
12. Appropriate authorities were directed to take prompt action against any person or body that issues or causes to be issued any advertisement in violation of section 22 of the Act.
13. Appropriate authorities were directed to take prompt action against all bodies specified in section 3 of the Act as also against persons who are operating without a valid certificate of registration under the Act.

In all its wisdom, with the object of preventing the misuse of such techniques for the purpose of pre-natal sex determination leading to female foeticide for matters connected therewith or incidental thereto, our Parliament enacted the PNDT Act 1994, but the immoral and unethical act to get rid of girl child before birth by misusing developed medical science as an offence could not be controlled by the Act. The government's initial step to rectify the declining sex ratio i.e. enactment of 1994 PNDT Act, by which all clinics with ultrasound machines were required to register themselves and performing a sex-determination test was made a cognizable, non-bailable offence, punishable with imprisonment and fine, proved to be extremely poor in its enforcement. Therefore, our Parliament gave more teeth to the Act of 1994 by amending and naming it as Pre-Conception and Pre-Natal Diagnostic Techniques (Prohibition of Sex Selection) Act, 2002. On International Women's Day, i.e., March 8, 2006, the Govt. reiterated its commitment to halt the alarming and continuous decline in the country's sex ratio and announced several measures to reverse the trend. Currently the national figure stands at 933 women to 1000 men, but what is most disturbing is that the number of girls per 1000 boys in the 0-6 age group has fallen from 945 in the 1991 census to 927 in the latest census.[11] To combat this 'high-tech sexism'[12] i.e. to abort a foetus after determining sex, the Union Health and Family Welfare Ministry is in the process of setting up a *'National Support and Monitoring Cell'* to curb female foeticide. The Ministry has undertaken training of people from State Judicial Academies to sensitize the judiciary on the issue. A National Inspection and Monitoring Committee with representatives from the Ministry of Women and Child Development, National Commission for Women, Indian Council for Medical Research as members, undertakes periodical visits to the districts with low child sex ratio (0-6 years) to oversee the implementation of the Act at the ground level and monitors the prosecutions launched against unregistered bodies and those violating the Act.[13] The sex ratio in the age group of 0-6 all over the country has come down from 976 in 1961 to 927 in 2001. Of the 591 districts, 16 have a sex ratio of less than 800, in 33 districts it is between 850 and 849, and it is between 850 and 899 in 72 districts. It is between 950-999 in 245 districts and 1,000-1,049 in only 21 districts.[14]

Of late making history, the country's first conviction on 28-3-2006, was made under the PNDT Act A Doctor practicing at Palwal in Faridabad district and his ultra-sound technician were sentenced for two years' imprisonment and a fine of Rs. 5,000/- each for conducting sex determination test This conviction showed that this Act is more powerful because the unborn girl is given a fair chance of life in our country, but the Act is UNDERUSED in the country.

The data above show that there exists a great gender imbalance in the country. The crime is rising in the Metropolis. The traditional system of female infanticide whereby the female baby was done away with after birth by throwing into water, poisoning or letting her choke on husk has changed with the advancement of science and technology. The purpose is now solved by taking advantage of advanced medical techniques i.e. female foeticide. Judiciary as well as legislature is keen to curb this social evil which can more appropriately be called an organized crime against the female foetus. However, in practice the simple procedures of the Act is not being followed nor the conviction can be ensured without full proof of evidences. Therefore some high-tech measures and social norms can be appreciated to prevent the crime of female foeticide:

1. Though the crime of female foeticide is a result of medical and scientific advancement it should be controlled scientifically by developing various methods such as completely locking the system through which sex could not be determined prenatal.

2. The medical practitioners involved in determining the, sex, their license to practice be cancelled for the whole life, not for a limited period, at the first instance.

3. The parents, involved in such act, if in government or semi-government jobs, should be terminated immediately. If doing own business their license be cancelled to carry on such business.

4. The persons giving information of such crime be awarded and particularly if the person informing of the crime is unemployed he or she be awarded with some suitable job in the area of unemployment. For this will create a creative public awareness also.

5. The persons involve in such crime either medical practitioner or potential parents be publicly reprimanded. In the area of show business, this mud slinging will lower down the reputation of persons involved. For this will also create a fear in their mind not to involve in such crime resulting in mental punishment.

6. The parents of girl child should be entitled for incentive and relief from Income Tax Department, subject to population policy. For this will ensure (to some extent) that girl child is not a *Binder*.

NOTES

1. Marriage problem, dowry' demand, inferiority in society being parents of a girl child etc. This is the Indian mentality.
2. B.A. Kullem, Infanticide in England in the later middle ages (1974) A History of Childhood Quarterly 371.
3. Landmarks in Indian Legal & Constitutional History, B.M. Gandhi 1989 at 246.
4. See Sections 412-418 of Indian Penal Code 1861.
5. See Article 14 of the Indian Constitution.
6. Priti Saxena, "Written Laws Unwritten Differentiation and Fair Sex" AIR 1997 Journal Section at 101.
7. Centre for Enquiry into Health and Allied Themes (CEHAT) v. Union of India (2001) 5 S.C.C. 577.
8. Proviso to section 9(1) of the Act of 1994.
9. Section 16(ii) of the Act of 1994.
10. Section 16 of the Act of 1994.
11. 2001 census, The Hindu, March, 17, 2006, at page 10
12. As called by Noble Prize winning economist, Prof. Amartya Sen.
13. The Hindu 19-4-06 at 13.
14. The Hindu 8-4-06.

SOCIAL SITUATION OF THE STREET CHILDREN IN A GROWING CITY OF EASTERN INDIA

R.P. Mohanty and N.K. Behura***

I

World population is growing rapidly. In developing countries like India, the situation has become alarming. It has created various social problems in manifold ways and hence it has become deleterious to the prosperity of the nation.

About 35 per cent (2001) of Indian population are illiterate and most of them are intrinsically attached 'to their age-old tradition. Their insight on the negative effects of unplanned family is very low. This, of course leads to overexploitation of the existing natural resources and in that case the demand for searching of alternative ways and means for livelihood always remains on the front line. For the poor and hapless people, when it becomes very difficult to sustain life, they migrate to the urban centers and lead a very wretched and pitiful life in slums. They struggle hard for their existence in the new ecological setting, i.e., slum and finally take to socially low and derogatory occupations, like rickshaw-pulling, wage-earning, construction work; domestic sundry work etc., either willingly or unwillingly by the compulsion of circumstances. By the way they become very individualistic and self-centric in nature and ask their minor children to work for themselves and often for the family members too. But since the children are not valued much for wage-earning, they come on to the streets to pick rags, beg alms, sweep railway platforms and train coaches, vend stuffs, shine shoes or to do similar jobs. Normally these works are very hazardous and involve high risks since they work for prolonged hours and not conscious of their rights even though they are very defensive in nature. Thus, these children

* Academic Member in Anthropology, Nabakrushna Choudhury Centre for Development Studies, Bhubaneswar-751013.

** Honorary Fellow in Anthropology, Nabakrushna Choudhury Centre for Development Studies, Bhubaneswar-751013.

comprise a major social problem in our country from various aspects and, therefore, the need of social intervention is very much essential for their well- being.

II

With a view to understand the field reality, a total number of 120 street children, below the age of 14 years were selected from different pockets of Bhubaneswar city, the state capital of Orissa, on the basis of simple random sampling procedure. First of all, 8 potential pockets namely, (i) Rajmahal/Market building/Kalpana area (ii) Railway station/Cuttack Road area, (iii) FCI Malgodown/Sriya Talkies area, (iv) Jayadev Vihar/ Salia Sahi area, (vii) Baramunda/CRPF area and (viii) Ainginia/ Dumudum area, were selected purposively where the street children are mostly concentrated. From each pocket, a total number of 15 samples were selected on the basis of simple random sampling giving weightage to cover at least 25 per cent of street girl children irrespective of taking equal proportion of sample of these children from each pocket. This restriction was imposed in the sampling procedure with a view to save time and complete the research project in time since locating street girl children was more time consuming.

In order to understand and focus the real problems of the street children; both quantitative as well as qualitative anthropological methods, like, collection of primary data through structured schedules, observations, personal interviews and documentation of case studies etc. were adopted.

III

Generally the parents of the street children are very poor. Educationally they are also very backward. There are 86.67 per cent of fathers as against as many as 96.67 per cent of mothers who are illiterate. Partly because of this and partly because of some other reasons, the street children remain deprived of their right to education. As a result, most (78%) of them are found to be illiterate (Table 1). This, together with utter poverty compel them to work and earn for themselves instead of attending to schools.

Generally, the street children take to such occupations that do not require any formal education. They do not bother about the social sanctity of the job they adopt and mind less for their social prestige in the public.

Hunger, the most vital propelling instinct, may compel a child to beg for alms or even snatch a piece of bread from the mouth of an animal but he/she does not normally adopt such occupations that are not approved by his/her parents or guardians. But if he/she is independent and has less or no contact with his/her parents, he/she enjoys absolute freedom to earn out of any work according to his/her own choice and interest that may be rag-picking, shoe-shining, collection of rotten fruits and vegetables, sorting of vegetables, cleaning of utensils at hotels or cleaning clothes or doing similar jobs as a domestic servant etc. Thus, a child of the street can take to any kind of sundry job depending upon his/her personal interest and the demand of the situation.

Table 1
Educational Status Among the Street Children

Level of Education	*Total Cases*	*% age*
(1)	(2)	(3)
Illiterate	93	77.50
Primary (I-V)	24	20.00
Middle (VI VII)	2	1.67
Upto High School but below Matriculation	1	0.83
Total	120	100.00

It is found that the street children of Bhubaneswar city are engaged in as many as 10 different occupations. These are: Collection of semi-burnt coal and green coconut fibres, domestic service, garage work and working in cycle-repairing shops, menial work in hotels, collection of strewn potatoes at storage sites, potato sorting, rag-picking, cleaning of railway platforms and train compartments and collection of tips and alms, shoe-shining, and vending of edible items at various market complexes, railway stations and public places. But surprisingly most of the street children (55.83%) are engaged in rag picking. They are followed by about 12 per cent of children who are engaged in collection of strewn potatoes form different potato storage sites. Next to them, 8.33 per cent of them are found to work as domestic servants. An equal percentage of these children are found to be self-employed with the business of shoes-shining at railway platforms, bus stations, foot-paths etc. A total number of 7 of them, accounting for 5.83 per cent, work in different automobile garages, work-shops and cycle-repairing shops followed by 3.33 per cent engaged in vending of various edible items, like egg, ground-nut, betel and cigarette, tea etc at railway platforms and in train compartments. Only 2 (1.67%) of them collect thrown out semi-burnt coal from tea shops and hotels and green coconut coir from road sides for selling or for personal use as fuel. Another group consisting of an equal percentage of street children work as roadside hotel assistants. Further, same number of street children work to sort out potatoes of different sizes and rotten potatoes at potato retail shops. The rest 2 (2.22) children are found to clean railway platforms and train compartments and beg for tips, alms etc (Table 2).

Table 2
Distribution of Street Children According to Sex and Occupation

Sl. No.	*Occupation*	*Boys*	*Girls*	*Total*
(1)	(2)	(3)	(4)	(5)
1.	Collection of semi-burnt coal and green coconut fibres	–	2 (6.67)	2 (6.67
2.	Domestic service	1 (1.11)	9 (30.00)	10 (8.33)
3.	Garage work/asst. at cycle repairing shop	7 (7.78)	–	7 (5.83)
4.	Hotal work	2 (2.22)	–	2 (1.67)
5.	Collection of strewn potato	12 (13.33)	2 (6.67)	14 (11.67)
6.	Potato sorting	1 (1.11)	1 (1.33)	2 (1.67)
7.	Rag-picking	52 (57.78)	15 (50.00)	67 (55.83)
8.	Cleaning of railway platform and train compartment and collection of tips and alms	2 (2.22)	–	2 (1.67)
9.	Shoe-shining	10 (11.11)	–	10 (8.33)
10.	Vending	3 (3.33)	1 (1.33)	4 (3.33)
	Total	90 (100.00)	30 (100.00)	120 (100.00)

So far as the sex-wise distribution of occupation among the street children is concerned, it is observed that in case of either sexes, adoption of rag-picking is found to be highest that comes to 57.78 per cent for the boys as against 50 per cent for the girls. But so far as the next important occupation is concerned, it is potato collection (13.33%) for boys, and domestic service (30.00%) for the girls.

The reasons that have compelled the street children to adopt these occupations, are found to be as many as 10 different types (Table 3). In most of the cases (77.5%) the street children say that they have adopted their present occupations as per the opinion, suggestion or instruction of their parents followed by a total number of 35 children, about 29 per cent, who say that they have taken to different jobs, because most of their peers are engaged in such activities. Interestingly, 20 per cent of them opine that their present jobs are more profitable than other jobs.

As a result of this, they have retained such occupations. About 12 per cent of them state that they happened to take up the present jobs as their brothers and sisters are already engaged in such activities. Among the rest 5 reasons, each one comprises below 10 per cent of the total sample, which in the descending order are; poverty or forced circumstances (9.17%), less hazardous and involvement of less risk (9.17%), tradition (6.67%), opinion or suggestion of relatives (2.50%) and death of parents; father or mother or both (2.50%).

Table 3
Factors Responsible for Taking to the Present Occupations
(N = 120)

Sl. No.	*Factors*	*Total Cases*	*% Age*
(1)	(2)	(3)	(4)
1.	As per the opinion/suggestion/ instruction of parents	93	77.5
2.	As per the opinion/suggestion of relatives	3	2.50
3.	As more peers are engaged in this work	35	29.17
4.	As brother (s)/sisters(s) are, engaged in this work	14	11.67
5.	As it is more profitable	24	20.00
6.	As it is less hazardous and involves less risk	11	9.17
7.	Death of parents	3	2.50
8.	Poverty/forced by circumstances	11	9.17
9.	Traditional occupation	11	6.67
10.	Decision by self to raise own money to spend independently.	12	10.00

In order to stay alive, each moment becomes challenging for the street children. The motive of 'struggle for survival' rings at the dawn of the morning and compels them to leave the bed as soon as they can. They are habituated to wake up early in the morning, and rush to the streets of the city to earn their daily bread. Throughout the day they are to remain on the streets and work hard, otherwise they remain starved.

A perusal of Table 4 reveals that maximum street children (34.17%) remain on streets for about 9-10 hours per day followed by 24.17 per cent remaining for 7-8 hours and 11.67 per cent for 5-6 hours. An equal percentage of them are compelled to work on the streets for about 11-12 hours per day. The situation of 12 (10.00%) street children, 10 per cent of the total sample, is found to be horrible who work for 13 or more hours per day on the street. But fortunately 8.33 per cent of them are found to be in a little better position who work only for about 2-4 hours a day. When one looks at certain occupations with regard to utilization of average time, it is observed that the street children who work in different hotels, toil for longer duration per day which comes to be about 14 hours on an average, and it is least, i.e., 3.5 hours per day in case of those who are engaged in collection of semi-burnt coal and green coconut fibres. Amongst the rest, the street children who clean railway platforms and train compartments and collect tips or alms, work for about 13 hours a day followed by garage boys and assistants in cycle repairing shops (12.86 hours), vendors (10.5 hours), rag-pickers (9.57 hours), shoes-shiners (9.05 hours), potato collectors (7.93 hours), potato graders (6.5 hours) and domestic servants (4.55 hours). The average working hours per street children irrespective of occupations comes to be 9.12 hours per day (Table 5).

Table 4
Working Hour of the Street Children per Day

Duration of work (In Hours)	*Total Cases*	*% age*
(1)	(2)	(3)
2-4	10	8.33
5-6	14	11.67
7-8	29	24.17
9-10	41	34.17
11-12	14	11.67
13 and More	12	10.00
Total	120	100.00

IV

The street children can, in one way, be treated as the by-product of population explosion, that stand against maintenance of good quality of life. Deterioration of quality of life starts soon after the poor and helpless immigrants are maladjusted in urban centers and their subjunctive hopes become futile. In this context it seems that both the parents as well as children struggle very hard for their survival and try to enhance their quality of life. But high rate of illiteracy among the parents of these

Table 5
Average Working Hour per day According to Occupations

Sl. No.	*Occupation*	*Total Persons*	*Total time spend in last working engaged day (in Hours)*	*Average*
(1)	(2)	(3)	(4)	(5)
1.	Collection of semi-burnt. coal and green coconut fibre	2	7	3.5
2.	Domestic service	10	45.5	4.55
3.	Garage work/asst. at cycle repairing shop	7	90	12.86
4.	Hotel assistant	2	28	14.00
5.	Potato collection	14	111	7.93
6.	Potato sorting	2	13	6.5
7.	Rag-picking	67	641.5	9.57
8.	Cleaning of railway platforms and train compartments	2	26	13.00
9.	Shoe-shining	10	90.5	9.05
10.	Vending	4	42	10.5
	Total	120	1094.5	9.12

children has necessitated them to adopt low income generating occupations in order to sustain their life in a highly competitive environment and to financially support their families. The families of these people normally constitute a large number of members per family. This leads to disorganization of familial ties between parents and children. In many cases (75.00%) parents become addicted to alcoholic drinks in order to get rid of hyper-tension, bodily pain and psychosocial and economic pressure of supporting their large family with their meager daily income. Apart from this, parents (19.01%) also suffer from various diseases, the most important ones being viral fever (33.33%), colic or abdominal pain (23.8%) etc compel them to ask their children to work for themselves as well as for their parents and other family members. Relating to this, as many as 87 (82.08%) children belonging to the first category of children, i.e., 'Children On Street' say that they are asked by their parents to work and earn daily (Table 6). Not only they are simply asked to work and earn daily rather in case of 27.59 per cent of children a large amount is fixed up by their parents for earning daily (Table 7) In most of the cases (37-50%) Rs.10/- per day is demanded by the parents of the street children and they are followed by 29.17 per cent of them for whom it is as high as Rs. 30/- (Table 8). When the street children do not work as per the instructions of their parents and earn accordingly, they

Table 6
Whether parents ask you to do work and earn daily (Among Children on Street)?

Responses	*Total Cases*	*% age*
(1)	(2)	(3)
Yes	87	82.08
No	19	17.92
Total	100	100.00

Table 7
If yes, do they fix up any target amount to earn daily?

Responses	*Total Cases*	*% age*
(1)	(2)	(3)
Yes	24	27.59
No	63	72.41
Total	87	100.00

Table 8
Target Amount Fixed to Earn for the Last Day

Target Among Fixed	*Total Cases*	*%age*
(1)	(2)	(3)
1-10	7	37.5
11-20	3	12.5
21-30	5	20.83
31+	7	29.17
Total	24	100.00

are scolded and are also beaten up (89.53%). At times, they are not given adequate food (30.23%), and even in many cases (20.93%) food is completely denied. For about 7 per cent of children, their parents close the doors and in such cases the children become disappointed and hopeless (Table 9). Because of these embarrassing situations about 18 per cent of the total children (Table 10) did not come to their respective homes at least for once during the last week out of fear of being scolded or beaten up when they had not worked so as to meet the demands of their parents. In this regard Table 11 illustrates that of the total 19 children, about 74 per cent had not come to their respective homes for about 1-2 days during the last week and they had spent their nights mostly at the railway platforms (73.68%), market complex premises (15.79%), community halls or meeting pendals of their hamlets (5.26%) etc. (Table 12).

Table 9
What happens when you do not work according to your parents (N = 86)?

Varieties	Total Cases	%age
(1)	(2)	(3)
At time adequate food is not given	26	30.23
At times food is denied	18	20.93
At times door is closed	6	6.8
Many times scolded and beaten up	77	89.53

Table 10
Have you ever not returned home out of fear during the last week?

Responses	*Total Cases*	*% age*
(1)	(2)	(3)
Yes	19	17.92
No	87	82.08
Total	106	100.00

Table 11
If yes, how many times last week?

No. of times (in days)	Total Cases	% age
(1)	(2)	(3)
1	7	36.84
2	7	36.84
3	3	15.89
4+	2	10.53
Total	19	100.00

Table 12
In such cases, where did you stay?

Places	*Total Cases*	*% age*
(1)	(2)	(3)
Railway platform	14	73.68
Community hall/meeting pendal or basti/ slum/village	1	5.26
Garage	1	5.26
Market complex premise	3	15.79
Total	19	100.00

Street children work hard and in most of the cases (90.1%), they give away a large share of their daily earnings to their parents and remain underfed. When a question on the ways of spending of their earnings by their parents was asked, 97.17 per cent of them opined that their parents spend it for the general purpose of family. But 34.91 per cent of them say that most often their fathers take it for consumption of alcohol followed by 29.25 per cent who said that at times their fathers do so, but for most of the times their money is spent for the day to day management of the family (Table 13).

Table 13
How your income is spent by your parents (N=106)?

Responses	*Total Cases*	*% age*
(1)	(2)	(3)
Spent for the general purpose of the family	103	97.17
For majority of times father takes it for consumption of alcoholic drinks	31	29.25
At times father takes it for consumption of alcohol	37	34.91
It is sent to village for education of bothers/sisters	1	0.94
It is saved for marriage purpose of self/sister	2	1.89
Adjusted towards food charges at relative's home	1	0.94

Food or nutritional intake is one of the three basic needs of life. But it is the most important requirement for sustenance of life and hence it has direct bearing with the physical and mental growth and also development of working ability. If a child takes required amount of food according to its age and bodily growth, it grows properly and works accordingly. But the poor economic condition of parents of a number of street children does not permit them to feed their children properly. On the other hand their poor economic condition demands hard labour daily from each of their children. At times some of the children remain unfed and often they remain underfed. Subsequently they suffer from malnutrition.

A perusal of Table 14 throws some light on the dietary pattern of the street children on the day before the interview was conducted with them. It is found that 13.33 per cent of children had not taken any breakfast before they went to the streets for earning their day's bread. Surprisingly 1.67 per cent of them had no other way than to spend the whole day without a lunch. Further 4.7 per cent of them could not have dinner before they went to sleep. In between the time of lunch and dinner, only about 56 per cent had taken tiffin and the rest remained hungry. When about 49 per cent had adequate breakfast, the rest were underfed. Still about 72 per cent were satisfied with lunch as against 75 per cent who had dinner to their hearts content. Tiffins were adequately available for only 69 per cent of these children (Table 15). Thus, since quite a sizable number of these children remained underfed, they starved. But still then they were not relieved from working daily on the streets.

Table 14
Status of Consumption of Food on Last Day (N=120)

Variables	*Whether consumed*			
	Yes	*% age*	*No*	*% age*
(1)	(2)	(3)	(4)	(5)
Breakfast	101	86.67	16	13.33
Lunch	118	98.33	2	1.67
Tiffin	67	55.83	53	44.17
Dinner	115	95.83	5	4.17

Table 15
Quantity of Consumption of Food on Last Day (N = 120)

Variables	*No. of Chindren consumed*	*Level of Consumption*			
		Adequate	*% age*	*Inadequate*	*% age*
(1)	(2)	(3)	(4)	(5)	(6)
Breakfast	104 (100.00)	51	49.04	53	50.96
Lunch	118 (100.00)	85	72.03	33	27.97
Tiffin	67 (100.00)	42	62.69	25	37.31
Dinner	115 (100.00)	86	74.78	29	25.22

Since most of the street children live in unhygienic environments, remain underfed and work hard in empty stomach, they suffer miserably form various diseases. It is found from the Table 16 that one-fourths of the street children are presently suffering from diseases, like scabies (30.00%), joint pain (20.00%), mild fever (10,00%), itching on feet and hand (6.67%), headache (3.33%), dog-bite (3.33%), polio (3.33%), and tuberculosis (3.33%) etc. These findings otherwise signify that working in unhygienic conditions and neglecting personal hygienic care cause scabies to a large number of street children, cold and cough affects a sizeable number of children as they remain exposed to sun, rain and cold for a major part of time. Joint-pain is quite obvious to them as each child is to cover a long distance by walk on every working day. Suffering from itching is a problem mainly with the girl street children who usually work as maid-servants and are supposed to do such works as cleaning utensils, house floors, clothes etc. Even though, these children suffer from these diseases, they (73.33%) do not take any remedial measure unless they become very serious. A total number of 4 (13.33%) diseased children are however found to have consulted the doctors and the local health workers as against 6.67 per cent who have just consulted the salesmen of medicine shops and purchased medicines as per their prescriptions. They have done so to avoid consultation fee with a doctor and also to save time. There are an equal percentage of these children whose parents are taking care to cure them through the local traditional healers (Table 17).

Table 16
Diseases among diseased street children (N=30)

Sl. No.	*Diseases*	*Total Cases*	*% age*
(1)	(2)	(3)	(4)
1.	Cold and Cough	7	23.33
2.	Dog Bite	1	3.33
3.	Headache	1	3.33
4.	Itching	2	6.67
5.	Joint pain	6	20.00
6.	Mild fever	3	10.00
7.	Polio	1	3.33
8.	Scabies	9	30.00
9.	Tuberculosis	1	3.33
10.	Wound on feet and body	8	26.67

Table 17
Types of Treatment Going on Among Diseased Street Children (N = 30)

Sl. No.	*Type of Treatment*	*Total Cases*	*% age*
(1)	(2)	(3)	(4)
1.	Consultation with doctor/health worker	4	13.33
2.	Consultation with sales men	2	6.67
3.	Consultation with traditional healer	2	6.67
4.	No treatment	22	73.33
	Total	30	100.00

Attitudinal aspects of the general public, municipal officials, railway and police officers towards the street children have been highlighted in Table 18. It points out that during the last year while 13.33 per cent of these children have been harassed by the general public, it is 7.5 per cent children who were put to trouble by the railway staff and police officials. A total number of 4 (3.33%) children say that they have been put in difficult situations by the municipal officials also. Generally these children (rag-pickers and domestic servants etc.) are often scolded and even beaten up by some public whenever there is a theft case. In many cases they are also handed over to the police even if they are not involved in such cases. The shoe-shiners who open their petty shops at roadsides or railway stations, are most often beaten up or their petty shops are thrown out by the railway police mainly during the peak business hours or during the arrival of ministers and other such VIPs. Sometimes municipal officers also create much problem for them by the way of seizing their shops and belongings.

Table 18
Harassment by Public, Police, Municipal Officials to the Street Children During Last Year (N = 120)

Variables	*Harassed*	*Not Harassed*
1	(2)	(3)
Public	16 (13.33)	104 (86.67)
Municipal Officials	4 (3.33)	116 (96.67)
Railway/Public Police	9 (7.5)	111 (92.50)

Note: Figures in brackets represent % age in all tables.

V

The root cause of any social problem lies on sustained persistence of an imbalance between population and available resources for utilization. In a populous country, like India, human population is growing very fast because of illiteracy, low level of awareness among the rural people and flexible implementation of family planning legislations. It exerts much pressure on the local resources, and when the resources become scarce, people face various problems and migrate to resource-rich areas in order to extract their livelihood. Developing urban centers are such resource-rich areas that attract a number of rural wage-earning people. But when the urban centers receive more of such people than required, the available resources are overexploited and in such situations most of the children of these people come on to the streets to work and earn their own livelihood. As a result, in order to have complete eradication of appearance of these children on streets of urban centers, our national family planning measures should be implemented with utmost sincerity on priority instead of being suggestive to have only one or two children per couple. This would, in the other way, minimize over migration of rural people to different developing urban centers and hence proper balance between population and resources for utilization could be maintained. The other related measures for immediate adoption for eradicating of street children would be as follows:

(a) That the Municipal corporations must develop their own strategies to restrict over immigration of rural wage-earners whose children most often come on to the streets for work. These corporate bodies must be very cautious to register each immigrant and not to accommodate more immigrants than required. It should endeavor to rehabilitate them properly.

(b) Those who are accommodated within the municipal area and are provided with 'Urban Basic Service' (UBS) facilities must be imparted awareness to strictly follow the family planning measures of the government. In no case a family residing within the municipal area be permitted to procreate more children than approved. Those who fail to follow it should be withdrawn from availing accommodation and land holding facility within the municipal boundary. If, for the time being, these suggestive recommendations are not possible for implementation, then the following measures be adopted for the development and welfare of the street children.

  (i) That a scientific survey be made on priority basis to identify street-child-households. In each slum, these children must be covered under universalisation of formal education and it should be ensured that they are not asked or forced by their parents to work as earners of bread either on streets or on any other pale. If it happens so, then their parents must be restricted from availing of ration-card facility or be withdrawn from poverty alleviation programmes if they are covered under any of such programmes.

  (ii) Each and every child of the slum must be provided with free education apart from free boarding facility, at least upto matriculation and there should be job guarantee for the matriculates. For the non-matriculates, need-based vocational training be provided according to their own choices and demand of the market. Provision should also be made for rehabilitation of successful trainees so that more and more street children as well as their parents would be interested and come forward to avail the opportunities. By this way, two-fold objectives of the nation, viz., improvement of literacy and reduction of unemployment among the Indian population would be considerably reduced.

(iii) The poorest of the poor or 'At-Risk' slum dwellers and those who lie on footpaths, backyard of urban residents, under open sky, railway platforms, market complex premises, office premises etc should be identified on priority basis and be covered under special poverty alleviation programmes in order to improve their economic condition. These children should be given more attention and be covered under the above job-guaranted educational and vocational training programmes.

(iv) Medical service should be provided at the doorstep of each and every slum dweller periodically, i.e., at least once in a week through public mobile-health-checkup-camps/vans. Emphasis must be given on health check-up of each child and nursing mothers without fail.

(v) Since the nature and working pattern of the street children vary from one place to another, government must work out some specific legislation for the welfare of each category of these children. For example, the working conditions and patterns of a domestic servant are not same as with a hotel boy or a garage worker. Hence, there must be specific legislations indicating their nature of work, hour of work, etc. Accordingly minimum wage rates also be fixed up and specified in order to protect them from exploitation.

(vi) The rag-pickers work hard throughout the day but they are exploited at various levels; one level being at the local godown keepers where they sell their collections. Since there is no uniformity in the rate charts for different scraps, the innocent rag-pickers fall prey to various godown keepers. So, government must take proper initiative to fix-up uniform rates for different scraps and the godown keepers must be instructed to display the rate charts for the knowledge of the public.

(vii) Relating to the above suggestions, there should be a special consumer court to which the children can have easy access and approach to file complaints.

(viii) As an alternative to the above suggestion it would be better if municipal corporate bodes fix up some collection localities/centers and collect rags from rag-pickers at such localities/centers through mobile collection vans. If it is done so, on one hand these corporate bodies would raise their own revenue and on the other hand the rag-pickers would get proper value of their collections and hence also get freed from being exploited by the local godown keepers.

(ix) As the street children are deprived of availing public parks, playgrounds etc for relaxation, slum-based recreational/ playgrounds be developed and game items be provided by the municipal corporate bodies or NGOs.

(x) Government should take immediate steps to identify the orphans who work on streets, railway stations etc. on priority basis and must try to accommodate them in orphanage homes financed by union or state governments or NGOs funded by foreign agencies.

(xi) Like the orphans, girl-street children should also be identified on priority basis and specific need-based self-employment programmes be formulated for them. Specifically, they should be imparted training on some vocational trades like sewing, applique work, terractotta work and other handicrafts out of which they can independently earn their livelihood. However, there must be a cooperative institution at the government level to procure the products from these children at a suitable cost fixed by the government. This would, in other way help them to get suitable life partners for marriage.

(xii) It is universally accepted that if we educate a man, we educate a person but if we educate a women, we educate a family. So, apart from providing vocational training, girl children should also be provided with formal or non-formal education depending upon their age and interest.

(xiii) Finally, a special committee be formed at the government level to facilitate proper implementation of the welfare schemes and to protect the street children form exploitation.

REFERENCES

Arimpoor, Joe (1992), *Street Children of Madras,* Noida: National Labour Institute.

Behura, N.K. & R.P. Mohanty (1998), *Socio-Economic Profile of Street Children in Bhubaneswar City* (Mimeographed), Bhubaneswar, NKC Centre for Development Studies.

G.o.O. (1995), *Orissa State Plan of Action for Children 2000* Orissa *A.D.* Bhubaneswar: Department of Women and Child Development.

——— (1996), *Orissa State Council for Child Welfare (Amendment) Rules,* Bhubaneswar: Department of Women and Child Development.

Mandal, M.N. (ed.) (1990), *Street Children and Slum Children in India,* Calcutta: Socio Legal Aid Research and Training Centre.

Mohsin, Nadeem (1994), *'Street Children and Working Children in* South Asia', (Working paper prepared for the *Independent Commission for Population and Quality* of *life,* UNESCO) Patna: A.N. Sinha Institute of Social Studies.

Orissa State Council for Child Welfare and UNICEF (1994), *'Brief Workshop report on Govt. & NGO Participation for Street and Working Children"* held on 15-16, 1994 and organized by and UNICEF OSCOW, Bhubaneswar.

Pandey, Rajendra (1991), *Street Children of India,* Allahabad: Chugh.

EDUCATIONAL STATUS OF CHILD GIRLS IN INDIA –AN EXPLORATORY STUDY

Akash S.B. and Subash C. Natekar***

INTRODUCTION

Education played vital role in overall development of human being, because it facilitates to increases the individual knowledge, help to aware of their rights, encourages to fighting for their rights, helps to overcome the traditional barriers and it is a powerful strategy for overall development of the country. More over the sound educational system plays active role in creation of skilled human resources to meet the changing requirements of the country and business community. However the developing country like India, the general economic situation of women being worst than that of men in respect of education, nutrition, freedom, health, life expectation, family support etc. In view of this government of India had launched special programmes viz., development of women's in five year plans, national policy on education 1986 on women education, national policy on education review committee 1990, programme of action 1992, national policy for empowerment of women 2001, in tenth plan adopted three fold of strategies for empowerment of women and in July 2006 a new policy was launched the inclusive education which means education of the children with special needs. The main aim of these policies are to access education and equality of learning, elimination of gender bias, providing vocational education, provide proper training to women teacher, for undertaking entrepreneurial activities and sound education facilities for sustainable development of women. Due to many policies and programmes the participation of girls at all stages of education has been increasing steadily. Since 1950-51 girls participation has increased many folds in primary (28.1% to 46.8%), middle primary (16.1% to 43.9%), secondary (13.3% to 41.3%), and higher secondary (10% to 40%). However many

* Faculty Member, Department of Studies in Commerce, Karnatak University, PG Centre, Karwar (Karnataka).

** Lecturer, GE, Arts/Commerce College, Kalgatgi (Karnataka).

scholars shown a great interest to study on different aspects of girls children and women like Kishore (1993), Murthi (1995), Miller (1987), Bounes and Walker (1991) and Akash S.B. (2006) they argue that the education is a key factor in reducing the discrimination against women's, increases the social status, improve the health condition, life expectancy, increases the women employment, increases the self confidence, increases the political participation, increases the economic condition, reduces the social problems like child marriages, dowry system, aids etc. and the study also pointed out that the status of girls child's and women's much worst than that of men.

OBJECTIVES OF THE STUDY

1. To study the role of educational policies in increases the status of women.
2. To examine the growth of education institutions, magnitude of girls' enrolment for education in rural area and percentage of girls enrolment to total enrolment in rural area.
3. To find out the reasons that responsible for dropout of girl children from schools.
4. To suggest suggestions in the light of the findings of the study.

HYPOTHESES

$Ho_{1.}$ There is no relation between caste back ground of girls' parents and girls school dropouts.

$Ho_{2.}$ There is no positive relation between occupational background of girls parents and girls school dropouts.

$Ho_{3.}$ There is no sound relation between level of educational back ground of girl's parents and girl school dropouts.

SOURCES OF DATA

The study based on primary data and secondary data. The primary data collected from the both school dropouts girls and their parents. The secondary data collected from different sources like selected educational statistics, Ministry of Human Resources Development, Government of India, Central Statistics Organization, Government of India, and the Census of India etc. In addition to that the study also used relevant sources like leading National and International journals and leading daily papers.

SAMPLE DESIGN

In Bijapur district the size of villages are very large and the size of school dropouts' girls also more. In view of this the study selected 10 villages for systematic study like Peerapur, Niraligi, Bhantanur, Karnur, Kodganur, Shellagi, Navadagi, Aski, Uavinahalli, and Gotaganiki. And each village taken 20 school dropout's girls and their parents for systematic study by adopting simple random sampling method, therefore the total sample size is 200.

TOOLS AND TECHNIQUE

The study used tools like tabular method, percentage, simple growth rate, and chi square were applied for draw the meaningful conclusions.

PROGRAMMES AND POLICIES

The Indian Constitution enshrined the principle of gender equality in its Preamble, Fundamental Rights, Fundamental Duties and Directive Principles. Moreover the Constitution of India grants equality to women, but also empowers the State to adopt measures of positive discrimination in favour of women. Within the framework of a democratic polity, our laws, development policies, Plans and programmes have aimed at women's advancement in different spheres.

FIVE YEARS PLANS AND STATUS OF WOMEN

Since first five year plans (1951-1956) have been receiving great attention to develop the status of women and in this five-year plan development of women treated, as a subject of welfare. The second to fifth five-year plan (1956-79) continued to reflect the same welfare approach besides giving priority to women education. In sixth five year plans (1980-85), the approach is shift from welfare to development of women and in this plan adopted a multi-disciplinary approach with a special thrust on three areas like health, education and employment. Under seventh plan (1985-90) the development programmes continued with major objective of increases their overall status of women. In eighth plans (1992-97) also continued to provide proper education and vocational training with view to overall development of women. In ninth plan (1997-2002) the primary objective of ninth plan is to empowerment of women and also convergence of existing services available in both women specific and women related sector. In tenth plan adopted entirely different approach of women empowerment as compared to earlier approach. It provides stronger platform for action with definite goals, targets and time frame and it adopted three fold strategies for increases the overall status of women such as social empowerment, economic empowerment and gender justice.

NATIONAL POLICY ON WOMEN EDUCATION 1986

In the year 1986, national policy on women education was enacted with view to increases the status of women. It assumed that education is a key factor in changing the status of women. In order to neutralize the accumulated desertions of the past, there will be a positive, interventionist role in empowerment of women. Through these policy women studies have been promoted as a part of different course and educational institutions encourages taking active programmes to further increases the women status. In view of this government of India have been initiated many programmes to develop the women status such as adult education for women development in age group of 15-35, increases the women access to vocational, technical, professional education and to existing emergent technologies, substantial contribution towards women equality towards crating of appropriate cell.

NATIONAL POLICY ON EDUCATION REVIEW COMMITTEE 1990

This policy has different objectives such as to provide access to education and equality of education to women, access to vocational education, ensuring adequate training and other educational facilities to women, encourages research and development of women studies, focuses on employment of women, encourages adult education, providing hostel facilities in all levels and ensure representative of women in the educational hierarchy.

THE PROGRAMME OF ACTION 1992

The export committee reported and felt that women empowerment possible through increases self-confidence and self-esteem, facilitates adequate information, knowledge and skill for economic independence, providing opportunity to women to make informed choice in the area like education, employment and health, special opportunity to ensure women to recruit and augment teacher training facilities to women.

ADEQUATE HOSTEL FACILITIES

Women and Child Development department implemented this scheme. The main objectives of this scheme are to provide adequate hostel facilities to workingwomen. This scheme facilitates to women to lead their life without fear, because, it provide dairy care. And it is encourages to women to under take active part in economic activities in different fields.

SERVA SHIKSH ABHIYAN

The programme was launched in the year 2000 in collaboration with the State with view to achieve the objectives of widening the scope of elementary education throughout the country. It is facilitates to bridge the gender inequality by giving due emphasis to promote education of girl child in the society and on a larger scale to afford them social justice, security and equality at par with the boy child. The programme has big ambitions like to provide quality education in the age group 6-14, years providing mid day meal and it also ensure additional support to women to increases the women literacy.

SUPPORT SERVICES FOR WOMEN

In the year 1997 Balika Samridhi Yojana was launched. The main aim of this project is to changes the community attitude towards the girl child. Through this programme given grants of Rs. 500 to deposit in interest bearing account in the name of girl child born after August 15, 1997 in a family below poverty line.

WOMEN STUDIES

The women studies now working in several universities and colleges and these institution encourages to women communities to under taking research, curriculum development, provide adequate information about availability of economic opportunities, extension services etc. The women study centre also encourages women to under take minor and major research projects and encourages women to conduct research on women issues such as literacy position of women in rural area and urban area, status of women in political field and other area.

The adequate educational institution played key role in meeting the educational requirement of the people of the country. Table 1 reveals the year wise growth of educational institution at different levels of education. At the primary level, during the year 1950-51 the total educational institutions were amounting 175999 and it increased by 573085 at the end of 2002-03. At the upper primary level the total educational institutions in the year 1950-51 amounting were 10413 and at the end of 2002-03 the total education institution amounting 193864 it means the education institution increased around 1761. % between 1950-51 to 2002-03. At the secondary and higher secondary level the total educational institution were 2827 in the year 1950-51 and it increased by 11.2% in the year 1980-81 as compared to 1950-51. Thus it is clear that the number of educational institution steadily increased over a period of time.

Table 1
Year-wise Growth of Educational Institution in Rural Areas

Year	*Primary*	*Upper Primary*	*Secondary / higher secondary*
1950-51	175999 (-)	10413 (-)	2827 (-)
1980-81	444752 (152.5)	94249 (805.1)	34668 (11.2)
1990-91	482628 (8.5)	117279 (24.4)	50415 (43.4)
2002-03	573085 (18.7)	193864 (65.3)	87380 (73.3)

Source: Selected Educational Statistics, MHRD, Government of India, 2002-03
Note: Figures in Parenthesis indicates percentage increased over previous year.

Table 2 provides information about size of enrolment by both girls and boys in primary school. During the year 1978-79 the size of enrolment by the boys 33.14 million and only 18.79 million girls were enrolled for primary education. However the table clearly indicates that in all years in study period girls were far beyond than boys in respect of enrolments for primary education. The table also shows that educational status of girls increased over a period of time due to many favourable policies and programmes towards women's education by the government.

Table 2
Size of Enrolment in Primary School (in million)

Year	*Boys*	*Girls*	*Total*
1978-79	33.14 (-)	18.79 (-)	51.93 (-)
1986-87	39.82 (20.15)	25.98 (38.2)	65.80 (13.8)
1993-94	42.06 (6.9)	30.14 (16.01)	72.47 (10.12)
2002-03	42.28 (.52)	38.09 (26.3)	80.37 (10.9)

Source: Selected Educational Statistics, MHRD, Government of India, 2002-03.
Note: Figures in Parenthesis indicates percentage increased over previous year.

Table 3 reveals the level of enrolment boys and girls at upper primary level. During the year 1978-79 7.91 million boys were enrolled and only just 3.05 million girls were enrolled. In the year 1986-87, 12.08 million boys were enrolled and 5.64 million girls were enrolled for upper primary education.

At the end of 2002-03 around 30 million boys and 24.31 girls were enrolled for upper primary education. Thus it is clear that at upper primary level also boys were more enrolled than girls.

Table 3
Level of Enrolment in Upper Primary School (in million)

Year	*Boys*	*Girls*	*Total*
1978-79	7.91 (-)	3.05 (-)	10.96 (-)
1986-87	12.08 (52.7)	5.64 (84.9)	17.72 (38.1)
1993-94	14.19 (17.4)	7.28 (9.1)	21.47 (21.1)
2002-03	29.83 (110.2)	24.31 (223.9)	54.14 (152.1)

Source: Selected Educational Statistics, MHRD, Government of India, 2002-03.
Note: Figures in Parenthesis indicates percentage increased over previous year.

Table 4 reveals the level of enrolment in secondary and higher secondary. During the year 1978-79 3.26 million boys and 0.90 girls were enrolled for higher secondary education. In the year 1986-87, 5.71 million boys and 2.08 million girls were enrolled. During the year 1993-94, 7.17 million boys and 3.33 girls were enrolled and it increases 25.5% and 60.1% enrolment of boys and girls respectively in the year 1993-94 as compared to 1986-87. Thus it is clear that the boys were more enrolled for higher secondary education; however the size of enrolment of girls were increased over a period of time.

Table 4
Level of Enrolment in Secondary/Higher Secondary (in million)

Year	*Boys*	*Girls*	*Total*
1978-79	3.26 (-)	0.90 (-)	4.16 (-)
1986-87	5.71 (75.1)	2.08 (131.1)	7.79 (87.2)
1993-94	7.17 (25.5)	3.33 (60.1)	10.50 (34.7)
2002-03	37.71 (425.9)	28.59 (7.5)	66.30 (531.4)

Source: Selected Educational Statistics, MHRD, Government of India, 2002-03.
Note: Figures in Parenthesis indicates percentage increased over previous year.

Table 5
Percentage of Girls Enrolment to total Enrolment (in million)

Year	*Primary*	*Middle Primary*	*Secondary*	*Higher secondary*
1980-81	38.6 (-)	32.9 (-)	29.6 (-)	26.7 (-)
1986-87	41.5 (7.5)	36.7 (11.5)	32.9 (11.1)	33.3 (24.7)
1993-94	43.7 (5.3)	40.9 (11.4)	38.6 (17.3)	39.4 (18.3)
2002-03	46.8 (7.1)	43.9 (7.3)	41.3 (6.9)	40.1 (1.7)

Source: Selected Educational Statistics, MHRD, Government of India, 2002-03.
Note: Figures in Parenthesis indicates percentage increased over previous year.

Table 5 reveals the percentage of girls' enrolment to total enrolment. At the primary level in the year 1980-81 (38.6%) million, middle primary (32.9%) million, secondary (29.6) million and higher secondary (26.7) million enrolment has taken place to total enrolment. At the end of 2002-03 at primary level 46.8 million, 43.9 million at middle primary, 41.3% at secondary and 40 millions at higher secondary. The table clearly indicates that at all level of education the enrolment of girls steadily increased.

Table 6 reveals the reasons that responsible for girl's school dropouts. 185 respondents amounting 33.3% stated that school dropouts due to economic backwardness, 170 respondents stated that school dropouts due to increases the family income and fallowed by to meet the household and farm work, other reasons, lack of knowledge about education and repeated fails.

Table 6
Reasons that Responsible for Girls School Dropouts

Reasons	*No of Respondents*	*Percentage*
Economic Backwardness	185	33.3
Lack of Knowledge about Education	25	4.5
Increases the Family Income	170	30.6
To meet the Household and Farm work	120	21.6
Repeated Fail	10	1.8
Other Reasons	45	8.2
Total	555	100

Source: Field Survey.
Note: 1. No. of response exceed 200 because of multiple answers. 2. Other reasons include, lack of infrastructure, lacking encourage able school environment, no school and not benefited immediately.

Table 7
Caste and Reasons that Responsible for Girls School Dropouts

Caste	*Reasons*					
	Lack of Knowledge about Education	*Economic Backwardness*	*Take part in household and farm work*	*Repeated fails*	*Other reasons*	*Total*
SC/ST	3 (3.1)	55 (57.8)	20 (21.1)	04 (4.2)	13 (13.8)	95 ( )
Muslims	10 (18.1)	13 (23.6)	27 (49.1)	5 (9.2)	–	55 ( )
Brahmins	–	03 (30)	07 (70)	–	–	10 ( )
Lingayat	7 (17.5)	19 (47.5)	11 (27.5)	1 (2.5)	2 (5)	40 ( )
Total	20 (10)	90 (45)	65(32.5	10(5)	15(7.5)	200( )

Source: Field Source Note1 Figures in Parenthesis indicate percentage to total.

Table 7 reveals the caste and reasons that responsible for girls' school dropouts. 55 SC/ST community girls amounting 57.8% dropouts schools due to economic backwardness. 27 Muslim community girls constituting

49.1% dropouts school due to take part in household and farm sector. 7 Brahmins community girls amounting 70% dropouts schools due to take part in household and farm activities. Among Lingayat community 19 girls constituting 47.5% dropouts school due to economic backwardness. At 5% level of significance the calculated value of chi-square amounting 48.7 and table value 21.03 for 12 degree of freedom, from this it can conclude that there is significant relation between girls' school dropouts and caste.

Table 8
Level of Income and Reasons that Responsible for Girls School Dropouts

Income (Rs 000)	*Reasons*					
	Lack of Knowledge about Education	*Economic Backward-ness*	*Take part in house-hold and farm work*	*Repeated fails*	*Other reasons*	*Total*
Below 20	12 (8.2)	76 (52.4)	48 (33.1)	04 (2.7)	5 (3.6)	145 (72.5)
20-30	8 (22.2)	12 (22.2)	18 (22.2)	3 (8.5)	5 (13.8)	36 (18)
31-40	_	02 (13.3)	07 (46.7)	2 (13.3)	4 (26.7)	15 (7.5)
above 41	-	-	02 (50)	1 (25)	2 (25)	04 (2)
Total	20 (10)	90 (45)	65 (32.5	10 (5)	15 (7.5)	200 (100)

Source: Field Source Note1 Figures in Parenthesis indicate percentage to total.

Table 8 reveals the level of income of girls' children parents and the reasons that responsible for girls' school dropouts. 145 respondents come under in the income group of Rs. below 20000, out of those 76 respondents constituting 52.4% stated that their children dropouts school due to economic backwardness. 36 respondents fall under in the income group of Rs. 21000 to 30000; among them the highest percentage (33.3%) stated that their children dropouts school due to economic backwardness. 15 respondents fall under in the income group Rs. 31000-40000, out of that 46.7% stated that their children dropouts school due to take part in household and farm work. 4 respondents come under in the income group of Rs. 41000 & above, among them 50% of the respondents stated that their children dropouts' school due to take part in household and farm sector. The calculated value of chi-square 22.1 and table value 21.03 at 5% level of significance for 12 degree of freedom and it can conclude from this the calculated value of chi-square is grater than table value, hence there is significant relation between level of income and girls school dropouts.

Table 9 reveals the educational levels of girls' parents and the reasons that responsible for girls' school dropouts. 70 respondents educated up to primary, among them 35% stated that their children dropouts school due to take part in house hold and farm work. 8 respondents educated up to SSLC, out of that the highest percentage (50%) stated that their children dropouts school due to economic backwardness. Among sample respondents 2 respondents educated up to degree, out of that 100% stated their children dropouts' school due to take part in household and farm work. 120 respondents belong to illiterate among them the highest percent (54.1) stated that their children dropouts school due to economic backwardness.

Table 9
Educational Level of Girls Parents and Reasons that Responsible for Girls School Dropouts

Education	*Reasons*					
	Lack of Knowledge about Education	*Economic Backward-ness*	*Take part in house-hold and farm work*	*Repeated fails*	*Other reasons*	*Total*
Primary	7 (10)	21 (30)	25 (35.8)	02 (2.8)	15 (21.4)	70 (35)
SSLC	1 (12.5)	4 (50)	03 (37.5)	-	-	8 (4)
Degree	_	-	02 (100)	-	-	2 (1)
Illiterate	12 (10)	65 (54.1)	35 (29.1)	8 (6.8)	-	120 (60)
Total	20 (10)	90 (45)	65 (32.5	10 (5)	15 (7.5)	200 ( )

Source: Field Source Note1 Figures in Parenthesis indicate percentage to total.

Table 10
Occupational Level and Reasons that Responsible for Girls School Dropouts

Occupation	*Reasons*					
	Lack of Knowledge about Education	*Economic Backward-ness*	*Take part in house-hold and farm work*	*Repeated fails*	*Other reasons*	*Total*
Cooli	15 (11.5)	68 (52.2)	40 (30.7)	04 (3.2)	3 (2.3)	130 (65)
Agriculture	5 (9.1)	16 (29..1)	22 (40)	6 (10.9)	6 (10.9)	55 (27.5)
Work-in factory	_	6 (46.1)	2 (15.3)	-	5 (38.6)	13 (6.5)
Other	-	-	1 (50)	-	1 (50)	2 (1)
Total	20 (10)	90 (45)	65 (32.5	10 (5)	15 (7.5)	200 (100)

Source: Field Source Note: 1 Figures in Parenthesis indicate percentage to total.

Table 10 reveals the occupation of children parents and the reasons that responsible for girl's dropout's school. Among cooli back ground respondents 68 amounting 52.2% stated that their girls' children dropouts' school due to economic backwardness. 40% agriculture background respondents stated that their girls' children's dropouts' school due to take part in household and economic activities. More than 46% working in factory respondents felt that their girl's child dropouts school due to economic backwardness. And 50% of other occupational back ground respondents opined their children dropouts' school due to take part in house hold and farm work. The calculated value of chi-square amounting 34.69 and table value 21.03 at 5% level of significance for 12 degree of freedom. It means there is a positive relation between occupational level of the respondents and girls school dropouts.

Table 11 reveals the nature of family and the reasons that responsible for girls' school dropouts. 160 sample respondents hail from nuclear family, among them 85% respondents constituting 53.1% stated that their girl child dropouts school due to economic backwardness. 40 respondents belong to joint family, out of those 18 respondents amounting 45% stated that their girl child dropouts school due to take part in house hold and farm work. At the 5% level of significance the calculated value of chi-square is 34.8 and table value 9.49 for 4 degree of freedom and it can conclude that there is a significant relation between nature of family and school dropouts.

Table 11
Nature of Family and Reasons that Responsible for Girls School Dropouts

Caste	*Reasons*					
	Lack of Knowledge about Education	*Economic Backward-ness*	*Take part in house-hold and farm work*	*Repeated fails*	*Other reasons*	*Total*
Nuclear	8 (5.3)	85 (53.1)	47 (29.3)	07 (4.2)	13 (8.1)	160 (80)
Joint	12 (30)	5 (12.5)	18 (45)	3 (7.5)	2 (5)	40 (20)
Total	20 (10)	90 (45)	65 (32.5)	10 (5)	15 (7.5)	200 (100)

Source: Field Source Note1 Figures in Parenthesis indicate percentage to total.

HYPOTHESES TESTING

Ho_1 There is no relation between caste back ground of girl's parents and girls school dropouts. At 5% level of significance the calculated value of chi square amounting 48.7 and table value 21.03 for 12 degree of freedom, from this it is clear that the table value of chi-square is much less than calculated value of chi-square, therefore the null hypothesis rejected. It means there is a positive relation between caste of girl's parents and girls school dropouts.

$Ho_{2.}$ There is no positive relation between occupational background of girls parents and girls school dropouts. The calculated value of chi-square amounting 34.69 and table value 21.03 at 5% level of significance for 12 degree of freedom. The calculated value of chi-square is much grater than table value hence the null hypotheses rejected. From this it can conclude that there is a significant relation between occupational level of the respondents and girls school dropouts.

$Ho_{3.}$ There is no sound relation between level of education of girl's parents and girl school dropouts. As the calculated value of chi-square 34.1 and table value 21.03 for 12 degree of freedom at 5% level of significance. The statistical date clearly indicates that the calculated value of chi-square is much greater than table value hence the null hypotheses rejected and it can conclude that there is a positive relation between levels of education of girl's parents and girls school dropouts.

SUGGESTIONS

1. Most of the of the primary school teachers felt that in rural area in schools suffers from in adequate infrastructure facilities, hence it is suggest that the government should provide adequate infrastructure facilities like roads, adequate rooms, sanitation facilities, play grounds and adequate size of teachers to encourage the girl children as well as boys to go school.
2. Most of the primary school teachers argue that due to recent government policies the teachers more involved other than teaching activities like arraigning mid day meals and preparing list of students up to data regarding attendance and dropouts etc. In view of this it is suggest that the government should recruit separate staff for meeting the work other than teaching it may helps the teacher to much concentrate on teaching.
3. Most of the illiterates have no adequate knowledge about the importance of education due to this reasons they not send their children to school and it is one of the important reasons that responsible for the girls dropouts from school, hence the NGO and Self-help groups should take active part to spread the message about importance of education among illiterates about role of education.
4. In rural area the government should open both girls and boys hostel and should create live able working environment, because most of the government and private hostels have no basic facilities it may helps to encourage the parents to send their children to school.

5. Most of the sample respondents felt that their children dropout's school due to many reasons among many reasons the important reasons is to take the household and farm work in order to increases the family income. This is only more occur those not have adequate knowledge about the education and economic backwardness, hence it is suggest that there is a need to initiate sound policies towards increases the awareness of education and economic income of illiterate.

CONCLUSIONS

The constitution of India guarantees free and compulsory education to all children irrespective of their status up to the age of fourteen due to many reasons such as the education is a vital instruments in not only increases the status of the women but also to make the best of economic opportunities, to under stand what is right and wrong, increases the knowledge of individuals, helps to aware their rights, to minimizes the traditional barriers, increases the socio- economic condition of human beings, facilitates skilled manpower and minimizes the social problems like aids child marriage, child labour and caste system and also it played role like bring about far reaching changes in stereotype gender status and relations between sexes and social attitudes etc. However from the above explanation it is clear that the educational status of girls not satisfactory, but the educational status of women steadily increased over a period of time.

REFERENCES

Gupta, M.D. (1987), Selective Discrimination Against Female Children in Rural Punjab, India Population Review, 13, No. 1, p. 77-100.

Kishore (1993), May God Give Sons to All: Gender and Child Mortality in India-American Sociological Review, 58, No. 2, p. 247.

Murthi (1995), Mortality Fertility and Gender Bias in India-A District level Analysis, Population and Development Review, 21, No. 4, p. 45.

Miller Barbara (1981), The Endangered Sex-Neglect of Female Children in Rural North India, Cornell University Press.

Akash, S.B. (2006), Impacts of SHG on Women Empowerment-With Special Reference to Karnataka State, Edited Book Entitled WTO and Globalization, Serial Publication, New Delhi, p. 567.

Sarkar, C.R. (2004), Poverty Education and Economic Development, University News, Delhi, Vol. 42, No. 2, p. 5.

United National Development Programmes World Development Report, Oxford University, 2004, Oxford.

BREAST FEEDING IS HUMAN RIGHTS OF THE CHILD

*Alok Pandey**

"A nation's children are its supremely important asset and the nation's future lies in their proper development. An investment in Children is indeed an investment in nation's future. A healthy and educated child of today is the active and intelligent citizen of tomorrow. Bestow blessing on these little innocent lives bloomed on earth, who have brought the message of Joy from heavenly garden".

—R.N. Tagore

Child development is integral to overall socio-economic development of a nation. Problems of child health and development present a formidable challenge. To meet this challenge every citizen of India has to make some contribution. It is obvious that hospitals or the medical staff alone would not be able to cope with the growing needs of our children, without the active and positive involvement of the community. It is the mother who has to assume the role of a frontline health worker; and the doctors and others have only supplement and support her efforts, whether the issue involved is diarrhoeal dehydration or vaccine-preventable disease, low birth weight or malnutrition, infant death or childhood disability or the lack of attainment of full mental faculties. Since independence, India nearly 59 years ago, many changes have been brought about from one five year plan to another. The problems of children are multi-faceted and multi-layered. They cover a wide range of fields from nutrition and education to development and protection so that they may8 become better human beings in later years.

The child has to be prepared for responsible life in a free society in the sprit of understanding, peace and tolerance, use of corporal punishment is antithetic to these values. We cannot subject the child to torture and still expect him to act with understanding, peace and

* Research Scholar of Law,Lucknow University, Lucknow (U.P.)

tolerance towards others and be a protagonist of peace and love. It was probably for this reason Mahatma Gandhi said that "If we are to reach real peace in this world, and if we are to carry on a real war against war, we shall have to begin with children. And if they will grow up in their natural innocence, we won't have to struggle, we won't have to pass fruitless idle resolutions, but we shall go from love to love and peace to peace, until at last all the corners of the world are covered with that peace and love for which consciously or unconsciously, the whole world is hungering".[1]

The major health problems of children and high rates of mortality and morbidity, generally result from three interrelated conditions malnutrition, infection and the consequences of ill-timed, closely spaced and too frequent pregnancies, without necessary health care.[2] The are often associated with poor socio-economic and social including scarcity of health and other social services. Breast-feeding has an important relevance to all these interlocking maternal and child health problems.

For the first few months of a child's life the best possible protection which any mother can provide for the baby's normal health and growth is exclusive breast-feeding. Breast-milk contains at least six anti-infective agents against some of the most common illness of infancy. It is also the most nutritious and hygienic food which any child can be given. So breast feeding is very important of the child for the first few months of life. Breast feeding is Human Rights of the Child.

Breast-feeding is a natural gifts and ideal type of feeding for the children, from birth to 6 months of life. Even in the most industrialized. Societies. It has not been possible to replace breast milk, with formula feeds, without health risks. But depending on bottle and formula milks by poor people, living in unsanitary environment, bottle-feeding can be dangerous to the children, exposing them to severe malnutrition and deadly infections besides the unbearable economic burden on the family.[3]

The infant who does not receive colostrums, a marked fall in I.G. levels occurred on the fifth day after birth as compared to levels at birth. On the fifth day, levels of immunoglobulin are significantly higher in the serum of colostrums-fed infants than in those who do not receive colostrums. The immunoglobulin present in colostrums are to a certain extent, absorbed from intestinal tract of new born infants, and this has got some physiological significance in the resistance to infection during the early neonatal period.[4]

Advantage of breast feeding to the nation reduce the incidence of marasmic-diarrhoea syndrome in the first 1½ years of life. During period brain growth may get retarded and reduce protein gap. Breast milk most hygienic, so save the child from infection e.g., Infantile eczema is much less in breast fed. It is a perfect food, so help in his growth and development and ready-made anti-bodies which protect against several common infectious diseases. Conductive to more healthy an happy relationship between the child an mother, leading to better personality development. It is economical and convenient and enjoyable and gives the emotional satisfaction to mothers. It helps in rapid involution of uterus and reduced the incidence of breast cancer among the mothers and very helpful of increasing the birth spacing.

Though breast feeding is a natural process and has been traditionally practiced since the origin of species there has been a decline in number of women (mothers) who go for in breast feeding due to the process of industrialization as well as the as the changing pattern of life style and also a large number of women now they work out side their homes, So they found feeding in convenient and impractical the availability of easy and attractive milk substitute contributed a lot towards the decline of breast-feeding practices. Maternity services and the attitude of health workers, however, unwittingly have created additional grounds for unblocking the process. Since the breast-feeding is a manifestation of human behavior it is evident that the changing pattern of breast feeding should be viewed with in the sphere of socio-economic dynamics and changes in economic society.[5]

INTERNATIONAL LAW SUPPORT OF THE BREAST FEEDING

There has been great concern for the welfare of children at the international level culminating in the declaration of the Rights of the child adopted by the general Assembly of the United Nations. The Declaration in its preamble points out that the child by reason of his physical and mental immunity needs special safeguards and that mankind owes to the child the best it has to give and formulated several principles. It provided—the child shall enjoy special protection and shall be given opportunities and facilities, by law and by other means to enable him to develop physically, mentally, morally, spiritually and socially in a health and normal manner and in conditions of freedom and dignity. In the enactment of law for this purpose, the best interests of the child shall be the paramount consideration. Child shall also be protected from all forms of neglect, cruelty and exploitation.[6]

The right to adequate nutrition has been accepted since long in the normative instruments of International Law. The league of nations in 1924 adopted the Geneva Declaration of Right of the child. In 1948

General Assembly adopted "Universal Declaration of Human Rights" The freedoms and right of children were implicitly included in this declarations which asserts, in Article 25(1), that "everyone has the right to standards of living adequate for the health and well being of himself and his family including the food". This right has been reaffirmed in two major binding international conventions.[7]

The Universal Declaration of Eradication of Hunger and Malnutrition 1974,[8] which asserts in Article 6(2) the inalienable right of every man, woman and child to be free from hunger and malnutrition in order to develop their physical and mental faculties and fixes responsibility on the Government to work together for higher production and for more equitable and for more efficient distribution of goods between the countries and with in the countries.

The convention of the Right of child in order to maintain the standard of living adequate for their growth and development.[9] The Innocent Declaration on the Protection 1990, Promotion and support of Breast feeding was adopted by participants at a meeting on breast feeding held at the International child Development centre in Florence, Italy. The declaration started a variety of specific global goals including the goal that all women should be enabled to practice exclusive breast feeding and all infants should fed exclusively on breast mile from birth to four-six months of age.

The world submit for children held in year 1990 called for Empowerment of all women to breast feed their children exclusively for 4 to 6 months and to continue breast feeding with complementary food, well into second year. In 1992 the International conference on nutrition in Rome Pledged to reduce substantially within the decade, social and other impediments to optimal breast feeding. The fourth world conference on women 1995 in Beijing, promoting the benefits of breast feeding and International code of marketing of Breast Milk substitutes and facilitating of breast feeding by working women. In 1999 the 12th Session of the U.N. committee on Economic Social and cultural Rights released its general comment 1-2 on the right to adequate food. This statement by the committee constitutes definite contribution to International Juris Prudence.[10]

THE RIGHT OF BREAST FEEDING UNDER INDIAN CONSTITUTION

Children's programme should find a prominent part in our National Plans for the development of human resources, so that our children grow up to become robust citizens, physically fit, mentally alert and morally healthy, endowed with skills and motivations needed by society. Equal opportunities for development to all children during the period of growth should be our aim, for this would serve our larger purpose of reducing inequality and ensuring social Justice.[11]

In Indian Societies breast-feeding used to continue as long as the mother's milk was not exhausted either in natural biological course or consequent on another pregnancy. Today, the duration of breast-feeding, timing of the introduction of supplementary foods and the extent of reliance on foods other than human milk have changed a great deal.

The right of breast feeding in Indian constitution as not directly accepted but the above right included in different United Nation Charters, conventions has been duly accepted and recognized by our state who is the party to those covenants by in cooperating in the Directive Principles of State Policy. Ordains that the children should be given opportunity and facility to develop in a healthy manner with proper freedom and degnity[12] Further, it reiterates by giving importance raising the level of nutrition and of living of the people and improvement of public health.[13] Through the mode of improving the nutritional status of child has not been explicitly mentioned as a fundamental right in the Indian constitution, the Judiciary by the harmonious construction of the fundamental rights and the Directive Principles of State Policy has prescribed modalities of access to nutritious food including breast feeding and Right to life in Art 21 give the fundamental right including the life of child to live so breast feeding of the right of child therefore breast feeding is the human right of child.

CONCLUSION

Best food for the child is the mother's milk. Mother's milk is natural gift of the child so breast feeding is right of the child. Don't feed the child artificially unless you are sure that you have the money to buy enough milk. It is now known that breast-milk contains at least six anti infective agents against some of the most common illness of infancy. Breast feeding also the most nutritious and hygienic food. For the first few months of a child, life, the best food and best protection which-provide mother can for the baby's normal health and growth is exclusive breast feeding. The breast feeding is the very important to child growth and development. Breast feeding is life line of the child and best life of child. Breast feeding is the Human Rights of the Child. The following Suggestion are enumerated for effectuating the right of child in respect of breast feeding.

1. The State should save the child from such unwarranted situation, by way making legislation for (specially the child respect of breast feeding).
2. Govt. N.G.O., Media, and Social workers, Religious Person, and famous person of the society Doctors etc. to create awareness to the importance of the breast feeding.
3. The Govt. should amend the existing maternity benefit by providing 6 months maternity leave benefits to the women, so that they can properly feed their children to meet their nutritional needs.
4. Embarrassment about burning the breast in front of other people. Working-class mothers are said to be more embarrassed by nudity. Breast-feeding break at work place should be provided and sufficient crèches should be created, so that the mother can be able to find sufficient time to breast feed their new born.
5. Generally women think that Breast feeding spoils the shape of the breast this is not true, for it is the enlargement of the breasts during pregnancy that stretches the skin and makes the breast more pendulous.
6. The Infant milk substitute feeding Bottle and Infant food (Regulation and control Act) 1992 should be implemented strictly and minimum sentence should be provided against those who violate the rules and condition prescribed in the Act. Simultaneously all the artificial milk product sold in the marked must contain a brand the "breast feed is the best feeding".[14]

NOTES AND REFERENCES

1. Parents forum of meaningful Education Vs. Union of India (AIR 2001 Del 212 at P. 218).
2. A.R. Omran: Health benefits of family planning, WHO MCH/71.
3. R. Kumar 'Child Development in India' Vol. I, 2002.
4. O.M. Ellander: Vahlquist-B : Melbin T. Breast feeding and Artificial feeding Acts paediac, Uppslain-1959.
5. Dr. L. Khanede-Breast feeding is the best feeding, orissa times-1994.
6. Satyavan Kottarakkara Vs. State, (AIR 1997 Ker. 133 at P. 137).
7. (i) International convent on Economic Social and cultural Right (1976),
   (ii) "convention of the right of child, 1989".
8. Adopted on 16th November, 1974 by the world food conference and endorsed by U.N. General Assembly in 1974.

9. Article 27(1) "Convention of the Right of Child, 1989".
10. G.K. Mishra, "Human Rights of Child V. Breast feeding" AIR 2002, Journal 342.
11. Supra-6.
12. Article 39(g) of the Indian Constitution.
13. Article 47 of the Indian Constitution.
14. Supra–10.

HOUSEHOLD CHARACTERISTICS OF CHILD LABOUR IN SELECTED STATES

*Shamim Akhtar**

INTRODUCTION

The issue of child labour in India attracted public attention and debate for the first time in 1985. However, it became the focus of major concern in the aftermath of globalisation in 1991, whereby India ushered in a new era of liberalisation and privatisation. With the signing of the agreement at Marrakesh, trade issues have focused on labour costs and the right of labour. The international community has clearly expressed through various conventions and declarations its belief that child labour needs to be climinated. Apart from ILO, other international agencies and the UN system as a whole pledged their full support to eliminate child labour and signed a joint declaration in New Delhi in August 1998.The government of India (Gol) and the United states department of labour (USDoL)launched a major project in October 2002 to eliminate child labour, especially in hazardous industries in certain states and districts.

In a country of India's size of well over one billion people and around 26.1 per cent of the population living in extreme poverty in 1999-2000, the issue of child labour is a complex one. Under the Indian Constitution, no child below 14 years of age shall be employed to work in any factor or in any hazardous employment (Article 24). "Childhood and growth are to be protected against exploitation and against moral and material abandonment" (Article 39F) and "the state shall endeavour to provide... free and compulsory education for all children until they complete the age of 14 years" (Article 45). The Child Labour (Prohibition and Regulation) Act was enacted in 1986 and a national policy on child labour was framed in August 1987.An MoU was also signed with ILO for the international programme on the Elimination of Child labour in 1992.

* Lecturer in Krishana College of low, Bijnor (UP)

India also signed the UN Convention on the Right of Child (CRC) in December 1992.The National Authority for the Elimination of Child Labour (NAEL) was also constituted by the union ministry of labour in September 1994. Despite these intentions and efforts lakhs of children still work in India. Two major schools of thought have dominated the debate on child labour. While the first school blames poverty as the main cause of child labour and believes in its regulation the second school argues the lack of educational outcomes as the reason for it and advocates the complete prohibition of child labour. The second school does not distinguish between child 'work' and child 'labour'. Anyone outside the school is a child labourer.

The first school reasons that children work out of necessity and without their earnings the standard of living of their families would decline further. They therefore, argue that it is not easy to eliminate child labour all of sudden due to the existing socio-economic situation. Regulation of employment in selected industries, improving working conditions, reducing working hours, ensuring minimum wages, providing facilities for health and education could reduce the plight of child labour [Bissell 2003, Basu 2003, Basu and Van 1998]. On the other hand, there are those who feel that the answer to the problem lay in compulsory primary education [Bhargava 2003, Misra 2000, Burra 1996, and Weiner 1991]. This group believes that non-formal education, which implies education with work (and earning with learning), is a myth as it is neither feasible nor desirable. Besides poverty and illiteracy, the other determinants of child labour which have been identified by scholars are migration, unemployment, deep social prejudices, unattractive education system, large family size, traditional family occupation, inadequate measures of social security, ineffective law enforcement machinery, low government expenditure on education and poverty reduction, and the wage structure of adult workers. There also exist factors that perpetuate the demand for child labour. These are: (1) children work for less pay; (2) they are more flexible; (3) they do not demand overtime; (4) they are easy to be disciplined, and (5) they have no unions and less absenteeism.

Any solution to the problem of child labour lies in essentially identifying working children, the magnitude and the place where they are working. The present exercise is aimed at four states, namely Madhya Pradesh, Maharashtra, Tamil Nadu and Utter Pradesh[1]. Within these states certain sectors have been selected on the basis of high visibility of working children-bidi, brassware, bricks, carpets, fireworks, footwear, glass bengles, locks, matches, silk, and stone quarrying.

CHILD LABOUR OF DATABASE

The entire computation of child labour[2] is based on the unit data of the 55th round (1999-2000) of the NSSO survey for employment and unemployment. The 55th round identifies the population on the basis of activity status of an individual and outs a person in one or a combination of the following three status during a reference period:

- Working or being engaged in economic activity (work), that is 'employed':
- Being not engaged in economic activity (work) and either making tangible efforts to seek 'work' or being available for 'work' if 'work' is available, that is, unemployed.
- Being not engaged in any economic activity (work) and also not available for 'work', that is, not being in the labour force.

Worker (or employed) is defined to be a person who is engaged in any economic activity. Unpaid helpers who assist in the operation of an economic activity in the household farm or non-farm activities are also considered as 'workers'. The coverage of economic activities in the 55th round of NSS has been kept the same as in the 50th round and it includes:

All market activities, that is, activities that involve remuneration to those who perform it, or activity performed for pay or profit these are essentially production of goods and services for the market including those of government services.

Non-market activities (a) activities relating to the agricultural sector (industry division 01 to 05 of NIC 1998), which result in production (including gathering of uncultivated crops, forestry, collection of firewood, hunting, fishing) of agricultural produce for own consumption, and (b) activities relating to the own-account production of fixed assets (including construction of own houses, roads, wells and of machinery tools, for household enterprise and also construction of any private or community facilities free of charge), either in the capacity of a labourer or a supervisor.

The estimates of child labour for the 55th round are based on the usual and subsidiary economic status (UPSS).[3] Since the estimated are based on the definitions used by NSSO, they may suffer from some definitional inadequacies. However since the emphasis of the current exercise is not only to find out the magnitude of child labour but also its relationship with child labour household characteristics, such inadequacies if any may not have much bearing on the final analysis.

DEMOGRAPHIC PROFILE AND TREND

Table 1, which presents some important demographic characteristics of the four states, highlights the large variations between them between males and females. Whereas Tamil Nadu (TN) is at one extreme with a low rate of growth of population (11.2 per cent), high sex ratio (986), high urbanization rate (43.86 per cent), high literacy rate (73.5 per cent), high WPR (44.8 per cent) and low proportion of population below poverty line (21.12 per cent) with HDI rank of 3, Uttar Pradesh has almost everything opposite to it, with HDI rank of 13, and MP, Maharashtra falling in between the two. It is also clear that in all four states there is social discrimination against women, as female literacy rates, their gross enrolment ratio, as well as their WPR for all age groups and adults are very low. The difference between the two sexes is high for UP and MP, which speaks of the traditions and culture of the two states.

Even after a decade of economic reforms and a relatively faster growth of the economy, India was home to 9.33 million child labourers of the age group 5-14 in 1999-2000, which constitutes 4.12 per cent of the child population. A majority, around 90 per cent (8.15 million), is in rural areas (with a percentage of 4.66 in rural areas and 2.27 in urban areas), and male child labour constitutes 4.98 million, (53.3 per cent) of total child labour. The age composition reveals that more than 93 per cent of the child labour belongs to the 10-14 age group. A comparison with 1991 NSS database estimates obtained by Chaudhri (1996), however, shows that there is an all-round (both in rural and urban sectors) fall in the number of child labourers in India, from 13.95 million to 9.33 million, a fall of almost one-third of the number in 1991. Table 4 also shows that the fall in the proportion of child labour between the 50th round and 55th round is across all age groups and all sectors. Though child labour has not been completely wiped out a sharp all has been seen in the absolute numbers and the proportion of child labour in the last decade.

The trends in child labour in the four states are presented in tables 2 to 4, from tables 2 and 3 we observe that between 1991 (census data estimates) and 1999-2000 (NSS 55th round based estimates), total child labour in the four states has dropped from 4.4 million to 3.3 million. It now ranges from 3.06 per cent in UP to 4.07 per cent in MP. The range is from 3.12 per cent for rural UP to 4.88 per cent in rural Maharashtra and from 1.03 per cent for urban Maharashtra to 2.81 per cent for urban UP (Table 3). Low and decelerating growth rate of population and high literacy rates in Maharashtra and Tamil Nadu suggests a decelerating potential of child labour in the two states, while it continues to be potentially strong in UP and MP. The bulk of the child labour belongs to

Table 1
Demographic and Educational Characteristics in MP, Maharashtra, TN and UP, 2001

States	*Population*	*Population Growth Rate*	*Sex Ratio*	*Urbanization*	*WPR (Total Workers as per cent to total Pop)*			*Adult WPR*[1]		*Poverty*[2] *HCR-*	*PCI at 80-81 Prices*
	Persons	*1991-2001*	*2001*		*Persons*	*Males*	*Females*	*Males*	*Females*	*1999-2000*	*1999-2000*
Madhya Pradesh	60385118	24.34	920	26.67	42.75	51.62	33.1	52.23	37.13	37.43	23.63
Maharashtra	96752247	22.57	922	42.4	43.46	53.49	32.59	51.97	42	25.02	6001
Tamil Nadu	62110839	11.19	986	43.86	44.78	58.06	31.32	58.59	41.51	21.12	3797
Uttar Pradesh	166052859	25.8	898	20.78	32.6	47.26	16.28	47.17	20.23	31.15	2067

States	*Literacy Rate*			*Adult Literacy Rate*[1]		*Gross Enrolment Ratio (1999-2000)*[3]					
						Primary Class I to V (6-11 Years)			*Upper Primary VI to VIII (11-14 Years)*		
	Persons	*Males*	*Females*	*Males*	*Females*	*Persons*	*Males*	*Females*	*Persons*	*Males*	*Females*
Madhya Pradesh	64.11	76.8	50.28	57.64	25.08	111.42	120.52	101.91	58.78	70.43	46.26
Maharashtra	77.27	86.27	67.51	73.12	44.98	110.41	112.86	107.84	85.2	89.66	80.49

Notes: 1. Refers to age 15+
2. Planning Commission (2001).
3. Selected Educational Statistics 2000-01, Ministry of HRD, GoI.
4. Selected Educational Statistics 1999-2000, Ministry of HRD, GoI.
5. National Human Development Report, 2002, OUP, New Delhi.

Table 2
Child Labour in 1991 (Census) and 1999-2000 (NSS)

State	*Sector*	*Age Group*	*1991 (Census-Official)*			*1999-2000 (NSS Estimates)*		
			Total Male Workers	*Total Female Workers*	*Total Male Workers*	*Total Male Workers*	*Total Female Workers*	*Total Workers*
MP	Total	5 to 9	67756	64921	132677	22524	1364	23888
		10 to 14	595936	623950	1219886	472656	312683	785339
		5 to 14	663692	688871	1352563	495180	314047	809227
	rural	5 to 9	62470	62220	124690	17451	1364	18815
		10 to 14	557249	603713	1160962	435243	295532	730775
		5 to 14	619719	665933	1285652	452694	296896	749590
	urban	5 to 9	5286	2701	7987	5073	0	5073
		10 to 14	38687	20237	58924	37413	17151	54564
		5 to 14	43973	22938	66911	42486	17151	59637
Maharashtra	Total	5 to 9	41299	49326	90625	22214	26947	49161
		10 to 14	429843	547950	977793	352202	313416	665618
		5 to 14	471142	597276	1068418	374416	340363	714779
	rural	5 to 9	35390	45656	81046	21844	26741	48585
		10 to 14	361406	520110	881516	302299	287942	590241
		5 to 14	396796	565766	962562	324143	314683	638826
	urban	5 to 9	5909	3670	9579	370	206	576
		10 to 14	68437	27840	96277	49903	25474	75377
		5 to 14	74346	31510	105856	50273	25680	75953
TN	Total	5 to 9	19974	19270	39244	621	6096	6717
		10 to 14	259210	280435	539645	203421	174318	377739
		5 to 14	279184	299705	578889	204042	180414	384456
	rural	5 to 9	15980	16870	32850	621	4674	5295
		10 to 14	200218	243665	443883	148454	139080	287534
		5 to 14	216198	260535	476733	149075	143754	292829

State	*Sector*	*Age Group*	*1991 (Census-Official)*			*1999-2000 (NSS Estimates)*		
			Total Male Workers	*Total Female Workers*	*Total Male Workers*	*Total Male Workers*	*Total Female Workers*	*Total Workers*
	urban	5 to 9	3994	2400	6394	0	1422	1422
		10 to 14	58992	36770	95762	54967	35238	90205
		5 to 14	62986	39170	102156	54967	36660	91627
UP	Total	5 to 9	97821	57008	154829	37293	19177	56470
		10 to 14	889761	365496	1255257	810783	508587	1319370
		5 to 14	987582	422504	1410086	848076	527764	1375840
	rural	5 to 9	84489	52233	136722	27639	14284	41923
		10 to 14	764560	342709	1107269	637604	450688	1088292
		5 to 14	849049	394942	1243991	665243	464972	1130215
	urban	5 to 9	13332	4775	18107	9654	4893	14547
		10 to 14	125201	22787	147988	173179	57899	231078
		5 to 14	138533	27562	166095	182833	62792	245625

Source: Census of India, 1991.

Table 3
Proportion of Child Labour in 1991 (Census) and 1999-2000 (NSS)

State	*Sector*	*Age Group*	*1991 (Census-Official)*			*1999-2000 (NSS Estimates)*		
			Total Male Workers	*Total Female Workers*	*Total Male Workers*	*Total Male Workers*	*Total Female Workers*	*Total Workers*
MP	Total	5 to 9	1.46	1.47	1.46	0.41	0.03	0.23
		10 to 14	14.72	17.20	15.89	9.16	7.09	8.21
		5 to 14	7.64	8.56	8.08	4.66	3.39	4.07
	rural	5 to 9	1.71	1.79	1.75	0.40	0.04	0.23
		10 to 14	18.01	21.83	19.81	10.69	8.51	9.69
		5 to 14	9.19	10.66	9.90	5.36	4.05	4.75
	urban	5 to 9	0.53	0.29	0.41	0.47	0.00	0.25
		10 to 14	4.05	2.35	3.24	3.43	1.83	2.69
		5 to 14	2.25	1.27	1.78	1.96	0.89	1.46
Maharashtra	Total	5 to 9	0.83	1.04	0.93	0.44	0.57	0.50
		10 to 14	9.26	12.79	10.95	6.14	6.35	6.24
		5 to 14	4.89	6.63	5.73	3.48	3.52	3.50
	rural	5 to 9	1.11	1.50	1.30	0.68	0.90	0.79
		10 to 14	12.40	19.30	15.72	8.08	9.10	8.55
		5 to 14	6.51	9.66	8.13	4.66	5.14	4.88
	urban	5 to 9	0.33	0.22	0.27	0.02	0.01	0.02
		10 to 14	3.95	1.75	2.90	2.51	1.43	2.00
		5 to 14	2.10	0.96	1.55	1.32	0.72	1.03
TN	Total	5 to 9	0.66	0.66	0.66	0.02	0.26	0.13
		10 to 14	8.44	9.54	8.98	7.12	6.27	6.70
		5 to 14	4.57	5.11	4.83	3.57	3.50	3.53
	rural	5 to 9	0.78	0.85	0.82	0.03	0.30	0.15
		10 to 14	9.72	12.48	11.06	8.08	8.07	8.07
		5 to 14	5.26	6.63	5.93	3.95	4.36	4.14

State	Sector	Age Group	1991 (Census-Official)			1999-2000 (NSS Estimates)		
			Total Male Workers	*Total Female Workers*	*Total Male Workers*	*Total Male Workers*	*Total Female Workers*	*Total Workers*
	urban	5 to 9	0.41	0.25	0.33	0.00	0.18	0.08
		10 to 14	5.82	3.73	4.79	5.40	3.33	4.35
		5 to 14	3.15	2.02	2.59	2.82	1.97	2.40
UP	Total	5 to 9	0.92	0.60	0.77	0.29	0.17	0.23
		10 to 14	9.64	4.74	7.41	7.32	5.26	6.36
		5 to 14	4.98	2.46	3.81	3.54	2.51	3.06
	rural	5 to 9	0.98	0.68	0.84	0.26	0.16	0.21
		10 to 14	10.35	5.64	8.23	7.24	5.91	6.62
		5 to 14	5.29	2.87	4.17	3.42	2.77	3.12
	urban	5 to 9	0.69	0.27	0.49	0.43	0.23	0.33
		10 to 14	6.77	1.40	4.25	7.62	2.84	5.36
		5 to 14	3.55	0.81	2.31	4.03	1.49	2.81

Source: Census of India 1991

the 10-14 age group but there are also a substantial number of children below 10 years of age who work. The fall in the number and proportion of child labour is substantial or the rural sector of MP, Maharashtra and TN for both age groups, 5-9 and 10-14. For UP, however, we learn that there has been an increase in female child labour in the age group 10-14 years for both rural (from 3.4 lakh to 4.5 lakh) and urban sectors (from 22,700 to 57,900) and in male child labour for the 10-14 age group for the urban sector (from 1.25 lakh to 1.73 lakh). So two distinct trends are visible-one is the increased number and proportion of child labour of both sexes in the 10-14 age group in urban UP (from 6.77 per cent to 7.62 per cent for males and from 1.4 per cent to 2.84 per cent for females). The second trend is the increase in the number and proportion of female child labour in the 10-14 age group in rural UP as well. Child labour in UP is lowest (3.06 per cent). Among the selected states, not because of any awareness or adoption of specific programmes to eliminate it. It is mainly because high poverty, low literacy and low economic development of the state did not provide ample employment opportunities to them.

Table 4
Child Labour in 50th and 55th NSS Rounds (Per 1000)

		NSS 50th Round (Official)				*NSS 55th Round (Estimates)*			
		Males	*Females*	*Males*	*Females*	*Males*	*Females*	*Males*	*Females*
		5-9	5-9	10-14	10-14	5-9	5-9	10-14	10-14
MP	Rural	15	7	191	150	4	0	107	85
	Urban	2	10	24	22	5	0	34	18
Maharashtra	Rural	7	12	103	151	7	9	61	91
	Urban	0	3	54	23	0	0	25	14
TN	Rural	13	30	147	221	0	3	81	81
	Urban	6	5	102	76	0	2	54	33
UP	Rural	4	6	124	79	3	2	72	59
	Urban	4	4	87	32	4	2	76	28
All India	Rural	11	14	139	142	6	7	89	92
	Urban	4	4	71	47	3	2	49	34

Source: NSS 50th Round.

In Table 4, a comparison is made between the estimates of the 50th NSS round with the 55th round. We find that except for boys in urban MP, child labour has reduced over the two rounds for all categories of age, sex and sectors. The differences in the census 1991 and NSS 50th round estimates account for the difference in trend in child labour for MP and UP. It is also evident from our estimates that the proportion of child labour in rural areas has been higher than in urban area. But the agewise and sexwise distribution reveals that in UP, except for females of age 10-14 in all other categories urban proportion is equal to or higher than the rural child labour. UP also shows the minimum gap between the proportion of child labour in rural and urban sectors because of its low urbanisation ratio. The peculiar characteristics of child labour behaviour in UP could easily be discerned from Table 1, where low values for all social and economic indicators are noticed, for the state.

HOUSEHOLD CHARACTERISTICS OF CHILD LABOUR

Analysis of the incidence of child labour boils down to their social and economic background, which includes composition of the household, its size, caste and religion, type of household, status of female, size of landholding/cultivated by the household, financial position, monthly per capita expenditure (MPCE), and educational and occupational background.

On the basis of evidence from developing countries, Lloyd (1994) suggests that larger households tend to have less children going to school and the relationship is influenced by family culture, level of social expenditure by the state, and the level of socio-economic development. Misra (2000: 28) argues that there is evidence that poor households tend to sent children to work in order to supplement family income, which is uncertain due to natural calamity, failed harvest and prolonged illness, among other factors. It is also proposed that if the education system is undeveloped and irrelevant, many parents may not prefer to send their children to school and prefer child labour as an option. It is in this context that we examine here the household characteristics of child labour for both rural and urban sectors.

RURAL SECTOR

The brief account of the household characteristics in the rural sector, both agewise and sexwise, is presented in Table 5(a) for MP and Maharashtra, and Table 5(b) for TN and UP. We have maintained the same classification as has been used by NSS in its 55th round in schedule 10. From the tables it is clear that in MP the maximum proportion of child labour, 37.53 per cent, belongs to households with size 4-6 and another 16.4 per cent to the households with size 0-4. Thus, 54 per cent of households belong to the average and smaller families. The concentration of child labour in large families (above 8) is only 22 per cent. In Maharashtra, almost two-thirds of child labour comes from households with average or below average size. Only around 12 per cent of the child labour comes from very large households (size above 8). In

Table 5(a)
Child Labour in 2001 (Household Characteristics)-Rural MP and maharashtra

		Madhya Pradesh							*Maharashtra*					
		Child Labour as a Percentage of Child Population				*Child Labour as a per cent of Total Child Population*	*Child Labour as a per cent of Total Child Labour (5-14)*		*Child Labour as a Percentage of Child Population*				*Child Labour as a per cent of Total Child Population*	*Child Labour as a per cent of Total Child Labour (5-14)*
		Male (5-9)	*Female (5-9)*	*Male (10-14)*	*Female (10-14)*				*Male (5-9)*	*Female (5-9)*	*Male (10-14)*	*Female (10-14)*		
		(1)	(2)	(3)	(4)	(5)	(6)		(1)	(2)	(3)	(4)	(5)	(6)
HH size	0-4	0.00	0.00	14.02	9.29	6.28	16.40	0-4	0.00	1.19	7.57	9.92	4.87	18.20
	4-6	0.37	0.09	9.07	8.61	4.34	37.53	4-6	0.80	0.94	9.06	7.68	4.88	48.85
	6-8	0.73	0.00	12.22	5.83	4.40	24.19	6-8	0.55	1.21	5.52	10.15	4.77	20.78
	8-10	0.65	0.00	10.34	14.82	6.54	13.82	8-10	3.42	0.00	14.08	14.68	7.56	10.50
	Above 10	0.00	0.00	9.26	7.57	3.68	8.06	Above 10	0.00	0.21	0.96	6.43	1.70	1.67
	Total	0.40	0.04	10.69	8.51	4.75	100.00	Total	0.68	0.90	8.08	9.10	4.88	100.00
Social group	ST	1.01	0.00	19.19	15.60	8.32	50.23	ST	1.55	2.11	14.48	12.72	7.39	28.12
	SC	0.50	0.20	9.01	4.65	3.49	12.54	SC	0.00	1.20	8.57	18.23	7.12	20.74
	OBC	0.00	0.00	7.69	7.49	3.69	32.44	OBC	0.54	0.63	7.02	9.23	4.61	27.17
	Others	0.06	0.00	5.00	1.68	1.81	4.79	Others	0.57	0.25	5.61	4.88	3.05	23.97
	Total	0.40	0.04	10.69	8.51	4.75	100.00	Total	0.68	0.90	8.08	9.10	4.88	100.00
Religion	Hindu	0.42	0.04	10.95	8.71	4.86	97.92	Hindu	0.80	1.07	8.43	8.66	4.98	87.32
	Islam	0.00	0.00	5.52	4.36	2.31	1.71	Islam	0.00	0.00	5.99	4.34	2.77	3.54
	Chrishtion	0.00	0.00	0.00	7.79	2.54	0.37	Chrishtion	0.00	0.00	0.00	11.12	3.76	0.28
	Sikh	0.00	0.00	0.00	0.00	0.00	0.00	Sikh	0.00	0.00	0.00	0.00	0.00	0.00
	Jain	0.00	0.00	0.00	0.00	0.00	0.00	Jain	0.00	0.00	0.00	0.00	0.00	0.00
	Buddhist	0.00	0.00	0.00	0.00	0.00	0.00	Buddhist	0.00	0.00	6.34	20.97	6.12	8.33
	Others	0.00	0.00	0.00	0.00	0.00	0.00	Others	0.00	0.00	0.00	10.62	2.61	0.53
	Total	0.40	0.04	10.69	8.51	4.75	100.00	Total	0.68	0.90	8.08	9.10	4.88	100.00
HH Type	SE : Non-ag	0.36	0.48	5.50	2.61	2.27	3.93	SE : Non-ag	0.00	0.00	3.19	5.56	2.23	3.82
	Ag Lab	0.16	0.00	10.39	8.69	4.48	35.17	Ag Lab	0.97	0.42	11.08	14.50	6.67	60.97
	Other Lab	0.83	0.00	14.16	18.53	7.22	8.00	Other Lab	0.00	0.00	1.01	3.44	1.11	1.57
	SE : Ag	0.62	0.00	12.09	9.25	5.49	50.24	SE : Ag	0.96	2.24	9.01	7.14	5.28	29.85

		Madhya Pradesh							*Maharashtra*					
		Child Labour as a Percentage of Child Population				*Child Labour as a per cent of Total Child Population*	*Child Labour as a per cent of Total Child Labour (5-14)*		*Child Labour as a Percentage of Child Population*				*Child Labour as a per cent of Total Child Population*	*Child Labour as a per cent of Total Child Labour (5-14)*
		Male (5-9)	*Female (5-9)*	*Male (10-14)*	*Female (10-14)*				*Male (5-9)*	*Female (5-9)*	*Male (10-14)*	*Female (10-14)*		
		(1)	(2)	(3)	(4)	(5)	(6)		(1)	(2)	(3)	(4)	(5)	(6)
	Others	0.00	0.00	7.00	1.21	2.17	2.66	Others	0.00	0.95	3.57	0.71	1.48	3.79
	Total	0.40	0.04	10.69	8.51	4.75	100.00	Total	0.68	0.90	8.08	9.10	4.88	100.00
Sex of HH	Male	0.41	0.04	10.43	8.22	4.60	93.41	Male	0.72	0.79	7.69	8.63	4.65	89.05
	Female	0.00	0.00	17.86	14.75	8.71	6.59	Female	0.00	2.78	12.94	12.45	8.10	10.95
	Total	0.40	0.04	10.69	8.51	4.75	100.00	Total	0.68	0.90	8.08	9.10	4.88	100.00
Land Cultivated (Hectares)	0.00	0.12	0.14	9.00	4.78	3.22	17.23	0.00	0.69	0.87	10.10	9.62	5.39	48.80
	0.01-0.4	0.00	0.00	9.62	9.55	4.51	8.41	0.01-0.4	0.00	0.00	1.49	8.71	2.82	4.51
	0.41-1.0	0.00	0.00	11.33	10.55	5.39	23.38	0.41-1.0	0.00	0.00	5.66	6.76	3.15	9.53
	1.01-2.0	1.37	0.00	11.00	13.00	6.31	25.99	1.01-2.0	0.00	2.14	7.68	9.83	5.18	17.65
	2.01-4.0	0.85	0.00	11.57	7.69	4.94	16.28	2.01-4.0	3.02	2.11	10.37	12.09	7.77	12.98
	Above 4.0	0.08	0.00	10.96	6.32	4.24	8.72	Above 4.0	1.26	1.02	9.80	11.18	6.23	6.53
	Total	0.42	0.04	10.56	8.72	4.76	100.00	Total	0.59	0.97	8.35	9.42	5.05	100.00
MPCE (Rs)	0-225	1.07	0.18	13.36	13.96	6.26	23.76	0-225	2.36	1.10	15.13	15.78	7.51	19.37
	225-255	0.92	0.00	14.91	10.40	5.49	12.74	225-255	0.00	1.71	13.53	12.49	6.03	9.93
	255-311.34	0.31	0.00	12.19	8.51	4.82	21.63	255-311.34	0.23	0.30	11.10	13.36	6.06	25.40
	311.34-340	0.00	0.00	4.62	6.20	2.51	5.35	311.34-340	0.00	4.11	4.68	13.33	5.87	9.18
	340-380	0.00	0.00	14.45	5.37	5.23	11.86	340-380	0.00	0.45	7.40	6.36	3.84	9.07
	380-420	0.00	0.00	6.49	12.73	4.74	7.29	380-420	3.29	0.00	12.02	6.46	6.29	12.37
	420-470	0.00	0.00	9.99	7.29	4.98	7.55	420-470	0.00	0.00	6.59	7.54	4.07	7.28
	470-525	0.17	0.00	4.84	4.55	2.52	2.65	470-525	0.00	0.00	4.60	4.05	2.71	3.37
	525-615	0.00	0.00	6.95	3.23	2.86	2.94	525-615	0.00	0.00	2.90	2.36	1.77	2.57
	615-775	0.00	0.00	15.07	0.00	4.47	2.28	615-775	0.00	0.00	0.90	0.00	0.31	0.30
	775-950	0.00	0.00	15.34	5.27	6.82	1.55	775-950	0.00	5.73	0.00	6.62	2.78	1.19
	950 & above	0.00	0.00	5.95	0.00	2.07	0.40	950 & above	0.00	0.00	0.00	0.00	0.00	0.00
	Total	0.40	0.04	10.69	8.51	4.75	100.00	Total	0.68	0.90	8.08	9.10	4.88	100.00

Contd...

		Madhya Pradesh							Maharashtra					
		Child Labour as a Percentage of Child Population				*Child Labour as a per cent of Total Child Population*	*Child Labour as a per cent of Total Child Labour (5-14)*		*Child Labour as a Percentage of Child Population*				*Child Labour as a per cent of Total Child Population*	*Child Labour as a per cent of Total Child Labour (5-14)*
		Male (5-9)	*Female (5-9)*	*Male (10-14)*	*Female (10-14)*				*Male (5-9)*	*Female (5-9)*	*Male (10-14)*	*Female (10-14)*		
		(1)	(2)	(3)	(4)	(5)	(6)		(1)	(2)	(3)	(4)	(5)	(6)
Loan (Rs)	0-300	0.44	0.00	10.71	8.59	7.78	92.67	0-300	0.77	0.90	8.40	8.32	4.86	88.33
	300-525	0.00	0.00	0.00	0.00	0.00	0.00	300-525	0.00	0.00	0.00	24.93	4.80	1.77
	525-1000	0.00	0.00	24.81	0.00	7.45	0.62	525-1000	0.00	0.00	0.00	56.13	5.50	0.48
	1000-2000	0.00	0.00	10.12	4.65	3.52	1.10	1000-2000	0.00	0.00	0.00	9.69	1.32	0.49
	2000-4000	0.00	0.00	6.73	3.64	2.59	1.10	2000-4000	0.00	0.00	4.18	36.57	5.68	2.39
	4000-6000	0.00	0.00	0.00	13.68	2.55	0.58	4000-6000	0.00	0.00	0.00	11.32	2.54	0.69
	Above 6000	0.00	0.00	16.63	11.25	6.74	3.93	Above 6000	0.00	3.04	15.44	11.15	7.48	5.85
	Total	0.40	0.04	10.69	8.51	4.75	100.00	Total	0.68	0.90	8.08	9.10	4.88	100.00
Average HH size						6.60							5.79	
Average MPCE (Rs)						368.00							442.00	
Average loan (Rs)						485.00							1134.00	

Notes: MPCE (Rs) is monthly per capita expenditure
HH Type is type of the household
HH size means household size
Se: Non-ag means self-employed in non-agriculatural activities
AG Lab is agriculture labour
Other lab is Other Labour
SE: Ag means self-employed in agricultural activities.
ST means scheduled caste
SC means scheduled tribe
OBC is other backward castes

Table 5 (b)
Child Labour in 2001 (Household Characteristics)-Rural TN and U.P.

		Tamil Nadu							*Uttar Pradesh*					
		Child Labour as a Percentage of Child Population				*Child Labour as a per cent of Total Child Population*	*Child Labour as a per cent of Total Child Labour (5-14)*		*Child Labour as a Percentage of Child Population*				*Child Labour as a per cent of Total Child Population*	*Child Labour as a per cent of Total Child Labour (5-14)*
		Male (5-9)	*Female (5-9)*	*Male (10-14)*	*Female (10-14)*				*Male (5-9)*	*Female (5-9)*	*Male (10-14)*	*Female (10-14)*		
		(1)	(2)	(3)	(4)	(5)	(6)		(1)	(2)	(3)	(4)	(5)	(6)
HH size	0-4	0.08	0.00	8.78	10.72	4.97	43.21	0-4	0.82	0.00	14.18	6.70	5.83	19.32
	4-6	0.00	0.59	7.30	7.25	3.79	43.21	4-6	0.24	0.13	7.08	6.37	3.08	32.30
	6-8	0.00	0.00	5.94	5.34	2.78	8.28	6-8	0.30	0.28	7.22	6.32	3.24	30.99
	8-10	0.00	0.00	6.58	5.69	2.91	1.84	8-10	0.09	0.00	5.19	5.81	2.59	10.99
	Above 10	0.00	0.00	37.79	0.00	10.20	2.83	Above 10	0.00	0.20	3.09	3.41	1.44	6.40
	Total	0.03	0.30	8.08	8.07	4.14	100.00	Total	0.26	0.16	7.24	5.91	3.12	100.00
Social group	ST	0.00	0.00	0.14	0.00	0.04	0.01	ST	0.00	0.00	6.67	13.40	3.80	1.40
	SC	0.00	0.20	4.76	9.19	3.47	28.92	SC	0.32	0.40	7.49	8.23	3.66	30.07
	OBC	0.05	0.39	9.95	7.99	4.75	69.11	OBC	0.32	0.06	7.97	6.97	3.49	49.53
	Others	0.00	0.00	6.95	2.23	2.09	1.96	Others	0.11	0.09	5.87	2.61	2.05	19.00
	Total	0.03	0.30	8.08	8.07	4.14	100.00	Total	0.26	0.16	7.24	5.91	3.12	100.00
Religion	Hindu	0.04	0.34	7.70	8.32	4.12	89.13	Hindu	0.24	0.14	7.05	5.73	3.03	82.25
	Islam	0.00	0.00	0.00	0.00	0.00	0.00	Islam	0.41	0.17	7.48	7.19	3.49	16.38
	Chrishtion	0.00	0.00	18.39	9.68	6.49	10.87	Chrishtion	0.00	0.00	70.99	0.00	24.26	1.01
	Sikh	0.00	0.00	0.00	0.00	0.00	0.00	Sikh	0.00	0.00	13.31	0.00	2.67	0.13
	Jain	0.00	0.00	0.00	0.00	0.00	0.00	Jain	0.00	0.00	0.00	0.00	0.00	0.00
	Buddhist	0.00	0.00	0.00	0.00	0.00	0.00	Buddhist	0.00	0.00	0.00	0.00	0.00	0.00
	Others	0.00	0.00	0.00	0.00	0.00	0.00	Others	0.00	0.00	19.85	0.00	3.30	0.23
	Total	0.03	0.30	8.03	8.07	4.14	100.00	Total	0.26	0.16	7.24	5.91	3.12	100.00
HH Type	SE : Non-ag	0.00	2.37	9.65	10.23	5.07	15.12	SE : Non-ag	0.48	0.20	10.17	6.90	3.92	20.83
	Ag Lab	0.07	0.15	8.87	9.53	4.66	53.39	Ag Lab	0.00	0.10	7.35	6.28	2.90	16.14

Contd...

		Tamil Nadu							Uttar Pradesh					
		Child Labour as a Percentage of Child Population				Child Labour as a per cent of Total Child Population	Child Labour as a per cent of Total Child Labour (5-14)		Child Labour as a Percentage of Child Population				Child Labour as a per cent of Total Child Population	Child Labour as a per cent of Total Child Labour (5-14)
		Male (5-9)	Female (5-9)	Male (10-14)	Female (10-14)				Male (5-9)	Female (5-9)	Male (10-14)	Female (10-14)		
		(1)	(2)	(3)	(4)	(5)	(6)		(1)	(2)	(3)	(4)	(5)	(6)
	Other Lab	0.00	0.00	6.75	4.46	2.82	8.82	Other Lab	0.54	0.00	6.85	5.43	3.05	5.51
	SE : Ag	0.00	0.00	9.79	10.00	5.31	22.34	SE : Ag	0.15	0.21	7.37	6.19	3.29	51.98
	Others	0.00	0.00	0.57	0.00	0.14	0.34	Others	0.72	0.00	2.62	3.12	1.55	5.56
	Total	0.03	0.30	8.08	8.07	4.14	100.00	Total	0.26	0.16	7.24	5.91	3.12	100.00
Sex of HH	Male	0.04	0.32	7.77	7.42	3.86	84.18	Male	0.25	0.14	7.22	6.02	3.10	90.36
	Female	0.00	0.00	10.65	13.27	6.87	15.82	Female	0.38	0.29	7.43	4.94	3.32	9.64
	Total	0.03	0.30	8.08	8.07	4.14	100.00	Total	0.26	0.16	7.24	5.91	3.12	100.00
Land Cultivated (Hectares)	0.00	0.05	0.46	7.54	7.35	3.73	61.18	0.00	0.46	0.22	7.99	6.13	3.24	24.99
	0.01-0.4	0.00	0.00	13.44	18.55	8.15	22.82	0.01-0.4	0.37	0.00	7.65	6.52	3.28	29.18
	0.41-1.0	0.00	0.00	6.25	5.35	3.28	9.07	0.41-1.0	0.13	0.32	6.23	6.98	3.17	25.70
	1.01-2.0	0.00	0.00	5.47	7.18	3.52	4.86	1.01-2.0	0.18	0.21	8.29	5.87	3.54	15.45
	2.01-4.0	0.00	0.00	16.27	0.11	4.64	2.03	2.01-4.0	0.00	0.00	5.12	1.69	1.69	3.96
	Above 4.0	0.00	0.00	0.44	0.70	0.30	0.03	Above 4.0	0.00	0.00	3.92	0.17	1.01	0.72
	Total	0.03	0.32	7.97	8.42	4.19	100.00	Total	0.27	0.16	7.17	5.94	3.11	100.00
MPCE (Rs)	0-225	0.00	0.00	7.19	11.43	4.29	15.94	0-225	0.00	0.00	6.23	7.66	2.84	6.94
	225-255	0.00	2.60	7.78	8.89	5.25	11.17	225-255	0.00	0.00	4.59	7.63	2.51	5.14
	255-317.64	0.20	0.00	12.36	6.13	4.60	19.23	255-317.64	0.34	0.47	4.51	7.13	2.64	12.07
	307.64-340	0.00	0.00	8.43	11.99	4.46	10.57	307.64-340	0.17	0.24	9.85	8.16	4.08	15.78
	340-380	0.00	0.00	5.41	0.23	1.52	3.40	340-380	0.57	0.37	6.39	5.41	3.04	13.69
	380-420	0.00	0.00	8.61	12.54	6.02	13.36	380-420	0.17	0.00	8.45	2.97	2.67	9.22
	420-470	0.00	0.00	2.51	11.72	3.50	6.23	420-470	0.31	0.06	9.03	5.84	3.46	11.34
	470-525	0.00	0.00	14.92	5.60	6.70	9.90	470-525	0.35	0.00	4.54	5.03	2.36	5.93
	525-615	0.00	0.00	10.36	8.93	4.83	6.91	525-615	0.44	0.00	8.88	6.01	4.06	9.80

		Tamil Nadu							Uttar Pradesh					
		Child Labour as a Percentage of Child Population				*Child Labour as a per cent of Total Child Population*	*Child Labour as a per cent of Total Child Labour (5-14)*		*Child Labour as a Percentage of Child Population*				*Child Labour as a per cent of Total Child Population*	*Child Labour as a per cent of Total Child Labour (5-14)*
		Male (5-9)	*Female (5-9)*	*Male (10-14)*	*Female (10-14)*				*Male (5-9)*	*Female (5-9)*	*Male (10-14)*	*Female (10-14)*		
		(1)	(2)	(3)	(4)	(5)	(6)		(1)	(2)	(3)	(4)	(5)	(6)
	615-775	0.00	1.29	2.49	3.74	1.67	2.34	615-775	0.00	0.00	8.57	4.06	3.11	5.76
	775-950	0.00	0.00	4.75	0.00	1.34	0.92	775-950	0.00	0.00	10.58	1.65	3.65	2.17
	950 & above	0.03	0.00	0.12	0.00	0.03	0.01	950 & above	0.00	0.00	8.28	5.31	4.10	2.18
	Total	0.04	0.30	8.08	8.07	4.14	100.00	Total	0.26	0.16	7.24	5.91	3.12	100.00
Loan (Rs)	0-300	0.00	0.36	8.11	7.93	4.17	87.32	0-300	0.27	0.16	6.90	5.89	3.04	93.25
	300-525	0.00	0.00	30.18	0.00	13.68	1.06	300-525	0.00	0.00	12.28	0.00	1.58	0.19
	525-1000	0.00	0.00	0.00	0.00	0.00	0.00	525-1000	0.00	0.00	2.97	14.42	3.42	0.51
	1000-2000	0.00	0.00	11.33	14.45	5.18	2.16	1000-2000	0.00	0.00	18.23	18.18	8.51	1.64
	2000-4000	0.00	0.00	0.00	0.00	0.00	0.00	2000-4000	0.00	0.00	16.06	3.64	4.23	1.09
	4000-6000	0.00	0.00	0.00	11.64	2.95	1.35	4000-6000	0.00	0.00	16.08	0.00	3.82	0.50
	Above 6000	0.00	0.00	10.81	10.79	5.71	8.10	Above 6000	0.00	0.00	15.69	1.59	5.26	2.83
	Total	0.03	0.30	8.08	8.07	4.14	100.00	Total	0.26	0.16	7.24	5.91	3.12	100.00
Average HH size														
Average MPCE (Rs)														
Average loan (Rs)														

Notes: MPCE (Rs) is monthly per capita expenditure
HH Type is type of the household
HH size means household size
Se: Non-ag means self-employed in non-agriculatural activities
AG Lab is agriculture labour
Other lab is Other Labour
SE: Ag means self-employed in agricultural activities.
ST means scheduled caste
SC means scheduled tribe
OBC is other backward castes

TN, child labour is mainly concentrated in households with size 0-4 (43.2 per cent) and 4-6 (43.84 per cent). In UP, more than half of the child labour belongs to households with size less than six, 31 per cent with household size of 6-8 and another 17 per cent with household size more than eight. However these households (with size above 8) are sending a very small proportion of their children to work. The estimates in Tables 5(a) and 5(b) reveal that the proportion of child labour to child population is high, that is, more than average for large households (size above 8) in all the states except UP and for small households (size 0-4) for MP, TN and UP. If households are poor and small in size, then they tend to supply more child labour so as to compensate for the otherwise lesser number of earning members. On the other hand, large households have more available supply of child labour, as well as the need to send children to work. Thus, we find limited support for the results obtained by Lloyd (1994).

A look at the social background of child labour households shows that child labour mainly comes from socially backward classes of SC, ST, and OBC In rural MP, while 50 per cent belongs to STs, another 47 per cent are from SC and OBC classes. It is also observed that among STs, child labour as a proportion of child population is highest at 8.32 per cent, almost 75 per cent more than the average of 4.75 per cent. While in Maharashtra 76 per cent belongs to these classes, in TN it is mainly OBCs (69 per cent) and SCs (29 per cent) who supply child labour in the state. In UP also, 80 per cent of the child labour belongs to SC and OBC households. It is observed from the ratio of child labor to child population that not only do these socially backward classes supply child labour but also a large proportion of their child population also joins the army of child labour.

The religion-based distribution of child labour shows that child labour mostly comes from the Hindu community, and the Islamic community has noteworthy contribution only in UP (16.38 per cent). It is to be noted that the proportion of child labour to child populations is higher for Hindus than Muslims in MP, Maharashtra, and TN. Only in UP's rural sector the Muslims proportion is slightly higher than Hindus but is very high for Christians (24.26 per cent). On examining the type of households, supplying child labour, it is learnt that child labour basically belongs to the agricultural households-that is, either the households are self-employed in agriculture or are agricultural labourers. The proportion ranges from 68 per cent in UP to 91 per cent in Maharashtra. The proportion of child labour to child population varies from 2.9 per cent in UP to 6.67 per cent in Maharashtra for agricultural labour. It indicates that in Maharashtra agricultural labour households are sending a high proportion of their children to the workplaces.

Analysis of household characteristics also informs us that most of the child labour belongs to male-headed household but the proportion of child labour to child population is much higher for female-headed households, at 8.71 per cent as compared with 4.6 per cent in male-headed households in MP; 8.1 per cent and 4.65 per cent for Maharashtra; 6.87 per cent and 3.86 per cent for TN and 3.32 per cent and 3.1 per cent respectively for UP. One can see from Table I that this gap between male-headed and female-headed households has a close positive link with adult female WPR, as the gap is more in states where adult female WPR is high and low for UP where both the female WPR and adult female WPR are quite low. It thus supports the contention that female-headed households supply more child labour.

To gather evidence for the view of 'poverty induced' child labour, we examine three available characteristics, namely, size of land cultivated by the households, monthly per capita expenditure (MPCE), and indebtedness of rural households. It is believed that it is poverty that causes child labour and perpetuates it. But child labour could itself add to poverty by increasing the supply of labour, which would depress adult wages and may put adults out of work. Child labour may itself be shaped by impressive economic growth and competition-as employers demand and use more poorly paid and casually employed workers such as children and women to stay in competition.

Misra (2000) gives the possibility of the link between child labour and size of landholding. The incidence of child labour increases with increase in the size of the farm, as land and labour are complementary inputs in agricultural production [Bhatty 1998]; but the trend may be reversed if the landlord leases out land instead of operating it himself. In order to ascertain the exact relationship, we have investigated the relationship of child labour with land cultivated rather than landholding. We observe that most of the child labour in Maharashtra and TN belongs to households that do not cultivate any land, which is supported by our earlier observation that most of the households in these two states are the agricultural labour type, that is, wage labour. On the contrary, in MP and UP we find that more child labour belongs to households with small size of cultivated land. It is also noticed that while in MP and UP, a higher proportion of male children work on the farm, it is the reverse in TN and Maharashtra. It shows how in MP and UP females are generally not encouraged to go out of the home and join the workforce because of social prejudices against females.

MPCE is an indication of the economic condition of the households. On the basis of NSS data for 1993-94. Thorat (1999) find a negative relationship between MPCE and child labour. The relationship for 1999-2000 has been examined here. The estimates obtained for 1999-2000 discloses[4] that the proportion of child labour which belongs to below poverty line[5] households in rural sectors is 58, 54.7, 46 and 40 for MP (Poverty line is Rs 311.34), Maharashtra (poverty line is Rs 318.63), TN (poverty line is Rs 307.64) and UP (poverty line is Rs 336.88), respectively. It is also evident that the proportion of child labour to child population is relatively high in low MPCE categories, especially in the first three states. Two interesting facts which must be noticed are, that one, while UP's per capita income is almost one-third that of Maharashtra, the difference in their average MPCE for the rural sectors [Tables 5(a) and 5(b)] is not much different. So rural Maharashtra may be income-rich but not consumption-rich compared with rural UP. Secondly, we can also notice that while in UP only 40 per cent of child labour comes from below poverty line households, the proportion is higher at 55 per cent for Maharashtra. So the poverty-induced child labour argument holds more for a richer state like Maharashtra rather than a poorer state like UP. This is also supported by the fact that a high proportion of child population is joining the labour force in Maharashtra (Table 5(a) than in UP (col 5, Table 5(b).

There is a lot of evidence on the link between poverty and indebtedness of households. Poor households tend to borrow more with increase in household size and would be compelled to send their children to work instead of school. The average indebtedness of rural households is Rs 485, Rs 1,134, Rs 1,109 and Rs 293 for MP, Maharashtrta, TN and UP respectively. Thus, we find that the indebtedness is higher in the richest state and lowest in the poorest state. This could be explained by the differences in the: (1) capacity of households, i.e, in income, to repay their debt, and (2) availability of loans to rural households in these states. Tables 5 (a) and 5(b) reveal that 87 to 93 per cent of rural households in the four stats have taken either no loan or just a small amount. In such households, the proportion of child labour to child population is low or just the average. It is evident from the two tables that whatever child labour exists among the 5-9 age group, it mostly belongs to such households. But for the households with huge loans, especially in relation to their average MPCE, we gather that more and more children are joining the labour force.

The agewise and sexwise distribution of child labour shows considerable variation between them and supports the already known fact that females enjoy a lower status in MP and UP. It is shown by a lower female WPR for age 5-9 as well as for 10-14 (Table 3). No such discrimination is, however, evident in TN at the aggregate level and a positive discrimination (That is, more females are forced to join the workforce) is visible in Maharashtra (also high adult female WPR in Table 1), A closer examination shows that among SCs a higher proportion of boys of age 10-14 work in MP but in the other three states the trend is the reverse, that is, a higher proportion of girls of age 10-14 years join the workforce. Among STs, there is uniformity in behaviour in all states-more boys go to work than girls. In case of OBCs also we find the same trend except in Maharashtra. It is also evident from the tables that whatever child labour exists for the age group 5-9 in these states, is more among the socially backward classes (ST (MP), SC (TN and UP), OBC (Maharashtra, TN and UP), belonging to poor households with no land, no loan and low MPCE.

Thus, we have some evidence for the link of economic factors with the proportion of child labour in the rural sector of the selected states. A child labourer in the rural sector of these states is more likely to be a Hindu male of 10-14 age, belonging to large households with no or small landholding, of a socially backward caste, headed by a male, who is employed either as agricultural labour or is self-employed in agriculture and his household MPCE being below the respective poverty line.

URBAN SECTOR

Table 6 (a) for MP and Maharashtra and 6(b) for TN and UP provide us the information about socio-economic characteristics of households contribution to child labour. We find that child labour as a proportion of child population varied from a low of 1.03 in urban Maharashtra to a high of 2.81 in urban UP. In MP, about 50 per cent of the child labour comes from households whose size is below 6, while in Maharashtra, TN and UP the corresponding percentages of child labour are 58, 75 and 48 respectively. It is also revealed by the two tables (column 5) that as the size of household increases, they send relatively a large proportion of child population to work, supporting the findings of Lloyd (1994).

The social background of child labour in the urban sectors of these four states shows that ST as a social class does not contribute much to child labour, except a bit in MP and Mahrashtra. However, SCs are significant contributors of child labour (from 15 to 26 per cent) and in these households a relatively large proportion of the child population joins the workforce. OBCs have been a major source of child labour in MP (37 per cent), TN (79.5 per cent) and UP (56 per cent). Thus, we find

Table 6 (a)
Child Labour in 2001 (Household Characteristics)-Urban MP and Maharashtra

		Madhya Pradesh							*Maharashtra*					
		Child Labour as a Percentage of Child Population				*Child Labour as a per cent of Total Child Population*	*Child Labour as a per cent of Total Child Labour (5-14)*		*Child Labour as a Percentage of Child Population*				*Child Labour as a per cent of Total Child Population*	*Child Labour as a per cent of Total Child Labour (5-14)*
		Male (5-9)	*Female (5-9)*	*Male (10-14)*	*Female (10-14)*				*Male (5-9)*	*Female (5-9)*	*Male (10-14)*	*Female (10-14)*		
		(1)	(2)	(3)	(4)	(5)	(6)		(1)	(2)	(3)	(4)	(5)	(6)
HH size	0-4	0.74	0.00	3.23	0.97	1.39	14.23	0-4	0.08	0.06	2.56	0.82	1.04	22.52
	4-6	0.83	0.00	1.95	2.21	1.22	35.22	4-6	0.00	0.00	1.76	1.45	0.86	35.20
	6-8	0.00	0.00	4.93	1.94	1.80	31.83	6-8	0.00	0.00	2.98	0.80	0.95	18.44
	8-10	0.00	0.00	7.40	1.88	2.16	11.48	8-10	0.00	0.00	6.95	4.82	2.71	22.77
	Above 10	0.00	0.00	4.02	0.85	1.12	7.24	Above 10	0.00	0.00	0.83	0.00	0.17	1.06
	Total	0.47	0.00	3.43	1.83	1.46	100.00	Total	0.02	0.01	2.51	1.43	1.03	100.00
Social group	ST	0.00	0.00	2.50	3.20	1.20	9.16	ST	0.00	0.00	1.76	0.00	0.47	2.19
	SC	3.01	0.00	3.11	4.28	2.58	25.74	SC	0.16	0.00	3.06	3.23	1.87	25.56
	OBC	0.00	0.00	4.13	1.59	1.60	37.18	OBC	0.00	0.00	0.57	1.23	0.47	8.58
	Others	0.00	0.00	3.10	0.79	1.01	27.92	Others	0.00	0.02	2.99	1.13	1.06	63.66
	Total	0.47	0.00	3.43	1.83	1.46	100.00	Total	0.02	0.01	2.51	1.43	1.03	100.00
Religion	Hindu	0.60	0.00	2.46	2.18	1.30	70.51	Hindu	0.03	0.02	1.72	1.40	0.83	53.43
	Islam	0.00	0.00	9.38	0.78	2.54	29.49	Islam	0.00	0.00	5.47	1.80	1.86	39.40
	Chrishtion	0.00	0.00	0.00	0.00	0.00	0.00	Chrishtion	0.00	0.00	0.00	0.00	0.00	0.00
	Sikh	0.00	0.00	0.00	0.00	0.00	0.00	Sikh	0.00	0.00	0.00	0.00	0.00	0.00
	Jain	0.00	0.00	0.00	0.00	0.00	0.00	Jain	0.00	0.00	0.00	0.00	0.00	0.00
	Buddhist	0.00	0.00	0.00	0.00	0.00	0.00	Buddhist	0.00	0.00	2.53	1.79	1.19	7.18
	Others	0.00	0.00	0.00	0.00	0.00	0.00	Others	0.00	0.00	0.00	0.00	0.00	0.00
	Total	0.47	0.00	3.43	1.83	1.46	100.00	Total	0.02	0.01	2.51	1.43	1.03	100.00
HH Type	SE	0.00	0.00	3.72	1.30	1.32	36.93	SE	0.06	0.03	2.76	1.48	1.13	36.94
	Sal Eam	1.00	0.00	2.55	1.55	1.28	30.72	Sal Eam	0.00	0.00	1.05	0.70	0.45	20.63
	C Labour	0.69	0.00	6.34	4.58	2.62	31.58	C Labour	0.00	0.00	7.18	3.41	2.57	36.89
	others	0.00	0.00	0.44	0.00	0.18	0.77	others	0.00	0.00	1.24	3.93	1.42	5.54
	Total	0.00	0.00	3.43	0.00	1.46	100.00	Total	0.00	0.00	2.51	0.00	1.03	100.00

		Madhya Pradesh							*Maharashtra*					
		Child Labour as a Percentage of Child Population				*Child Labour as a per cent of Total Child Population*	*Child Labour as a per cent of Total Child Labour (5-14)*		*Child Labour as a Percentage of Child Population*				*Child Labour as a per cent of Total Child Population*	*Child Labour as a per cent of Total Child Labour (5-14)*
		Male (5-9)	*Female (5-9)*	*Male (10-14)*	*Female (10-14)*				*Male (5-9)*	*Female (5-9)*	*Male (10-14)*	*Female (10-14)*		
		(1)	(2)	(3)	(4)	(5)	(6)		(1)	(2)	(3)	(4)	(5)	(6)
Sex of HH	Male	0.36	0.00	3.26	1.93	1.40	90.98	Male	0.02	0.00	2.33	1.47	0.99	89.63
	Female	3.22	0.00	0.00	0.00	2.72	9.02	Female	0.00	0.00	0.00	0.90	1.80	10.37
	Total	0.47	0.00	3.43	1.83	1.46	100.00	Total	0.02	0.01	2.51	1.43	1.03	100.00
MPCE (Rs)	0-300	0.00	0.00	3.45	7.70	2.44	29.12	0-300	0.00	0.00	1.63	3.28	1.09	11.02
	300-350	0.00	0.00	9.99	1.86	2.65	21.10	300-350	0.35	0.00	9.70	2.07	3.12	20.07
	350-425	0.00	0.00	2.84	1.59	1.18	11.41	350-425	0.00	0.00	6.19	2.08	2.03	20.14
	425-481.65	0.00	0.00	4.33	0.00	1.39	10.03	425-481.65	0.00	0.00	2.98	1.32	1.07	9.78
	481.65-575	0 91	0.00	1.94	0.00	0.82	7.29	481.65-575	0.00	0.00	2.01	2.41	1.17	7.71
	575-665	3.38	0.00	7.23	0.42	2.78	19.31	575-665	0.00	0.08	2.24	1.27	0.92	13.66
	665-775	0.00	0.00	0.77	0.00	0.20	0.97	665-775	0.00	0.00	0.00	2.74	0.62	6.01
	775-915	0.00	0.00	0.56	0.00	0.18	0.77	775-915	0.00	0.00	1.23	0.00	0.34	2.86
	915 & above	0.00	0.00	0.00	0.00	0.00	0.00	915 & above	0.00	0.00	1.32	0.00	0.41	8.76
	Total	0.47	0.00	3.43	1.83	0.46	100.00	Total	0.02	0.01	2.51	1.43	1.03	100.00
Average HH size							6.40							5.80
Average MPCE (Rs)							612.00							859.50

Notes: MPCE (Rs) is monthly per capita expenditure
HH Type is type of the household
HH size means household size
Se: self-amployed
C Lab is casual labour
Other means scheduled caste
ST: means scheduled tribe
OBC is other backward castes
Sal Eam means salary earner
Other means other labour

Table 6 (b)
Child Labour in 2001 (Household Characteristics)-Urban TN and UP

		Tamil Nadu							Uttar Pradesh					
		Child Labour as a Percentage of Child Population				*Child Labour as a per cent of Total Child Population*	*Child Labour as a per cent of Total Child Labour (5-14)*		*Child Labour as a Percentage of Child Population*				*Child Labour as a per cent of Total Child Population*	*Child Labour as a per cent of Total Child Labour (5-14)*
		Male (5-9)	*Female (5-9)*	*Male (10-14)*	*Female (10-14)*				*Male (5-9)*	*Female (5-9)*	*Male (10-14)*	*Female (10-14)*		
		(1)	(2)	(3)	(4)	(5)	(6)		(1)	(2)	(3)	(4)	(5)	(6)
HH size	0-4	0.00	0.00	3.82	3.32	1.95	34.94	0-4	0.00	0.00	8.60	1.80	2.86	15.34
	4-6	0.00	0.40	4.89	3.64	2.40	39.97	4-6	0.63	0.00	7.26	2.63	2.60	32.34
	6-8	0.00	0.00	6.82	3.91	3.10	13.32	6-8	0.15	0.89	6.92	4.09	3.09	28.26
	8-10	0.00	0.00	30.47	0.91	5.13	9.91	8-10	0.84	0.00	5.50	2.26	2.22	12.41
	Above 10	0.00	0.00	13.79	0.00	2.38	1.86	Above 10	0.41	0.17	13.27	1.63	3.79	11.64
	Total	0.00	0.18	5.40	3.33	2.40	100.00	Total	0.43	0.23	7.62	2.84	2.81	100.00
Social group	ST	0.00	0.00	0.00	0.00	0.00	0.00	ST	0.00	0.00	0.00	0.00	0.00	0.00
	SC	0.00	0.00	5.25	4.57	2.67	15.29	SC	0.00	0.70	6.16	4.37	2.80	15.87
	OBC	0.00	0.25	6.22	3.63	2.75	79.51	OBC	0.89	0.36	12.45	3.69	4.39	56.21
	Others	0.00	0.00	1.54	1.46	0.80	5.20	Others	0.20	0.00	4.66	1.73	1.68	27.92
	Total	0.00	0.18	5.40	3.33	2.40	100.00	Total	0.43	0.23	7.62	2.84	2.81	100.00
Religion	Hindu	0.00	0.22	3.96	2.98	1.92	64.34	Hindu	0.09	0.18	6.73	2.09	2.33	55.45
	Islam	0.00	0.00	16.88	5.88	6.01	32.77	Islam	1.10	0.33	9.76	4.37	3.82	43.96
	Chrishtion	0.00	0.00	1.37	3.18	1.29	2.89	Chrishtion	0.00	0.00	0.00	0.00	0.00	0.00
	Sikh	0.00	0.00	0.00	0.00	0.00	0.00	Sikh	0.00	0.00	0.00	0.00	0.00	0.00
	Jain	0.00	0.00	0.00	0.00	0.00	0.00	Jain	0.00	0.00	0.00	0.00	0.00	0.00
	Buddhist	0.00	0.00	0.00	0.00	0.00	0.00	Buddhist	0.00	0.00	42.22	0.00	42.22	0.59
	Others	0.00	0.00	0.00	0.00	0.00	0.00	Others	0.00	0.00	0.00	0.00	0.00	0.00
	Total	0.00	0.18	5.40	3.33	2.40	100.00	Total	0.43	0.23	7.62	2.84	2.81	100.00
HH Type	SE	0.00	0.00	6.33	3.24	2.40	36.13	SE	0.67	0.24	11.22	3.46	3.79	70.72
	Sal Eam	0.00	0.00	2.89	2.98	1.60	25.45	Sal Eam	0.00	0.00	3.38	0.24	1.01	10.85
	C Labour	0.00	0.87	10.75	5.45	4.52	37.04	C Labour	0.55	0.78	7.37	9.38	4.11	15.75
	others	0.00	0.00	1.32	0.00	0.61	1.38	others	0.00	0.00	3.48	0.00	1.13	2.68
	Total	0.00	0.18	5.40	3.33	2.40	100.00	Total	0.00	0.00	7.62	0.00	2.81	100.00

		Tamil Nadu							*Uttar Pradesh*					
		Child Labour as a Percentage of Child Population				*Child Labour as a per cent of Total Child Population*	*Child Labour as a per cent of Total Child Labour (5-14)*		*Child Labour as a Percentage of Child Population*				*Child Labour as a per cent of Total Child Population*	*Child Labour as a per cent of Total Child Labour (5-14)*
		Male (5-9)	*Female (5-9)*	*Male (10-14)*	*Female (10-14)*				*Male (5-9)*	*Female (5-9)*	*Male (10-14)*	*Female (10-14)*		
		(1)	(2)	(3)	(4)	(5)	(6)		(1)	(2)	(3)	(4)	(5)	(6)
Sex of HH	Male	0.00	0.00	4.96	0.00	2.12	80.67	Male	0.46	0.00	7.87	2.77	2.84	95.56
	Female	0.00	0.00	10.58	8.35	5.49	19.33	Female	0.00	0.00	0.00	3.89	2.30	4.44
	Total	0.00	0.00	0.00	3.33	2.40	100.00	Total	0.43	0.23	7.62	2.84	2.81	100.00
MPCE (Rs)	0-300	0.00	0.00	4.04	4.21	1.94	7.23	0-300	0.00	0.00	6.93	6.63	3.06	17.29
	300-350	0.00	2.49	6.00	7.05	4.28	12.46	300-350	0.85	0.78	7.16	4.76	3.24	13.09
	350-425	0.00	0.00	8.70	5.22	3.80	20.25	350-425	0.43	0.28	9.74	3.74	3.90	21.78
	425-481.65	0.00	0.00	12.54	4.42	4.86	16.45	425-481.65	0.52	0.00	10.19	1.68	2.95	18.43
	481.65-575	0.00	0.00	9.94	5.48	3.90	26.33	481.65-575	0.00	0.23	6.84	2.03	2.32	7.87
	575-665	0.00	0.00	4.10	2.67	1.66	6.30	575-665	0.00	0.00	4.58	1.99	1.43	4.84
	665-775	0.00	0.00	5.49	3.74	2.68	9.05	665-775	0.00	0.00	6.01	0.00	1.67	3.34
	775-915	0.00	0.00	0.98	0.00	0.31	0.88	775-915	0.00	0.00	0.97	0.00	0.24	0.41
	915 & above	0.00	0.00	0.04	0.34	0.11	1.06	915 & above	0.00	0.93	8.70	0.54	3.58	12.94
	Total	0.00	0.18	5.40	3.33	2.40	100.00	Total	0.43	0.23	7.62	2.84	2.81	100.00
Average HH size							4.85							6.60
Average MPCE (Rs)							809.00							613.00

Notes: MPCE (Rs) is monthly per capita expenditure
HH Type is type of the household
HH size means household size
Se: self-amployed
C Lab is casual labour
Other means scheduled caste
ST: means scheduled tribe
OBC is other backward castes
Sal Eam means salary earner
Other means other labour

a repetition of the rural trend-the socially backward classes contributing a large proportion, ranging from 37 per cent in Maharashtra to 95 per cent in TN to the total urban child labour in the states.

Unlike the rural sector, we notice that in the urban sector a larger proportion of the child population of Muslim households joins the labour force compared with other households. This indicates their relatively low status in urban areas. The type of households to which child labourers belong is mainly either casual labour or self-employed, But in casual labour households, the maximum proportion of children are forced to work-it being almost 75 per cent to 150 per cent more than the average for the state. We also find that female-headed households supply almost double the ration of child labour to child population in the first three states, while in UP male-headed households supply more child labour.

The role of poverty in child labour is analysed with the help of MPCE. We learn that in the urban sector, proportion of child labour which comes from below poverty line households, is 71.7, 68.7, 56.4 and 52.2 respectively, for the selected four states. These proportions are very high official poverty lines[6] [Deaton 2003] for the urban sector, like the rural sector, it is observed that the proportion of child labour to child population is quite high for lower MPCE classes. It is also seen that whereas female child labour in the age group 10-14 is higher for the poorest of the poor households that is, with MPCE of 0-300, male child labour (age 10-14) is substantial in higher MPCE categories also. The analysis gives evidence to the fact that in all the four states child labour to child population is higher among the poor households and supports the 'poverty induced' child labour hypothesis and the findings of Thorat (1999).

The age and sexwise distribution of child labour in the urban sector shows that a larger proportion of males have worked compared with females, except for 5-9 age group females in TN. The gap between the two sexes is maximum for UP and minimum for TN, for reasons already explained for the rural sector. Like the rural sector, a lot of variation is observed between the two age groups. It is also evident from the tables that child labour that exists among the age group 5-9 in these states, is more among the socially backward classes [SC(MP, Maharashtra), and OBC (TN and UP)], belonging to poor households, low MPCE and employed as casual labour or salary earner or self-employed.

It is thus observed that a typical child labourer in the urban sector is likely to be a male of the 10-14 age group with the average household size less than 8, headed by a male, belonging to the social group SC or

OBC, is most likely to be a Hindu or a Muslim working as casual labour or self-employed with MPCE less than Rs. 500.

However, it may be mentioned that the analysis of rural and urban sectors in this section may indicate that poverty has a role in shaping the supply of child labour, but it does not mean that poverty is the only or a single major cause of child labour. Child labour also comes from households that are not so poor and whose MPCE and size of land cultivated are relatively quite high. It could be due to other reasons, like social exclusion-that is, belonging to backward classes, large size of households, lack of education and the traditional occupational pattern of the households.

EDUCATIONAL AND OCCUPATIONAL PROFILE

In this section, an attempt has been made to ascertain the answer to the basic questions: where are the children working and are they literate? Scholars have argued that education as an alternative to child labour can be a well-established strategy, but it will work only if we ensure full enrolment and retention of children in the formal education system. But study after study has shown that in India, in most of the states, enrolment is poor and universalising education and ensuring that every child is in school is still not a reality. There are still high proportions of school dropouts, especially in higher age groups. The poor enrolment and high dropouts could in turn be due to non-availability of schools, poor and irrelevant course curriculum, lack of teachers and other relevant infrastructure (like buildings, classrooms, desks, blackboards), and lack of employment opportunities after completing school. All these factors make returns from education very low and makes it unattractive for households to send their children to school.

However, the evidence suggests the due to efforts by individuals, NGOs and government agencies, the literacy rate in general and gross enrolment rates in the primary class (I to V, age 6-11 years) and upper primary class (VI to VIII, age 11-14 years) have improved over the last two NSS rounds, from 81.9 per cent to 94.9 per cent for primary and 54.2 per cent to 58.8 per cent for upper primary class. But the huge gap between the primary and upper primary class point at the high dropout rates over the period. There is, however a lot of variation between the selected four states (Table 1) in the gross enrolment rates. The information about the educational and occupational profile of child labour in the selected states is summarised for the rural sectors in Tables 7(a) (for MP and Maharashtra) and 7(b) (for TN and UP), and for the urban sector in 8(a) and 8(b) respectively.

Table 7 (a)
Child Labour in 1999-2000 (Educational and Occupational Profile)-Rural MP and Maharashtra

		Madhya Pradesh					*Maharashtra*				
		Males 5-9	*Females 5-9*	*Males 10-14*	*Females 10-14*	*Total*	*Males 5-9*	*Females 5-9*	*Males 10-14*	*Females 10-14*	*Total*
Education Profile of child Labour	Illiterate	120009	1364	255928	168993	438294	20194	21732	149169	126891	317986
	up to primary	5442	0	161112	123594	290148	1650	5009	114952	125728	247339
	up to secondary	0	0	18203	2945	21148	0	0	31334	35323	66657
	Total	17451	01364	435243	295532	749590	21844	26741	295455	287942	631982
Principal industryof child labour	I	16087	0	414622	256029	686738	21844	26091	285047	287942	620924
	II	0	0	3921	8324	12245	0	0	2455	0	2455
	III	0	0	0	3010	3010	0	0	0	0	0
	IV	1364	1364	6173	14466	23367	0	0	4808	0	4808
	V	0	0	0	7744	7744	0	650	2254	0	2904
	VI	0	0	5166	1534	6700	0	0	722	0	722
	VII	0	0	1589	0	1589	0	0	6632	0	6632
	VIII	0	0	0	0	0	0	0	0	0	0
	IX	0	0	3772	4425	8197	0	0	381	0	381
	Total	17451	1364	435243	295532	749590	21844	26741	302299	287942	638826

Notes: I - Agriculture
II - Fishing
III - Mining and quarrying
IV - Manufacturing electricity and gas
V - Construction
VI - Trade and commerce
VII - Hotels and restaurants, etc.
VIII - Transport, storage, etc
IX - Other services

Table 7 (b)
Child Labour in 1999-2000 (Educational and Occupational Profile)-Rural NT and UP

		Tamil Nadu					*Uttar Pradesh*				
		Males	*Females*	*Males*	*Females*	*Total*	*Males*	*Females*	*Males*	*Females*	*Total*
		5-9	*5-9*	*10-14*	*10-14*		*5-9*	*5-9*	*10-14*	*10-14*	
Education Profile of child Labour	Illiterate	621	4674	36269	32454	74018	16096	9245	290876	278530	594747
	up to primary	0	0	103247	83136	186383	11543	5039	292204	158021	466807
	up to secondary	0	0	8938	23490	32428	0	0	54524	11711	66235
	Above Secondary	0	0	0	0	0	0	0	0	0	0
	Total	621	4674	148454	139080	292829	27639	14284	637604	448262	112789
Principal industry of child labour	I	621	0	86324	89151	176096	24517	13682	471674	369535	879408
	II	0	0	180	0	180	0	0	0	0	0
	III	0	0	0	0	0	0	0	0	0	0
	IV	0	3555	43465	49037	96057	3122	0	70768	76298	150188
	V	0	1119	11612	148	12879	0	0	12886	0	12886
	VI	0	0	6873	0	6873	0	0	59832	0	59832
	VII	0	0	0	139	139	0	0	0	0	0
	VIII	0	0	0	0	0	0	0	9920	0	9920
	IX	0	0	0	0	0	0	602	11035	4855	16492
	Total	621	4674	148454	138475	292224	27639	14284	636115	450688	1128726

Notes: I - Agriculture; II - Fishing; III - Mining and quarrying; IV - Manufacturing electricity and gas; V - Construction; VI - Trade and commerce; VII - Hotels and restaurants, etc.; VIII - Transport, storage, etc; IX - Other services

RURAL SECTOR

It is observed from Table 7(a) and most of the child labour in the states is illiterate, the percentages being 58.5, 50.3 and 52.7 for MP, Maharashtra and UP respectively. It is only in TN that the percentage of illiterates is only 25.3 and 64 per cent are literate up to the primary level. Up to the secondary level literacy is very low among child labour and ranged from 2.82 per cent in MP to 11 per cent in TN. The illiteracy rate is more among the 5-9 age group than the 10-14 age group. Within the latter age group, illiteracy is more among boys in TN and Maharashtra, and among girls in MP and UP., for reasons already stressed.

It is obvious that when children of the 5-9 age group join the labour force they are not able to go to school and remain illiterate. On the other hand, in the 10-14 age group there is a possibility that some of the children may continue school up to the primary level or upper primary level and then opt out of school and join the workforce. So literacy is more among this age group.

The occupational profile of child labour in the rural sector shows that most of the child labour is engaged in agriculture, possibly with other members of the household, though the proportion varies from 97 per cent in Maharashtra to 60 per cent in TN. Manufacturing is an important source of employment of child labour only in TN and UP, where almost 33 per cent and 13 per cent respectively of the child labour is employed in the sector. It is due to the availability of more employment opportunities that is, their greater demand in some industries of the states where child labour is widely used. A typical child labourer in the rural sector of the four states is thus either illiterate or at best literate up to the primary level, and is employed primarily in agriculture.

Urban Sector: The analysis of estimates in Table 8(a) and 8(b) shows that unlike the rural sector, the number and the proportion of illiterate child labour is less than those who are literate up to primary level, except in UP, where we notice that 60 per cent of the child labour is illiterate. It is also evident that except MP, in all other states the proportion of illiterates among the 5-9 age group is higher. In MP, which now claims to have attained universal education, it seems the 5-9 age group child labour is combining literacy with work. The gross enrolment ratios in Table-1 also support the link between literacy and child labour. It show how the rate is very low in UP for both the primary and upper primary classes, which accounts for the predominance of illiterate child labour in both the rural and urban sector of UP.

Table 8 (a)

Child Labour in 1999-2000 (Educational and Occupational Profile)-Urban MP and Maharashtra

		Madhya Pradesh					*Maharashtra*				
		Males	*Females*	*Males*	*Females*	*Total*	*Males*	*Females*	*Males*	*Females*	*Total*
		5-9	*5-9*	*10-14*	*10-14*		*5-9*	*5-9*	*10-14*	*10-14*	
Education Profile of child Labour	Illiterate	0	0	17034	9082	26116	370	206	15846	8626	25048
	up to primary	5073	0	16713	7034	28820	0	0	29351	8626	37977
	up to secondary	0	0	3666	1035	4701	0	0	3804	8222	12026
	Above Secondary	0	0	0	0	0	0	0	0	0	0
	Total	5073	0	37413	17151	59637	370	206	49001	25474	75051
Principal industry of child labour	I	0	0	6630	6323	13003	370	0	5671	2546	8587
	II	0	0	0	0	0	0	0	0	0	0
	IV	0	0	3375	4215	7590	0	0	8469	3393	11862
	V	0	0	1714	0	1714	0	0	5487	6712	12199
	VI	5073	0	16769	0	21842	0	206	19622	3327	23155
	VII	0	0	4344	1035	5379	0	0	4988	0	4988
	VIII	0	0	4092	0	2092	0	0	0	0	0
	IX	0	0	439	5578	6017	0	0	1141	8260	9401
	Total	5073	0	37413	17151	59637	370	206	45378	24238	70192

Notes: I - Agriculture
II - Fishing
III - Mining and quarrying
IV - Manufacturing electricity and gas
V - Construction
VI - Trade and commerce
VII - Hotels and restaurants, etc.
VIII - Transport, storage, etc
IX - Other services

Table 8(b)
Child Labour in 1999-2000 (Educational and Occupational Profile)-Urban TN and UP

		Tamil Nadu					*Uttar Pradesh*				
		Males	*Females*	*Males*	*Females*	*Total*	*Males*	*Females*	*Males*	*Females*	*Total*
		5-9	*5-9*	*10-14*	*10-14*		*5-9*	*5-9*	*10-14*	*10-14*	
Education Profile of child Labour	Illiterate	0	1422	4867	9665	15954	8375	3051	105395	29997	146818
	up to primary	0	0	43470	21766	65236	1279	1842	61853	25636	90610
	up to secondary	0	0	6630	3807	10437	0	0	5931	2266	8197
	Above Secondary	0	0	0	0	0	0	0	0	0	0
	Total	0	1422	54967	35238	91627	9654	4893	173179	57899	245625
Principal industry of child labour	I	0	0	1442	0	1442	0	0	15217	4492	19709
	II	0	0	1074	0	1074	0	0	0	0	0
	III	0	0	0	1063	1063	0	0	0	0	0
	IV	0	1422	10517	22452	34391	4768	3051	32855	45550	86224
	V	0	0	5927	3073	9000	0	0	4045	617	4662
	VI	0	0	31881	3504	35385	3607	1467	70829	4241	80144
	VII	0	0	2972	532	3504	1279	375	23941	750	26345
	VIII	0	0	0	0	0	0	0	4828	0	4828
	IX	0	0	1154	1073	2228	0	0	8121	1099	9220
	Total	0	1422	54967	31698	88087	9654	4893	159836	56749	231132

Notes : I - Agriculture
II - Fishing
III - Mining and quarrying
IV - Manufacturing electricity and gas
V - Construction
VI - Trade and commerce
VII - Hotels and restaurants, etc.
VIII - Transport, storage, etc
IX - Other services

The main occupations of urban child labour are manufacturing, and trade and commerce, with trade accounting for 30 to 40 per cent of.the total in the four stats. While girls are mainly employed in factories and agriculture (in MP and UP), boys are more into trade and commerce, and manufacturing. So unlike rural areas, a child labourer in urban areas is more likely to be literate up to primary level and employed in some non-agricultural activity.

CHILD LABOUR IN SELECTED INDUSTRIES

Employment of child labour in hazardous industries has been completely banned. In India, however, surveys have shown that it is prevalent in many such industries. Estimates have been obtained for certain hazardous industries, which have been identified by ILO for immediate intervention. The estimates are summarized in Table 9 for the 5-14 age group for both rural and urban sectors. It is observed that more of the female child labour in the age group 10-14 is employed in these hazardous industries, except urban UP. The major hazardous industries where child labour is employed in the four states are bidi and bricks (in MP, TN and UP), stone quarrying in MP, silk (in urban MP. TN and UP), footwear (in TN and urban UP), matches in TN, locks and glass bangles in urban UP and carpets in UP. The NSS 55th round estimates do not provide any evidence of child labour in these selected hazardous industries in Maharashtra. It can also be ascertained from the Tables 7(a) and 8(a) that in Maharashtra most of the child labour in the rural as well as urban sector is employed either in agriculture or in trade and commerce.

It is seen from the table that bidi making has the highest number of child labourers in the four states. Its employment varied from approximately 11,000 in MP to 29,000 in UP. Next in size of employment is the silk industry in UP, which employs 24,000 child labourers and match industry in TN employing 23,500 child labourers. A comparison of Table 9 with Tables 7(a) to 8(b) shows that in rural MP, out of a total of around 23,000 child labourers in manufacturing, more than half that is, 13,000 are employed in these hazardous industries, the bulk of them in bidi making. A similar situation is prevails in urban MP where the bulk of child labour (4,000 out of 7,500, Table 8(a) is in hazardous industries, 74 per cent in bidi making. In TN, the NSS estimates tell us that almost half of the, child labour (47,500 out of 96,000) in rural TN and 35 per cent in urban TN who are employed in the manufacturing sector are in the hazardous industries-mainly in bidi and matches. The 55th round estimates based on unit data do not reveal the presence of child labour of the age group 5-14 in Maharashtra and in the fireworks

Table 9
Child Labour in Specific Industries, 2001

Industry	Rural Sector					Urban Sector			
	Males 10-14	Females 10-14	Total	Per Cent	Industry	Males 10-14	Females 10-14	Total	Per Cent
Madhya Pradesh					**Madhya Pradesh**				
Bidi	4041	4119	8150	61.27	Bidi	916	2064	2976	74.2
Stone quarrying	0	3010	3010	22.63	Stone quarrying	0	0	0	0
Silk	0	0	0	0	Silk	0	1035	1035	25.8
Bricks	2142	0	2142	16.1	Bricks	0	0	0	0
Total	6173	7129	13302	100	Total	916	3095	4011	100
Tamil Naidu					**Tamil Naidu**				
Bidi	5378	11190	16568	34.83	Bidi	0	4009	4009	33.02
Silk	7104	0	7104	14.94	Silk	0	907	907	7.47
Matches	3924	13975	17899	37.63	Matches	0	5802	5802	47.79
Bricks	3627	0	3627	7.63	Carpets	0	0	0	0
Footwear	2366	0	2366	4.97	Footwear	1422	0	1422	11.71
Total	22399	25165	47564	100	Total	1422	10718	12140	100
Uttar Pradesh					**Uttar Pradesh**				
Bidi	2567	19118	21685	36.7	Bidi	2266	9583	11849	53.26
Silk	8582	13980	22562	38.19	Silk	1448	0	1448	6.51
Bricks	5271	0	5271	8.92	Locks	2580	0	2580	11.6
Glass Bangles	0	0	0	0	Bricks	1308	0	1308	5.88
Carpets	4247	5316	9563	16.19	Glass Bangles	944	0	944	4.24
Total	20667	38414	59081	100	Carpets	0	1312	1312	5.9
					Footwear	2806	0	2806	12.61
					Total	11352	10895	22247	100

Note: Belongs to boys of age 5-9.

industry of TN, which many individual surveys cite as the most hazardous industry in which a large number of children are employed. This may put a question mark on the reliability of the NSS data for estimating child labour, especially in these industries. In UP, the per centaes of child labour in hazardous industries are lower at 39 per cent for rural sector and 26 per cent for the urban sector. As stated earlier, the lower percentage in UP is not a reflection of better social and economic status of the state but due to lack of sufficient employment opportunities. In UP, there is enough potential of child labour supply but demand constraint has restricted the actual employment of child labour.

CONCLUSION

The analysis of child labour in the four states gives us its broad features. It shows that the supply of child labour generally tends to come from households in rural areas, are landless, have low MPCE, are average in size, are Hindus, belong to socially backward classes, are headed by a male and employed as labourers or self-employed. However, a higher proportion of the child population is sent to the job market by female-headed households, by those who have large-size households and by those who are deep in debt. It is noticed that the literacy rate in general and of females in particular, along with their dropout rates and gross enrolment rates is an important determinant of child labour. The dropout rates for girls for class I to VIII (Table I) is around 57 per cent for both MP and UP in 1998-99) and only 44 per cent and 34.8 per cent for Maharashtra and TN respectively. Accessibility to primary and upper primary schools in 1993 in rural areas was also quite low for MP and UP compared with the other two states (Table I). However, it may be noticed (Table 2) that the fall in child labour between 1991 and 1999-2000 is slowest in UP and fastest in MP. It is due to the fact that during the same period literacy and per capita income at 1993-94 prices increased relatively faster in MP (by 20 percentage points and 2.42 times) than in UP (by 16.6 percentage points and 2.36 times). It indicates a link between child labour and the educational and economic attainment of the state. With these attainments, one may expect that the problem of child labour may at least be contained, if not eliminated all together.

However, certain positive interventions by the community including the government, NGOs and other national and international organisations are called for in order to reduce child labour, Experience has shown that such efforts do bear fruit. Also there is no either or situation between the two approaches property versus illiteracy and both are to be attacked. The third approach advocated by Basu (2003) may be more appropriate as it recognises that child labour is a reality in India and it may not be feasible, at least in the near future, to completely ban it. It is also argued that 'product labelling' or banning child labour either under domestic or international pressure may not serve any worthwhile objective, as child labour then may just shift to alternative jobs. Bissell (2000) also advocated a balance between the right to education and the right to adequate standard of living. Deprivation from jobs may put children in more exploitative forms of economic activity. So a more appropriate policy could be to make education more meaningful and rewarding so that it not only provides incentive to households to send their children to school but may also help in reducing the high dropout rates. The strategy must aim at getting the 'nowhere children' into school and attempting to retain a much larger proportion of children from primary to middle school stage. Emphasis on women's education and some kind of stipend to students may also help to reduce child labour. Efforts also need to be made to simultaneously provide non-formal education, vocational education and training for child workers and income generating alternatives for families.

Though the role of the market may be important in the changed scenario of globalisation and competition, the state has to remain the main provider of education, particularly at the primary level and especially for the poor. Policy measures aimed at poverty reduction, and physical and social infrastructure development, may also reduce child labour. Interventions like micro credit for households, food for work, and enforcement of labour laws may also work towards achieving this goal. Increased community participation and government expenditure on education and poverty reductions a most for the solution to the problem.

NOTES

1. These four states have been selected under the GoI and USDoL project on 'Preventing and eliminating child labour in identified hazardous sectors' started in October 2002. The four states together have 35.56 per cent of the total 11.2 million child labour (5-14 years) in 1991 as per census estimates.
2. The estimates are provided only for the usual age group of 5-14 years, but on the request of ILO we also obtained estimates for older children and adolescent workers (15-18 years), as the project puts special emphasis on providing skill training to them. The estimates can be supplied to any interested researcher on request.
3. The activity status on which a person spent relatively longer time (major time criterion) during the 365 days preceding the date of survey is considered

the principal usual activity status of the person. A person whose principal usual status is determined on the basis of the major time criterion may have pursued some economic activity for a relatively shorter time (minor time) during the reference period of 365 days preceding the date of survey. The status in which such economic activity is pursued is the subsidiary economic activity status of the person. Thus, any person who is employed in any principal usual activity and/or in any subsidiary economic activity is clubbed into employed on the usual and subsidiary economic status (UPSS), and the same definition is used for estimating child labour.

4. The MPCE categories are the same as used by NSSO, except for the two categories in which the respective poverty line falls and its adjacent category. This adjustment has been done to accurately estimate the proportion of child labour in below poverty line households.

5. The poverty lines used in the current paper are the ones provide officially by the Planning Commission. Though they have been criticised and alternative estimates have been provided by Deaton (2003) and others, we decide not to take sides. An alternative poverty line may change the total proportion of child labour belonging to below poverty line households but the relationship of MPCE with child labour remains unaffected.

6. Respective official poverty lines for the urban sectors of the four states are Rs. 481.65 for MP Rs. 539.71 for Maharashtra, Rs. 475.60 for TN and Rs 416.29 for UP.

REFERENCES

Basu, Kaushik (2003), 'International Labour Standards and Child Labour' in Naila Kabeer, et al (ed), *Child Labour and the Right to Education in South Asia: Needs Vs Rights?* Sage Publications, New Delhi.

Basu, Kaushik and Pham Hoang Van (1998), 'The Economics of Child Labour', *American Economic Review, 88 (3),* June 412-27.

Bhargava, Pramila H. (2003), *The Elimination of Child Labour: Whose Responsibility?* Sage Publication, New Delhi.

Bhatty, K. (1998), 'Education Deprivation in India: A survey of Field Investigations, *Economic and Political Weekly, XXXIII,* (27 and 28), pp. 1731-40, 1858-69.

Bissel, S.L. (2000), *Manufacturing Childhood: The Lives and Livelihood of Children in Dhaka's Slums,* PhD Dissertation, Key Centre for Women's Health in Society, University of Melbourne, Australia.

Agarwal. S.C. (2004), Child a Labour in Selected State, Political Weekly 10 January, Pg. 173 to 185.

Burra, Neera (1995), *Born to Work: Child Labour in India,* Oxford University Press, New Delhi.

Chaudhri D.P. (1996), *Dynamic Profile of Child Labour in India 1951-1991,* ILO, New Delhi.

Deaton, Angus (2003), Prices and Poverty in India, 1987-2000, *Economic and Political Weekly, XXXVIII, (4),* pp. 362-68.

Lloyd, Tim (1994), *Poverty, Inequality and Rural Development,* St. Martins Press, New York. Misra, L.D. (2000): *Child Labour in India,* Oxford University Press, New Delhi.

Throat, S.K. (1999), 'Poverty, Caste and Child Labour in India: The Plight of Dalit and Adivasi Children', in K. Voll (ed.), *Against Child Labour: India and International Dimensions and Strategies,* pp. 154-75, Berlin Studies in International Polities, Mosaic Books, New Delhi.

Weiner, Myron (1991), The Child and the State in India: Child Labour and Education Policy in Comparative Perspective, Princeton University Press, Princeton.